MONEY MANAGEMENT STRATEGIES FOR FUTURES TRADERS

MONEY MANAGEMENT STRATEGIES FOR FUTURES TRADERS

Nauzer J. Balsara

Associate Professor
Northeastern Illinois University

JOHN WILEY & SONS, INC.

New York • Chichester • Brisbane • Toronto • Singapore

Library of Congress Cataloging-in-Publication Data

Balsara, Nauzer, 1954
    Money management strategies for futures traders / Nauzer Balsara.
        p.   cm. — (Wiley finance editions)
    Includes index.
    ISBN 0-471-52215-5 (cloth)
    1. Futures market. 2. Futures. 3. Investments. I. Title.
    II. Series.
    HG6024.A3B35   1992
    332.64'5—dc20   91-38287

10   9   8   7   6   5

WILEY FINANCE EDITIONS

FINANCIAL STATEMENT ANALYSIS
Martin S. Fridson

DYNAMIC ASSET ALLOCATION
David A. Hammer

INTERMARKET TECHNICAL ANALYSIS
John J. Murphy

INVESTING IN INTANGIBLE ASSETS
Russell L. Parr

FORECASTING FINANCIAL MARKETS
Tony Plummer

PORTFOLIO MANAGEMENT FORMULAS
Ralph Vince

TRADING AND INVESTING IN BOND OPTIONS
M. Anthony Wong

THE COMPLETE GUIDE TO CONVERTIBLE SECURITIES WORLDWIDE
Laura A. Zubulake

MANAGED FUTURES IN THE INSTITUTIONAL PORTFOLIO
Charles B. Epstein, Editor

ANALYZING AND FORECASTING FUTURES PRICES
Anthony F. Herbst

CHAOS AND ORDER IN THE CAPITAL MARKETS
Edgar E. Peters

INSIDE THE FINANCIAL FUTURES MARKETS, 3RD EDITION
Mark J. Powers and Mark G. Castelino

RELATIVE DIVIDEND YIELD
Anthony E. Spare

SELLING SHORT
Joseph A. Walker

THE FOREIGN EXCHANGE AND MONEY MARKETS GUIDE
Julian Walmsley

CORPORATE FINANCIAL RISK MANAGEMENT
Diane B. Wunnicke, David R. Wilson, Brooke Wunnicke

MONEY MANAGEMENT STRATEGIES FOR FUTURES TRADERS
Nauzer J. Balsara

Dedicated to my mother, Dolly, and the memory of my late father, Jehangir

Preface

This book on money management is a primer on conservative speculation. Although this phrase might sound contradictory, it is possible and even desirable to be a defensive speculator. If aggressiveness is confused with recklessness, speculation could soon degenerate into gambling and inevitably lead to financial ruin. This book does not pretend to develop techniques for making a killing in the markets. Instead, it shows how to avoid getting annihilated through disciplined risk taking. If the book helps the reader sidestep even one of the many pitfalls in the futures markets, it will have achieved its purpose.

The book is as nonmathematical as possible: The reader is not expected to know any math beyond basic algebra. Introducing complex mathematics would not help the exposition, nor would it make the reader a better trader.

Acknowledgments

This book has drawn heavily on the goodwill, patience, and understanding of many individuals, whom I wish to thank here collectively. However, a few debts are simply too big for a general thank-you!

My biggest debt is due Minu Patel for his statistical insight and expert programming assistance. But for his help and encouragement, this book would never have been completed. Thank you, Minu. A special thank-you also goes to Dave Lowdon of Logical Systems Inc. for programming support and to Mark Wiemeler and Ken McGahan for the charts presented in the book. Thanks are also due to graduate assistants Daniel Snyder and V. Anand for their untiring efforts. Special thanks are due to John Oleson for introducing me to chart-based risk and reward estimation techniques.

My debt to these individuals parallels the enormous debt I owe to Dean Olga Engelhardt for encouraging me to write the book and Associate Dean Kathleen Carlson for providing valuable administrative support. My chairperson, Professor C. T. Chen, deserves special commendation for creating an environment conducive to thinking and writing. I also wish to thank the Northeastern Illinois University Foundation for its generous support of my research endeavors.

Finally, I wish to thank Karl Weber, Associate Publisher, John Wiley & Sons, for his infinite patience with and support of a first-time writer.

Contents

MONEY MANAGEMENT STRATEGIES FOR FUTURES TRADERS

1

Understanding the Money Management Process

In a sense, every successful trader employs money management principles in the course of futures trading, even if only unconsciously. The goal of this book is to facilitate a more conscious and rigorous adoption of these principles in everyday trading. This chapter outlines the money management process in terms of market selection, exposure control, trade-specific risk assessment, and the allocation of capital across competing opportunities. In doing so, it gives the reader a broad overview of the book.

A signal to buy or sell a commodity may be generated by a technical or chart-based study of historical data. Fundamental analysis, or a study of demand and supply forces influencing the price of a commodity, could also be used to generate trading signals. Important as signal generation is, it is not the focus of this book. The focus of this book is on the decision-making process that follows a signal.

STEPS IN THE MONEY MANAGEMENT PROCESS

First, the trader must decide whether or not to proceed with the signal. This is a particularly serious problem when two or more commodities are vying for limited funds in the account. Next, for every signal accepted, the trader must decide on the fraction of the trading capital that he or she is willing to risk. The goal is to maximize profits while protecting the bankroll against undue loss and overexposure, to ensure participation in future major moves. An obvious choice is to risk a fixed dollar amount every time. More simply, the trader might elect to trade an equal number of contracts of every commodity traded. However, the resulting allocation of capital is likely to be suboptimal.

For each signal pursued, the trader must determine the price that un-equivocally confirms that the trade is not measuring up to expectations. This price is known as the stop-loss price, or simply the *stop price*. The dollar value of the difference between the entry price and the stop price defines the maximum permissible risk per contract. The risk capital allocated to the trade divided by the maximum permissible risk per contract determines the number of contracts to be traded. Money management encompasses the following steps:

1. Ranking available opportunities against an objective yardstick of desirability
2. Deciding on the fraction of capital to be exposed to trading at any given time
3. Allocating risk capital across opportunities
4. Assessing the permissible level of loss for each opportunity accepted for trading
5. Deciding on the number of contracts of a commodity to be traded, using the information from steps 3 and 4

The following paragraphs outline the salient features of each of these steps.

RANKING OF AVAILABLE OPPORTUNITIES

There are over 50 different futures contracts currently traded, making it difficult to concentrate on all commodities. Superimpose the practical constraint of limited funds, and selection assumes special significance. Ranking of competing opportunities against an objective yardstick of desirability seeks to alleviate the problem of virtually unlimited opportunities competing for limited funds.

The desirability of a trade is measured in terms of (a) its expected profits, (b) the risk associated with earning those profits, and (c) the investment required to initiate the trade. The higher the expected profit for a given level of risk, the more desirable the trade. Similarly, the lower the investment needed to initiate a trade, the more desirable the trade. In Chapter 3, we discuss chart-based approaches to estimating risk and reward. Chapter 5 discusses alternative approaches to commodity selection.

Having evaluated competing opportunities against an objective yardstick of desirability, the next step is to decide upon a cutoff point or benchmark level so as to short-list potential trades. Opportunities that fail to measure up to this cutoff point will not qualify for further consideration.

CONTROLLING OVERALL EXPOSURE

Overall exposure refers to the fraction of total capital that is risked across all trading opportunities. Risking 100 percent of the balance in the account could be ruinous if every single trade ends up a loser. At the other extreme, risking only 1 percent of capital mitigates the risk of bankruptcy, but the resulting profits are likely to be inconsequential.

The fraction of capital to be exposed to trading is dependent upon the returns expected to accrue from a portfolio of commodities. In general, the higher the expected returns, the greater the recommended level of exposure. The optimal exposure fraction would maximize the overall expected return on a portfolio of commodities. In order to facilitate the analysis, data on completed trade returns may be used as a proxy for expected returns. This analysis is discussed at length in Chapter 7.

Another relevant factor is the correlation between commodity returns. Two commodities are said to be positively correlated if a change in one is accompanied by a similar change in the other. Conversely, two commodities are negatively correlated if a change in one is accompanied by an opposite change in the other. The strength of the correlation depends on the magnitude of the relative changes in the two commodities.

In general, the greater the positive correlation across commodities in a portfolio, the lower the theoretically safe overall exposure level. This safeguards against multiple losses on positively correlated commodities. By the same logic, the greater the negative correlation between commodities in a portfolio, the higher the recommended overall optimal exposure. Chapter 4 discusses the concept of correlations and their role in reducing overall portfolio risk.

The overall exposure could be a fixed fraction of available funds. Alternatively, the exposure fraction could fluctuate in line with changes in trading account balance. For example, an aggressive trader might want to increase overall exposure consequent upon a decrease in account balance. A defensive trader might disagree, choosing to increase overall exposure only after witnessing an increase in account balance. These issues are discussed in Chapter 7.

ALLOCATING RISK CAPITAL

Once the trader has decided the total amount of capital to be risked to trading, the next step is to allocate this amount across competing trades. The easiest solution is to allocate an equal amount of risk capital to each commodity traded. This simplifying approach is particularly helpful when the trader is unable to estimate the reward and risk potential of a trade. However, the implicit assumption here is that all trades represent equally good investment opportunities. A trader who is uncomfortable with this assumption might pursue an allocation procedure that (a) identifies trade potential differences and (b) translates these differences into corresponding differences in exposure or risk capital allocation.

Differences in trade potential are measured in terms of (a) the probability of success and (b) the reward/risk ratio for the trade, arrived at by dividing the expected profit by the maximum permissible loss, or the payoff ratio, arrived at by dividing the average dollar profit earned on completed trades by the average dollar loss incurred. The higher the probability of success, and the higher the payoff ratio, the greater is the fraction that could justifiably be exposed to the trade in question. Arriving at optimal exposure is discussed in Chapter 7. Chapter 8 discusses the rules for increasing exposure during a trade's life, a technique commonly referred to as pyramiding.

ASSESSING THE MAXIMUM PERMISSIBLE LOSS ON A TRADE

Risk in trading futures stems from the lack of perfect foresight. Unanticipated adverse price swings are endemic to trading; controlling the consequences of such adverse swings is the hallmark of a successful speculator. Inability or unwillingness to control losses can lead to ruin, as explained in Chapter 2.

Before initiating a trade, a trader should decide on the price action which would conclusively indicate that he or she is on the wrong side of the market. A trader who trades off a mechanical system would calculate the protective stop-loss price dictated by the system. This is explained in Chapter 9. If the trader is strictly a chartist, relying on chart patterns to make trading decisions, he or she must determine in advance the precise point at which the trade is not going the desired way, using the techniques outlined in Chapter 3.

It is always tempting to ignore risk by concentrating exclusively on reward, but a trader should not succumb to this temptation. There are no guarantees in futures trading, and a trading strategy based on hope rather than realism is apt to fail. Chapter 6 discusses alternative strategies for controlling unrealized losses.

THE RISK EQUATION

Trade-specific risk is the product of the permissible dollar risk per contract multiplied by the number of contracts of the commodity to be traded. Overall trade exposure is the aggregation of trade-specific risk across all commodities traded concurrently. Overall exposure must be balanced by the trader's ability to lose and willingness to accept a loss. Essentially, each trader faces the following identity:

$$\text{Overall trade exposure} = \frac{\text{Willingness to assume risk}}{\text{backed by the ability to lose}}$$

The ability to lose is a function of capital available for trading: the greater the risk capital, the greater the ability to lose. However, the willingness to assume risk is influenced by the trader's comfort level for absorbing the "pain" associated with losses. An extremely risk-averse person may be unwilling to assume any risk, even though holding the requisite funds. At the other extreme, a risk lover may be willing to assume risks well beyond the available means.

For the purposes of discussion in this book, we will assume that a trader's willingness to assume risk is backed by the funds in the account. Our trader expects not to lose on a trade, but he or she is willing to accept a small loss, should one become inevitable.

DECIDING THE NUMBER OF CONTRACTS TO BE TRADED: BALANCING THE RISK EQUATION

Since the trader's ability to lose and willingness to assume risk is determined largely by the availability of capital and the trader's attitudes toward risk, this side of the risk equation is unique to the trader who alone can define the overall exposure level with which he or she is truly comfortable. Having made this determination, he or she must balance this desired exposure level with the overall exposure associated with the trade or trades under consideration.

Assume for a moment that the overall risk exposure outweighs the trader's threshold level. Since exposure is the product of (a) the dollar risk per contract and (b) the number of contracts traded, a downward adjustment is necessary in either or both variables. However, manipulating the dollar risk per contract to an artificially low figure simply to suit one's pocketbook or threshold of pain is ill-advised, and tinkering with one's own estimate of what constitutes the permissible risk on a trade is an exercise in self-deception, which can lead to needless losses. The dollar risk per contract is a predefined constant. The trader, therefore, must necessarily adjust the number of contracts to be traded so as to bring the total risk in line with his or her ability and willingness to assume risk. If the capital risked to a trade is $1000, and the permissible risk per contract is $500, the trader would want to trade two contracts, margin considerations permitting. If the permissible risk per contract is $1000, the trader would want to trade only one contract.

CONSEQUENCES OF TRADING AN UNBALANCED RISK EQUATION

An unbalanced risk equation arises when the dollar risk assessment for a trade is not equal to the trader's ability and willingness to assume risk. If the risk assessed on a trade is greater than that permitted by the trader's resources, we have a case of overtrading. Conversely, if the risk assessed on a trade is less than that permitted by the trader's resources, he or she is said to be undertrading.

Overtrading is particularly dangerous and should be avoided, as it threatens to rob a trader of precious trading capital. Overtrading typically stems from a trader's overconfidence about an impending move. When he is convinced that he is going to be proved right by subsequent events, no risk seems too big for his bankroll! However, this is a case of emotions winning over reason. Here speculation or reasonable risk taking can quickly degenerate into gambling, with disastrous consequences.

Undertrading is symptomatic of extreme caution. While it does not threaten to ruin a trader financially, it does put a damper on performance. When a trader fails to extend himself as much as he should, his performance falls short of optimal levels. This can and should be avoided.

CONCLUSION

Although futures trading is rightly believed to be a risky endeavor, a defensive trader can, through a series of conscious decisions, ensure that the risks do not overwhelm him or her. First, a trader must rank competing opportunities according to their respective return potential, thereby determining which opportunities to trade and which ones to pass up. Next, the trader must decide on the fraction of the trading capital he or she is willing to risk to trading and how he or she wishes to allocate this amount across competing opportunities. Before entering into a trade, a trader must decide on the latitude he or she is willing to allow the market before admitting to be on the wrong side of the trade. This specifies the permissible dollar risk per contract. Finally, the risk capital allocated to a trade divided by the permissible dollar risk per contract defines the number of contracts to be traded, margin considerations permitting.

It ought to be remembered at all times that the futures market offers no guarantees. Consequently, never overexpose the bankroll to what might appear to be a "sure thing" trade. Before going ahead with a trade, the trader must assess the consequences of its going amiss. Will the loss resulting from a realization of the worst-case scenario in any way cripple the trader financially or affect his or her mental equilibrium? If the answer is in the affirmative, the trader must lighten up the exposure, either by reducing the number of contracts to be traded or by simply letting the trade pass by if the risk on a single contract is far too high for his or her resources.

Futures trading is a game where the winner is the one who can best control his or her losses. Mistakes of judgment are inevitable in trading; a successful trader simply prevents an error of judgment from turning into a devastating blunder.

2
The Dynamics of Ruin

It is often said that the best way to avoid ruin is to have experienced it at least once. Having experienced devastation, the trader knows firsthand what causes ruin and how to avoid similar debacles in future. However, this experience can be frightfully expensive, both financially and emotionally. In the absence of firsthand experience, the next best way to avoid ruin is to develop a keen awareness of what causes ruin. This chapter outlines the causes of ruin and quantifies the interrelationships between these causes into an overall probability of ruin.

Failure in the futures markets may be explained in terms of either (a) inaction or (b) incorrect action. Inaction or lack of action may be defined as either failure to enter a new trade or to exit out of an existing trade. Incorrect action results from entering into or liquidating a position either prematurely or after the move is all but over. The reasons for inaction and incorrect action are discussed here.

INACTION

First, the behavior of the market could lull a trader into inaction. If the market is in a sideways or congestion pattern over several weeks, then a trader might well miss the move as soon as the market breaks out of its congestion. Alternatively, if the market has been moving very sharply in a particular direction and suddenly changes course, it is almost impossible to accept the switch at face value. It is so much easier to do nothing, believing that the reversal is a minor correction to the existing trend rather than an actual change in the trend.

Second, the nature of the instrument traded may cause trader inaction. For example, purchasing an option on a futures contract is quite different from trading the underlying futures contract and could evoke markedly different responses. The purchaser of an option is under no obligation to close out the position, even if the market goes against the option buyer. Consequently, he or she is likely to be lulled into a false sense of complacency, figuring that a panic sale of the option is unwarranted, especially if the option premium has eroded dramatically.

Third, a trader may be numbed into inaction by fear of possible losses. This is especially true for a trader who has suffered a series of consecutive losses in the marketplace, losing self-confidence in the process. Such a trader can start second-guessing himself and the signals generated by his system, preferring to do nothing rather than risk sustaining yet another loss.

The fourth reason for not acting is an unwillingness to accept an error of judgment. A trader who already has a position may do everything possible to convince himself that the current price action does not merit liquidation of the trade. Not wanting to be confused by facts, the trader would ignore them in the hope that sooner or later the market will prove him right!

Finally, a trader may fail to act in a timely fashion simply because he has not done his homework to stay abreast of the markets. Obviously, the amount of homework a trader must do is directly related to the number of commodities followed. Inaction due to negligence most commonly occurs when a trader does not devote enough time and attention to each commodity he tracks.

INCORRECT ACTION

Timing is important in any investment endeavor, but it is particularly crucial in the futures markets because of the daily adjustments in account balances to reflect current prices. A slight error in timing can result in serious financial trouble for the futures trader. Incorrect action stemming from imprecise timing will be discussed under the following broad categories: (a) premature entry, (b) delayed entry, (c) premature exit, and (d) delayed exit.

Premature Entry

As the name suggests, premature entry results from initiating a new trade before getting a clear signal. Premature entry problems are typically the result of unsuccessfully trying to pick the top or bottom of a strongly trending market. Outguessing the market and trying to stay one step ahead of it can prove to be a painfully expensive experience. It is much safer to stay in step with the market, reacting to market moves as expeditiously as possible, rather than trying to forecast possible market behavior.

Delayed Entry or Chasing the Market

This is the practice of initiating a trade long after the current trend has established itself. Admittedly, it is very difficult to spot a shift in the trend just after it occurs. It is so much easier to jump on board after the commodity in question has made an appreciably big move. However, the trouble with this is that a very strong move in a given direction is almost certain to be followed by some kind of pullback. A delayed entry into the market almost assures the trader of suffering through the pullback.

A conservative trader who believes in controlling risk will wait patiently for a pullback before plunging into a roaring bull or bear market. If there is no pullback, the move is completely missed, resulting in an opportunity forgone. However, the conservative trader attaches a greater premium to actual dollars lost than to profit opportunities forgone.

Premature Exit

A new trader, or even an experienced trader shaken by a string of recent losses, might want to cash in an unrealized profit prematurely. Although understandable, this does not make for good trading. Premature exiting out of a trade is the natural reaction of someone who is short on confidence. Working under the assumption that some profits are better than no profits, a trader might be tempted to cash in a small profit now rather than agonize over a possibly bigger, but much more uncertain, profit in the future.

While it does make sense to lock in a part of unrealized profits and not expose everything to the vagaries of the marketplace, taking profits in a hurry is certainly not the most appropriate technique. It is good policy to continue with a trade until there is a definite signal to liquidate it. The futures market entails healthy risk taking on the part of speculators, and anyone uncomfortable with this fact ought not to trade.

Yet another reason for premature exiting out of a trade is setting arbitrary targets based on a percentage of return on investment. For example, a trader might decide to exit out of a trade when unrealized profits on the trade amount to 100 percent of the initial investment. The 100 percent return on investment is a good benchmark, but it may lead to a premature exit, since the market could move well beyond the point that yields the trader a 100 percent return on investment. Alternatively, the market could shift course before it meets the trader's target; in which case, he or she may well be faced with a delayed exit problem.

Premature liquidation of a trade at the first sign of a loss is very often a characteristic of a nervous trader. The market has a disconcerting habit of deviating at times from what seems to be a well-established trend. For example, it often happens that if a market closes sharply higher on a given day, it may well open lower on the following day. After meandering downwards in the initial hours of trading, during which time all nervous longs have been successfully gobbled up, the market will merrily waltz off to new highs!

Delayed Exit

This includes a delayed exit out of a profitable trade or a delayed exit out of a losing trade. In either case, the delay is normally the result of hope or greed overruling a carefully thought-out plan of action. The successful trader is one who (a) can recognize when a trade is going against him and (b) has the courage to act based on such recognition. Being indecisive or relying on luck to bail out of a tight spot will most certainly result in greater than necessary losses.

ASSESSING THE MAGNITUDE OF LOSS

The discussion so far has centered around the reasons for losing, without addressing their dollar consequences. The dollar consequence of a loss depends on the size of the bet or the fraction of capital exposed to trading. The greater the exposure, the greater the scope for profits, should prices unfold as expected, or losses, should the trade turn sour. An illustration will help dramatize the double-edged nature of the leverage sword.

It is August 1987. A trader with $100,000 in his account is convinced that the stock market is overvalued and is due for a major correction. He decides to use all the money in his account to short-sell futures contracts on the Standard and Poor's (S&P) 500 index, currently trading at 341.30. Given an initial margin requirement of $10,000 per contract, our trader decides to short 10 contracts of the December S&P 500 index on August 25, 1987, at 341.30. On October 19, 1987, in the wake of Black Monday, our trader covers his short positions at 201.30 for a profit of $70,000 per contract, or $700,000 on 10 contracts! This story has a wonderful ending, illustrating the power of leverage.

Now assume that our trader was correct in his assessment of an overvalued stock market but was slightly off on timing his entry. Specifically, let us assume that the S&P 500 index rallied 21 points to 362.30, crashing subsequently as anticipated. The unexpected rally would result in an unrealized loss of $10,500 per contract or $105,000 over 10 contracts. Given the twin features of daily adjustment of equity and the need to sustain the account at the maintenance margin level of $5,000 per contract, our trader would receive a margin call to replenish his account back to the initial level of $100,000. Assuming he cannot meet his margin call, he is forced out of his short position for a loss of $105,000, which exceeds the initial balance in his account. He ruefully watches the collapse of the S&P index as a ruined, helpless bystander! Leverage can be hurtful: in the extreme case, it can precipitate ruin.

THE RISK OF RUIN

A trader is said to be ruined if his equity is depleted to the point where he is no longer able to trade. The risk of ruin is a probability estimate ranging between 0 and 1. A probability estimate of 0 suggests that ruin is impossible, whereas an estimate of 1 implies that ruin is ensured. The risk of ruin is a function of the following:

1. The probability of success
2. The payoff ratio, or the ratio of the average trade win to the average trade loss
3. The fraction of capital exposed to trading

Whereas the probability of success and the payoff ratio are trading system–dependent, the fraction of capital exposed is determined by money management considerations.

Let us illustrate the concept of risk of ruin with the help of a simple example. Assume that we have $1 available for trading and that this entire amount is risked to trading. Further, let us assume that the average win, $1, equals the average loss, leading to a payoff ratio of 1. Finally, let us assume that past trading results indicate that we have 3 winners for every 5 trades, or a probability of success of 0.60. If the first trade is a loser, we end up losing our entire stake of $1 and cannot trade any more. Therefore, the probability of ruin at the end of the first trade is 2/5, or 0.40.

If the first trade were to result in a win, we would move to the next trade with an increased capital of $2. It is impossible to be ruined at the end of the second trade, given that the loss per trade is constrained to $1. We would now have to lose the next two consecutive trades in order to be ruined by the end of the third trade. The probability of this occurring is the product of the probability of winning on the first trade times the probability of losing on each of the next two trades. This works out to be 0.096 (0.60 × 0.40 × 0.40).

Therefore, the risk of ruin on or before the end of three trades may be expressed as the sum of the following:

1. The probability of ruin at the end of the first trade
2. The probability of ruin at the end of the third trade

The overall probability of these two possible routes to ruin by the end of the third trade works out to be 0.496, arrived at as follows:

0.40 + 0.096 = 0.496

Extending this logic a little further, there are two possible routes to ruin by the end of the fifth trade. First, if the first two trades are wins, the next three trades would have to be losers to ensure ruin. Alternatively, a more circuitous route to ruin would involve winning the first trade, losing the second, winning the third, and finally losing the fourth and the fifth. The two routes are mutually exclusive, in that the occurrence of one precludes the other.

The probability of ruin by the end of five trades may therefore be computed as the sum of the following probabilities:

1. Ruin at the end of the first trade
2. Ruin at the end of the third trade, namely one win followed by two consecutive losses
3. One of two possible routes to ruin at the end of the fifth trade, namely (a) two wins followed by three consecutive losses, or (b) one win followed by a loss, a win, and finally two successive losses

Therefore, the probability of ruin by the end of the fifth trade works out to be 0.54208, arrived at as follows:

$$0.40 + 0.096 + 2 \times (0.02304) = 0.54208$$

Notice how the probability of ruin increases as the trading horizon expands. However, the probability is increasing at a decreasing rate, suggesting a leveling off in the risk of ruin as the number of trades increases.

In mathematical computations, the number of trades, n, is assumed to be very large so as to ensure an accurate estimate of the risk of ruin. Since the calculations get to be more tedious as n increases, it would be desirable to work with a formula that calculates the risk of ruin for a given probability of success. In its most elementary form, the formula for computing risk of ruin makes two simplifying assumptions: (a) the payoff ratio is 1, and (b) the entire capital in the account is risked to trading.

Under these assumptions, William Feller[1] states that a gambler's risk of ruin, R, is

$$R = \frac{(q/p)^a - (q/p)^k}{(q/p)^a - 1}$$

where the gambler has k units of capital and his or her opponent has $(a - k)$ units of capital. The probability of success is given by p, and the complementary probability of failure is given by q, where $q = (1 - p)$. As applied to futures trading, we can assume that the probability of winning, p, exceeds the probability of losing, q, leading to a fraction

[1] William Feller, *An Introduction to Probability Theory and its Applications,* Volume 1 (New York: John Wiley & Sons, 1950).

(q/p) that is smaller than 1. Moreover, we can assume that the trader's opponent is the market as a whole, and that the overall market capitalization, a, is a very large number as compared to k. For practical purposes, therefore, the term $(q/p)^a$ tends to zero, and the probability of ruin is reduced to $(q/p)^k$.

Notice that the risk of ruin in the above formula is a function of (a) the probability of success and (b) the number of units of capital available for trading. The greater the probability of success, the lower the risk of ruin. Similarly, the lower the fraction of capital that is exposed to trading, the smaller the risk of ruin for a given probability of success.

For example, when the probability of success is 0.50 and an amount of $1 is risked out of an available $10, implying an exposure of 10 percent at any time, the risk of ruin for a payoff ratio of 1 works out to be $(0.50/0.50)^{10}$, or 1. Therefore, ruin is ensured with a system that has a 0.50 probability of success and promises a payoff ratio of 1. When the probability of success increases marginally to 0.55, with the same payoff ratio and exposure fraction, the probability of ruin drops dramatically to $(0.45/0.55)^{10}$ or 0.134! Therefore, it certainly does pay to invest in improving the odds of success for any given trading system.

When the average win does not equal the average loss, the risk-of-ruin calculations become more complicated. When the payoff ratio is 2, the risk of ruin can be reduced to a precise formula, as shown by Norman T. J. Bailey.[2]

Should the probability of losing equal or exceed twice the probability of winning, that is, if $q \geq 2p$, the risk of ruin, R, is certain or 1. Stated differently, if the probability of winning is less than one-half the probability of losing and the payoff ratio is 2, the risk of ruin is certain or 1. For example, if the probability of winning is less than or equal to 0.33, the risk of ruin is 1 for a payoff ratio of 2.

If the probability of losing is less than twice the probability of winning, that is, if $q < 2p$, the risk of ruin, R, for a payoff ratio equal to 2 is defined as

$$R = \left\{ \left(0.25 + \frac{q}{p}\right)^{0.5} - 0.5 \right\}^k$$

[2] Norman T. J. Bailey, *The Elements of Stochastic Processes with Applications to the Natural Sciences* (New York: John Wiley & Sons, 1964).

where q = probability of loss

   p = probability of winning

   k = number of units of equal dollar amounts of capital available for trading

The proportion of capital risked to trading is a function of the number of units of available trading capital. If the entire equity in the account, k, were to be risked to trading, then the exposure would be 100 percent. However, if k is 2 units, of which 1 is risked, the exposure is 50 percent. In general, if 1 unit of capital is risked out of an available k units in the account, $(100/k)$ percent is the percentage of capital at risk. The smaller the percentage of capital at risk, the smaller is the risk of ruin for a given probability of success and payoff ratio.

Using the above equation for a payoff ratio of 2, when the probability of winning is 0.60, and there are 2 units of capital, leading to a 50 percent exposure, the risk of ruin, R, is 0.209. With the same probability of success and payoff ratio, an increase in the number of total capital units to 5 (a reduction in the exposure level from 50 percent to 20 percent) leads to a reduction in the risk of ruin from 0.209 to 0.020! This highlights the importance of the fraction of capital exposed to trading in controlling the risk of ruin.

When the payoff ration exceeds 2, that is, when the average win is greater than twice the average loss, the differential equations associated with the risk of ruin calculations do not lend themselves to a precise or closed-form solution. Due to this mathematical difficulty, the next best alternative is to simulate the probability of ruin.

SIMULATING THE RISK OF RUIN

In this section, we simulate the risk of ruin as a function of three inputs: (a) the probability of success, p, (b) the percentage of capital, k, risked to active trading, given by $(100/k)$ percent, and (c) the payoff ratio. For the purposes of the simulation, the probability of success ranges from 0.05 to 0.90 in increments of 0.05. Similarly, the payoff ratio ranges from 1 to 10 in increments of 1.

The simulation is based on the premise that a trader risks an amount of $1 in each round of trading. This represents $(100/k)$ percent of his initial capital of k. For the simulation, the initial capital, k, ranges between $1, $2, $3, $4, $5 and $10, leading to risk exposure levels of 100%, 50%, 33%, 25%, 20%, and 10%, respectively.

The Logic of the Simulation Process

A fraction between 0 and 1 is selected at random by a random number generator. If the fraction lies between 0 and $(1 - p)$, the trade is said to result in a loss of $1. Alternatively, if the fraction is greater than $(1 - p)$ but less than 1, the trade is said to result in a win of W, which is added to the capital at the beginning of that round.

Trading continues in a given round until such time as either (a) the entire capital accumulated in that round of trading is lost or (b) the initial capital increases 100 times to $100k$, at which stage the risk of ruin is presumed to be negligible.

Exiting a trade for either reason marks the end of that round. The process is repeated 100,000 times, so as to arrive at the most likely estimate of the risk of ruin for a given set of parameters. To simplify the simulation analysis, we assume that there is no withdrawal of profits from the account. The risk of ruin is defined by the fraction of times a trader loses the entire trading capital over the course of 100,000 trials. The Turbo Pascal program to simulate the risk of ruin is outlined in Appendix A. Appendix B gives a BASIC program for the same problem. Both programs are designed to run on a personal computer.

The Simulation Results and Their Significance

The results of the simulation are presented in Table 2.1. As expected, the risk of ruin is (a) directly related to the proportion of capital allocated to trading and (b) inversely related to the probability of success and the size of the payoff ratio. The risk of ruin is 1 for a payoff ratio of 2, regardless of capital exposure, up to a probability of success of 0.30. This supports Bailey's assertion that for a payoff ratio of 2, the risk of ruin is 1 as long as the probability of losing is twice as great as the probability of winning.

The risk of ruin drops as the probability of success increases, the magnitude of the drop depending on the fraction of capital at risk. The risk of ruin rapidly falls to zero when only 10 percent of available capital is exposed. Table 2.1 shows that for a probability of success of 0.35, a

TABLE 2.1   Probability of Ruin Tables

Available Capital = $1; Capital Risked = $1 or 100%

Probability of Success

Probability of Success	Payoff Ratio									
	1	2	3	4	5	6	7	8	9	10
0.05	1.000	1.000	1.000	1.000	1.000	1.000	1.000	1.000	1.000	1.000
0.10	1.000	1.000	1.000	1.000	1.000	1.000	1.000	0.998	0.991	0.978
0.15	1.000	1.000	1.000	1.000	0.999	0.979	0.946	0.923	0.905	0.894
0.20	1.000	1.000	1.000	0.990	0.926	0.886	0.860	0.844	0.832	0.822
0.25	1.000	1.000	0.990	0.887	0.834	0.804	0.788	0.775	0.766	0.761
0.30	1.000	1.000	0.881	0.794	0.756	0.736	0.720	0.715	0.708	0.705
0.35	1.000	0.951	0.778	0.713	0.687	0.671	0.663	0.659	0.655	0.653
0.40	1.000	0.825	0.691	0.647	0.621	0.611	0.609	0.602	0.601	0.599
0.45	1.000	0.714	0.615	0.579	0.565	0.558	0.554	0.551	0.551	0.550
0.50	0.989	0.618	0.541	0.518	0.508	0.505	0.504	0.499	0.499	0.498
0.55	0.819	0.534	0.478	0.463	0.453	0.453	0.453	0.453	0.453	0.453
0.60	0.667	0.457	0.419	0.406	0.402	0.402	0.402	0.400	0.400	0.400
0.65	0.537	0.388	0.363	0.356	0.349	0.349	0.349	0.349	0.349	0.347
0.70	0.430	0.322	0.306	0.300	0.300	0.300	0.300	0.300	0.300	0.300
0.75	0.335	0.266	0.252	0.252	0.252	0.252	0.250	0.249	0.249	0.249
0.80	0.251	0.205	0.201	0.201	0.198	0.198	0.198	0.198	0.198	0.198
0.85	0.175	0.153	0.151	0.151	0.150	0.150	0.150	0.150	0.150	0.150
0.90	0.110	0.101	0.101	0.101	0.101	0.101	0.101	0.100	0.100	0.100

Available Capital = $2; Capital Risked = $1 or 50%

Probability of Success

Probability of Success	Payoff Ratio									
	1	2	3	4	5	6	7	8	9	10
0.05	1.000	1.000	1.000	1.000	1.000	1.000	1.000	1.000	1.000	1.000
0.10	1.000	1.000	1.000	1.000	1.000	1.000	1.000	1.000	0.990	0.962
0.15	1.000	1.000	1.000	1.000	1.000	0.966	0.897	0.850	0.819	0.798
0.20	1.000	1.000	1.000	0.990	0.858	0.781	0.737	0.714	0.689	0.680
0.25	1.000	1.000	0.991	0.789	0.695	0.645	0.615	0.601	0.590	0.581
0.30	1.000	1.000	0.773	0.631	0.572	0.541	0.523	0.511	0.503	0.500
0.35	1.000	0.906	0.606	0.511	0.470	0.451	0.440	0.433	0.428	0.426
0.40	1.000	0.678	0.479	0.416	0.392	0.377	0.368	0.366	0.363	0.363
0.45	1.000	0.506	0.378	0.337	0.321	0.312	0.306	0.305	0.304	0.302
0.50	0.990	0.382	0.295	0.269	0.260	0.253	0.251	0.251	0.251	0.251
0.55	0.672	0.289	0.229	0.212	0.208	0.205	0.203	0.203	0.203	0.203
0.60	0.443	0.208	0.174	0.166	0.161	0.161	0.161	0.161	0.161	0.159
0.65	0.289	0.151	0.130	0.125	0.125	0.125	0.123	0.123	0.122	0.122
0.70	0.185	0.106	0.093	0.090	0.090	0.090	0.090	0.090	0.090	0.088
0.75	0.112	0.071	0.064	0.063	0.063	0.063	0.063	0.063	0.063	0.063
0.80	0.063	0.044	0.042	0.040	0.040	0.040	0.040	0.040	0.039	0.039
0.85	0.032	0.023	0.023	0.023	0.023	0.023	0.023	0.023	0.023	0.022
0.90	0.012	0.010	0.010	0.010	0.010	0.010	0.010	0.010	0.010	0.010

Table 2.1 *continued*

Available Capital = $3; Capital Risked = $1 or 33.33%

Probability of Success	Payoff Ratio									
	1	2	3	4	5	6	7	8	9	10
0.05	1.000	1.000	1.000	1.000	1.000	1.000	1.000	1.000	1.000	1.000
0.10	1.000	1.000	1.000	1.000	1.000	1.000	1.000	1.000	0.990	0.942
0.15	1.000	1.000	1.000	1.000	1.000	0.951	0.852	0.782	0.744	0.714
0.20	1.000	1.000	1.000	0.990	0.796	0.692	0.635	0.599	0.576	0.560
0.25	1.000	1.000	0.991	0.699	0.581	0.518	0.485	0.467	0.455	0.441
0.30	1.000	1.000	0.680	0.501	0.428	0.395	0.374	0.367	0.357	0.352
0.35	1.000	0.862	0.474	0.365	0.324	0.303	0.292	0.284	0.281	0.278
0.40	1.000	0.559	0.332	0.269	0.243	0.232	0.226	0.220	0.219	0.219
0.45	1.000	0.364	0.230	0.195	0.179	0.173	0.171	0.168	0.168	0.168
0.50	0.990	0.236	0.161	0.139	0.133	0.127	0.127	0.126	0.126	0.126
0.55	0.551	0.151	0.110	0.100	0.096	0.092	0.092	0.092	0.092	0.092
0.60	0.297	0.095	0.072	0.068	0.064	0.064	0.064	0.063	0.063	0.063
0.65	0.155	0.058	0.047	0.044	0.044	0.042	0.042	0.042	0.042	0.042
0.70	0.079	0.035	0.029	0.028	0.028	0.028	0.027	0.027	0.027	0.025
0.75	0.037	0.019	0.017	0.016	0.016	0.016	0.016	0.016	0.016	0.016
0.80	0.016	0.008	0.008	0.008	0.008	0.008	0.008	0.008	0.008	0.008
0.85	0.006	0.004	0.004	0.003	0.003	0.003	0.003	0.003	0.003	0.003
0.90	0.001	0.001	0.001	0.001	0.001	0.001	0.001	0.001	0.001	0.001

Available Capital = $4; Capital Risked = $1 or 25%

Probability of Success	Payoff Ratio									
	1	2	3	4	5	6	7	8	9	10
0.05	1.000	1.000	1.000	1.000	1.000	1.000	1.000	1.000	1.000	1.000
0.10	1.000	1.000	1.000	1.000	1.000	1.000	1.000	1.000	0.990	0.926
0.15	1.000	1.000	1.000	1.000	1.000	0.936	0.805	0.727	0.673	0.638
0.20	1.000	1.000	1.000	0.990	0.736	0.612	0.546	0.503	0.477	0.459
0.25	1.000	1.000	0.991	0.620	0.487	0.422	0.383	0.358	0.346	0.337
0.30	1.000	1.000	0.599	0.399	0.327	0.290	0.271	0.260	0.254	0.250
0.35	1.000	0.820	0.366	0.264	0.222	0.201	0.194	0.187	0.185	0.180
0.40	1.000	0.458	0.229	0.174	0.152	0.142	0.135	0.133	0.132	0.130
0.45	1.000	0.259	0.142	0.111	0.102	0.097	0.094	0.092	0.092	0.092
0.50	0.990	0.147	0.086	0.072	0.067	0.064	0.063	0.063	0.062	0.062
0.55	0.447	0.082	0.052	0.045	0.044	0.043	0.042	0.042	0.041	0.041
0.60	0.195	0.043	0.030	0.027	0.027	0.025	0.025	0.025	0.025	0.025
0.65	0.083	0.023	0.016	0.016	0.015	0.015	0.015	0.015	0.015	0.015
0.70	0.036	0.011	0.009	0.008	0.008	0.008	0.008	0.008	0.008	0.008
0.75	0.013	0.005	0.004	0.004	0.004	0.004	0.004	0.004	0.004	0.004
0.80	0.004	0.002	0.002	0.002	0.002	0.002	0.002	0.002	0.002	0.001
0.85	0.001	0.001	0.001	0.001	0.001	0.001	0.001	0.001	0.001	0.001
0.90	0.000	0.000	0.000	0.000	0.000	0.000	0.000	0.000	0.000	0.000

Table 2.1 *continued*

Available Capital = $5; Capital Risked = $1 or 20%

Probability of
Success

					Payoff Ratio					
	1	2	3	4	5	6	7	8	9	10
0.05	1.000	1.000	1.000	1.000	1.000	1.000	1.000	1.000	1.000	1.000
0.10	1.000	1.000	1.000	1.000	1.000	1.000	1.000	1.000	0.990	0.908
0.15	1.000	1.000	1.000	1.000	1.000	0.921	0.763	0.668	0.611	0.573
0.20	1.000	1.000	1.000	0.990	0.683	0.543	0.471	0.425	0.398	0.378
0.25	1.000	1.000	0.989	0.554	0.402	0.336	0.300	0.279	0.267	0.257
0.30	1.000	1.000	0.526	0.317	0.247	0.213	0.197	0.185	0.179	0.176
0.35	1.000	0.779	0.287	0.187	0.153	0.138	0.128	0.123	0.121	0.119
0.40	1.000	0.376	0.159	0.113	0.094	0.088	0.083	0.083	0.079	0.079
0.45	1.000	0.183	0.087	0.065	0.058	0.053	0.053	0.051	0.050	0.050
0.50	0.990	0.090	0.047	0.038	0.034	0.033	0.033	0.033	0.032	0.031
0.55	0.368	0.044	0.025	0.021	0.020	0.019	0.019	0.019	0.019	0.018
0.60	0.130	0.020	0.013	0.011	0.010	0.010	0.010	0.010	0.010	0.010
0.65	0.046	0.008	0.006	0.005	0.005	0.005	0.005	0.005	0.005	0.005
0.70	0.015	0.004	0.003	0.003	0.003	0.003	0.003	0.003	0.003	0.002
0.75	0.004	0.001	0.001	0.001	0.001	0.001	0.001	0.001	0.001	0.001
0.80	0.001	0.000	0.000	0.000	0.000	0.000	0.000	0.000	0.000	0.000
0.85	0.000	0.000	0.000	0.000	0.000	0.000	0.000	0.000	0.000	0.000
0.90	0.000	0.000	0.000	0.000	0.000	0.000	0.000	0.000	0.000	0.000

Available Capital = $10; Capital Risked = $1 or 10%

Probability of
Success

					Payoff Ratio					
	1	2	3	4	5	6	7	8	9	10
0.05	1.000	1.000	1.000	1.000	1.000	1.000	1.000	1.000	1.000	1.000
0.10	1.000	1.000	1.000	1.000	1.000	1.000	1.000	1.000	0.990	0.822
0.15	1.000	1.000	1.000	1.000	1.000	0.849	0.579	0.449	0.371	0.325
0.20	1.000	1.000	1.000	0.990	0.467	0.297	0.220	0.178	0.159	0.144
0.25	1.000	1.000	0.990	0.303	0.162	0.113	0.090	0.078	0.069	0.067
0.30	1.000	1.000	0.277	0.102	0.060	0.045	0.039	0.034	0.033	0.031
0.35	1.000	0.608	0.082	0.036	0.023	0.018	0.016	0.015	0.014	0.014
0.40	1.000	0.143	0.025	0.013	0.008	0.008	0.007	0.007	0.006	0.006
0.45	1.000	0.033	0.008	0.004	0.003	0.003	0.003	0.002	0.002	0.002
0.50	0.990	0.008	0.002	0.001	0.001	0.001	0.001	0.001	0.001	0.001
0.55	0.132	0.002	0.001	0.001	0.000	0.000	0.000	0.000	0.000	0.000
0.60	0.017	0.000	0.000	0.000	0.000	0.000	0.000	0.000	0.000	0.000
0.65	0.002	0.000	0.000	0.000	0.000	0.000	0.000	0.000	0.000	0.000
0.70	0.000	0.000	0.000	0.000	0.000	0.000	0.000	0.000	0.000	0.000
0.75	0.000	0.000	0.000	0.000	0.000	0.000	0.000	0.000	0.000	0.000
0.80	0.000	0.000	0.000	0.000	0.000	0.000	0.000	0.000	0.000	0.000
0.85	0.000	0.000	0.000	0.000	0.000	0.000	0.000	0.000	0.000	0.000
0.90	0.000	0.000	0.000	0.000	0.000	0.000	0.000	0.000	0.000	0.000

payoff ratio of 2, and a capital exposure level of 10 percent, the risk of ruin is 0.608. The risk of ruin drops to 0.033 when the probability of success increases marginally to 0.45.

Working with estimates of the probability of success and the payoff ratio, the trader can use the simulation results in one of two ways. First, the trader can assess the risk of ruin for a given exposure level. Assume that the probability of success is 0.60 and the payoff ratio is 2. Assume further that the trader wishes to risk 50 percent of capital to open trades at any given time. Table 2.1 shows that the associated risk of ruin is 0.208.

Second, he or she can use the table to determine the exposure level that will translate into a prespecified risk of ruin. Continuing with our earlier example, assume our trader is not comfortable with a risk-of-ruin estimate of 0.208. Assume instead that he or she is comfortable with a risk of ruin equal to one-half that estimate, or 0.104. Working with the same probability of success and payoff ratio as before, Table 2.1 suggests that the trader should risk only 33.33 percent of his capital instead of the contemplated 50. This would give our trader a more acceptable risk-of-ruin estimate of 0.095.

CONCLUSION

Losses are endemic to futures trading, and there is no reason to get despondent over them. It would be more appropriate to recognize the reasons behind the loss, with a view to preventing its recurrence. Is the loss due to any lapse on the part of the trader, or is it due to market conditions not particularly suited to his or her trading system or style of trading?

A lapse on the part of the trader may be due to inaction or incorrect action. If this is true, it is imperative that the trader understand exactly the nature of the error committed and take steps not to repeat it. Inaction or lack of action may result from (a) the behavior of the market, (b) the nature of the instrument traded, or (c) lack of discipline or inadequate homework on the part of the trader. Incorrect action may consist of (a) premature or delayed entry into a trade or (b) premature or delayed exit out of a trade. The magnitude of loss as a result of incorrect action depends upon the trader's exposure. A trader must ensure that losses do not overwhelm him to the extent that he cannot trade any further.

Ruin is defined as the inability to trade as a result of losses wiping out available capital. One obvious determinant of the risk of ruin is the probability of trading success: the higher the probability of success, the lower the risk of ruin. Similarly, the higher the ratio of the average dollar win to the average dollar loss—known as the payoff ratio—the lower the risk of ruin. Both these factors are trading system–dependent.

Yet another crucial component influencing the risk of ruin is the proportion of capital risked to trading. This is a money management consideration. If a trader risks everything he or she has to a single trade, and the trade does not materialize as expected, there is a high probability of being ruined. Alternatively, if the amount risked on a bad trade represents only a small proportion of a trader's capital, the risk of ruin is mitigated.

All three factors interact to determine the risk of ruin. Table 2.1 gives the risk of ruin for a given probability of success, payoff ratio, and exposure fraction. Assume that the trader is aware of the probability of trading success and the payoff ratio for the trades he has effected. If the trader wishes to fix the risk of ruin at a certain level, he or she can estimate the proportion of capital to be risked to trading at any given time. This procedure allows the trader to control his or her risk of ruin.

3

Estimating Risk and Reward

This chapter describes the estimation of reward and permissible risk on a trade, which gives the trader an idea of the potential payoffs associated with that trade. Technical trading is based on an analysis of historical price, volume, and open interest information. Signals could be generated either by (a) a visual examination of chart patterns or (b) a system of rules that essentially mechanizes the trading process. In this chapter we restrict ourselves to a discussion of the visual approach to signal generation.

THE IMPORTANCE OF DEFINING RISK

Regardless of the technique adopted, the practice of predefining the maximum permissible risk on a trade is important, since it helps the trader think through a series of important related questions:

1. How significant is the risk in relation to available capital?
2. Does the potential reward justify the risk?
3. In the context of questions 1 and 2 and of other trading opportunities available concurrently, what proportion of capital, if any, should be risked to the commodity in question?

THE IMPORTANCE OF ESTIMATING REWARD

Reward estimates are particularly useful in capital allocation decisions, when they are synthesized with margin requirements and permissible risk to determine the overall desirability of a trade. The higher the estimated reward for a given margin investment, the higher the potential return on investment. Similarly, the higher the estimated reward for a permissible dollar risk, the higher the reward/risk ratio.

ESTIMATING RISK AND REWARD ON COMMONLY OBSERVED PATTERNS

Mechanical systems are generally trend-following in nature, reacting to shifts in the underlying trend instead of trying to predict where the market is headed. Therefore, they do not lend themselves easily to reward estimation. Accordingly, in this chapter we shall restrict ourselves to a chart-based approach to risk and reward estimation. The patterns outlined by Edwards and Magee[1] form the basis for our discussion. The measuring objectives and risk estimates for each pattern are based on the authors' premise that the market "goes right on repeating the same old movements in much the same old routine."[2] While the measuring objectives are good guides and have solid historical foundations to back them, they are by no means infallible. The actual reward may under- or overshoot the expected target.

With this qualifier, we begin an analysis of the most commonly observed reversal and continuation (or consolidation) patterns, illustrating how risk and reward can be estimated in each case. First, we will cover four major reversal patterns:

1. Head-and-shoulders formation
2. Double or triple tops and bottoms
3. Saucers or rounded tops and bottoms
4. V-formations, spikes, and island tops and bottoms

[1] Robert D. Edwards and John Magee, *Technical Analysis of Stock Trends,* 5th ed. (Boston: John Magee Inc., 1981).
[2] Edwards and Magee, *Technical Analysis* p. 1.

Next, we will focus on the three most commonly observed continuation or consolidation patterns:

1. Symmetrical and right-angle triangles
2. Wedges
3. Flags

HEAD-AND-SHOULDERS FORMATION

Perhaps the most reliable of all reversal patterns, this formation can occur either as a head-and-shoulders top, signifying a market top, or as an inverted head-and-shoulders, signifying a market bottom. We shall concentrate on a head-and-shoulders top formation, with the understanding that the principles regarding risk and reward estimation are equally applicable to a head-and-shoulders bottom.

A theoretical head-and-shoulders top formation is described in Figure 3.1. The first clue of weakness in the uptrend is provided by prices reversing at 1 from their previous highs to form a left shoulder. A second rally at 2 causes prices to surpass their earlier highs established at 1, forming a head at 3. Ideally, the volume on the second rally to the head should be lower than the volume on the first rally to the left shoulder. A reaction from this rally takes prices lower, to a level near 2, but in any event to a level below the top of the left shoulder at 1. This is denoted by 4.

A third rally ensues, on decidedly lower volume than that accompanying the preceding two rallies, which helped form the left shoulder and the head. This rally fails to reach the height of the head before yet another pullback occurs, setting off a right shoulder formation. If the third rally takes prices above the head at 3, we have what is known as a broadening top formation rather than a head-and-shoulders reversal. Therefore, a chartist ought not to assume that a head-and-shoulders formation is in place simply because he observes what appears to be a left shoulder and a head. This is particularly important, since broadening top formations do not typically obey the same measuring objectives as do head-and-shoulders reversals.

Minimum Measuring Objective

If the third rally fizzles out before reaching the head, and if prices on the third pullback close below an imaginary line connecting points

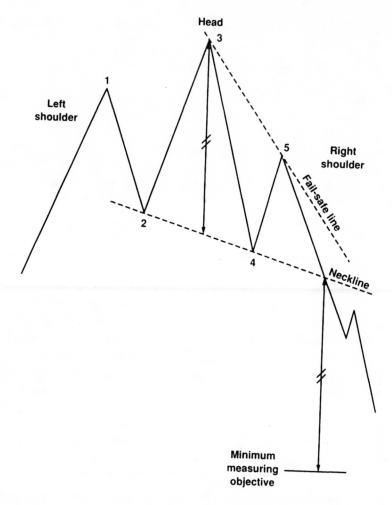

Figure 3.1   Theoretical head-and-shoulders pattern.

2 and 4, known as the "neckline," on heavy volume and increasing open interest, a head-and-shoulders top is in place. If prices close below the neckline, they can be expected to fall from the point of penetration by a distance equal to that from the head to the neckline. This is a minimum measuring objective.

While it is possible that prices might continue to head downward, it is equally likely that a pullback might occur once the minimum measuring objective has been met. Accordingly, at this point the trader might want to lighten the position if he or she is trading multiple contracts.

Estimated Risk

The trend line connecting the head and the right shoulder is called a "fail-safe line." Depending on the shape of the formation, either the neckline or the fail-safe line could be farther from the entry point. A protective stop-loss order should be placed just beyond the farther of the two trendlines, allowing for a minor retracement of prices without getting needlessly stopped out.

Two Examples of Head-and-Shoulders Formations

Figure 3.2a gives an example of a head-and-shoulders bottom formation in July 1991 silver. Here we have a downward-sloping neckline, with the distance from the head to the neckline approximately equal to 60 cents. Measured from a breakout at 418 cents, this gives a minimum measuring objective of 478 cents. The fail-safe line (termed fail-safe line 1 in Figure 3.2a) connecting the bottom of the head and the right shoulder (right shoulder 1) recommends a sell-stop at 399 cents. At the breakout of 418 cents, we have the possibility of earning 60 cents while assuming a 19-cent risk. This yields a reward/risk ratio of 3.16. The breakout does occur on April 18, but the trader is promptly stopped out the same day on a slump to 398 cents.

After the sharp plunge on April 18, prices stabilize around 390 cents, forming yet another right shoulder (right shoulder 2) between April 19 and May 6. Extending the earlier neckline, we have a new breakout point of 412 cents. The new fail-safe line (termed fail-safe line 2 in Figure 3.2a) recommends setting a sell-stop of 397 cents. At the breakout of 412 cents, we now have the possibility of earning 60 cents while assuming a 15-cent risk, for a reward/risk ratio of 4.00. In subsequent action, July silver rallies to 464 cents on July 7, almost meeting the target of the head-and-shoulders bottom.

In Figure 3.2b, we have an example, in the September 1991 S&P 500 Index futures, of a possible head-and-shoulders top formation that did not unfold as expected. The head was formed on April 17 at 396.20,

28

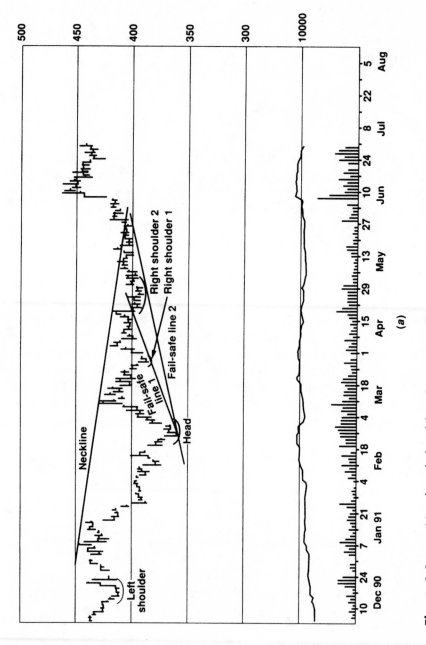

Figure 3.2a   Head-and-shoulders formations: (a) bottom in July 1991 silver.

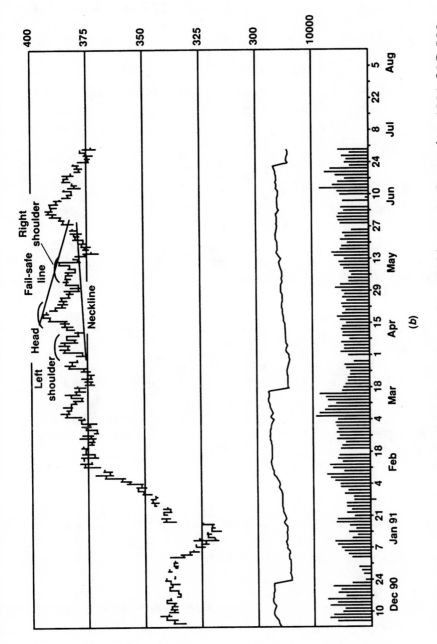

Figure 3.2b Head-and-shoulders formations: (*b*) possible top in September 1991 S&P 500 Index.

29

with a possible left shoulder formed at 387.75 on April 4 and the right shoulder formed on May 9 at 387.80. The head-and-shoulders top was set off on May 14 on a close below the neckline. However, prices broke through the fail-safe line connecting the head and the right shoulder on May 28, stopping out the short trade and negating the hypothesis of a head-and-shoulders top.

DOUBLE TOPS AND BOTTOMS

A double top is formed by a pair of peaks at approximately the same price level. Further, prices must close below the low established between the two tops before a double top formation is activated. The retreat from the first peak to the valley is marked by light volume. Volume picks up on the ascent to the second peak but falls short of the volume accompanying the earlier ascent. Finally, we see a pickup in volume as prices decline for a second time. A double bottom is simply a double top turned upside down, with the foregoing rules, appropriately modified, equally applicable.

As a rule, a double top formation is an indication of bearishness, especially if the right half of the double top is lower than the left half. Similarly, a double bottom formation is bullish, particularly if the right half of the double bottom is higher than the left half. The market unsuccessfully attempted to test the previous peak (trough), signalling bearishness (bullishness).

Minimum Measuring Objective

In the case of a double top, it is reasonable to expect that the decline will continue at least as far below the imaginary support line connecting the two tops as the distance from the higher of the twin peaks to the support line. Therefore, the greater the distance from peak to valley, the greater the potential for the impending reversal. Similarly, in the case of a double bottom, it is safe to assume that the upswing will continue at least as far up from the imaginary resistance line connecting the two bottoms as the height from the lower of the double bottoms to the resistance line. Once this minimum objective has been met, the trader might want to set a tight protective stop to lock in a significant portion of the unrealized profits.

Estimated Risk

The imaginary line drawn as a tangent to the valley connecting two tops serves as a reliable support level. Similarly, the tangent to the peak connecting two bottoms serves as a reliable resistance level. Accordingly, a trader might want to set a stop-loss order just above the support level, in case of a double top, or just below the resistance level, in case of a double bottom. The goal is to avoid falling victim to minor retracements, while at the same time guarding against unanticipated shifts in the underlying trend.

If the closing price of the day that sets off the double top or bottom formation substantially overshoots the hypothetical support or resistance level, the potential reward on the trade might barely exceed the estimated risk. In such a situation, a trader might want to wait for a pullback before initiating the trade, in order to attain a better reward/risk ratio.

Two Examples of a Double Top Formation

Consider the December 1990 soybean oil chart in Figure 3.3. We have a top at 25.46 cents formed on July 2, with yet another top formed on August 23 at 25.55. The valley high on July 23 was 23.39 cents, representing a distance of 2.16 cents from the peak of 25.55 on August 23. This distance of 2.16 cents measured from the valley high of 23.39 cents, represents the minimum measuring objective of 21.23 cents for the double top. The double top is set off on a close below 23.39 cents. This is accomplished on October 1 at 22.99. The buy stop for the trade is set at 23.51, just above the high on that day, for a risk of 0.52 cents.

The difference between the entry price, 22.99 cents, and the target price, 21.23 cents, gives a reward estimate of 1.76 cents for an associated risk of 0.52 cents. A reward/risk ratio of 3.38 suggests that this is a highly desirable trade. After the minimum reward target was met on November 6, prices continued to drift lower to 19.78 cents on November 20, giving the trader a bonus of 1.45 cents.

Although the comments for each pattern discussed here are illustrated with the help of daily price charts, they are equally applicable to weekly charts. Consider, for example, the weekly Standard & Poor's 500 (S&P 500) Index futures presented in Figure 3.4. We observe a double top formation between August 10 and October 5, 1987, labeled A and B in the figure. Notice that the left half of the double top, A, is higher than

32

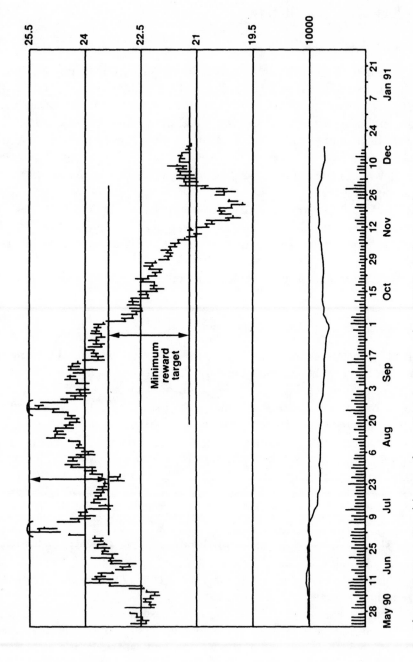

Figure 3.3 Double top formation in December 1990 soybean oil.

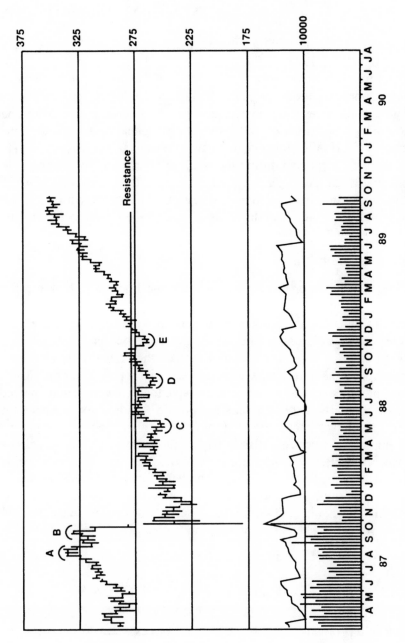

Figure 3.4 Double top and triple bottom formation in weekly S&P 500 Index futures.

33

the right half, B. The failure to test the high of 339.45, achieved by A on August 24, 1987, is the first clue that the market has lost upside momentum. A bearish close for the week of October 5, just below the valley connecting the twin peaks, confirms the double top formation. The minimum measuring objective is given by the distance from peak A to valley, approximately 20 index points. Measured from the entry price of 312.20 on October 5, we have a reward target of 292.20. This objective was surpassed during the week of October 12, when the index closed at 282.25. Accordingly, the buy stop could be lowered to 292.20, locking in the minimum anticipated reward. The meltdown that ensued on October 19, Black Monday, was a major, albeit unexpected, bonus!

Triple Tops and Bottoms

A triple top or bottom works along the same lines as a double top or bottom, the only difference being that we have three tops or bottoms instead of two. The three highs or lows need not be equally spaced, nor are there any specific guidelines as regards the time that ought to elapse between them. Volume is typically lower on the second rally or dip and even lower on the third. Triple tops are particularly powerful as indicators of impending bearishness if each successive top is lower than the preceding top. Similarly, triple bottoms are powerful indicators of impending bullishness if each successive bottom is higher than the preceding one.

In Figure 3.4, we see a classic triple bottom formation developing in the weekly S&P 500 Index futures between May and November 1988, marked C, D, and E. Notice how E is higher than D, and D higher than C, suggesting strength in the stock market. This is substantiated by the speed with which the market rallied from 280 to 360 index points, once the triple bottom was established at E and resistance was surmounted at 280.

SAUCERS AND ROUNDED TOPS AND BOTTOMS

A saucer top or bottom is formed when prices seem to be stuck in a very narrow trading range over an extended period of time. Volume should gradually ebb to an extreme low at the peak of a saucer top or at the trough of a saucer bottom if the pattern is to be trusted. As the market seems to lack direction, a prudent trader would do well to stand aside. As soon as a breakout occurs, the trader might want to enter a position. Saucers are not too commonly observed. Moreover, they are difficult to trade, because they develop at an agonizingly slow pace over an extended period of time.

Minimum Measuring Objective and Permissible Risk

There are no precise measuring objectives for saucer tops and bottoms. However, clues may be found in the size of the previous trend and in the magnitude of retracement from previous support and resistance levels. The length of time over which the saucer develops is also important. Typically, the longer it takes to complete the rounding process, the more significant the subsequent move is likely to be. The risk for the trade is evaluated by measuring the distance between the entry price and the stop-loss price, set just below (above) the saucer bottom (top).

An Example of a Saucer Bottom

Consider the October 1991 sugar futures chart in Figure 3.5. We have a saucer bottom developing between the beginning of April and the first week of June 1991, as prices hover around 7.50 cents. The breakout past 8.00 cents finally occurs in mid-June, at which time a long position could be established with a sell stop just below the life of contract lows at 7.45 cents. After two months of lethargic action, a rally finally ignited in early July, with prices testing 9.50 cents.

V-FORMATIONS, SPIKES, AND ISLAND REVERSALS

As the name suggests, a V-formation represents a quick turnaround in the trend from bearish to bullish, just as an inverted V-formation signals a sharp reversal in the trend from bullish to bearish. As Figure 3.6 illustrates, a V-formation could be sharply defined as a spike, as in Figure 3.6a, or as an island reversal, as in Figure 3.6b. Alternatively, the formation may not be so sharply defined, taking time to develop over a number of trading sessions, as in Figure 3.6c.

The chief prerequisite for a V-formation is that the trend preceding it is very steep with few corrections along the way. The turn is characterized by a reversal day, a key reversal day, or an island reversal day on very heavy volume, as the V-formation causes prices to break through

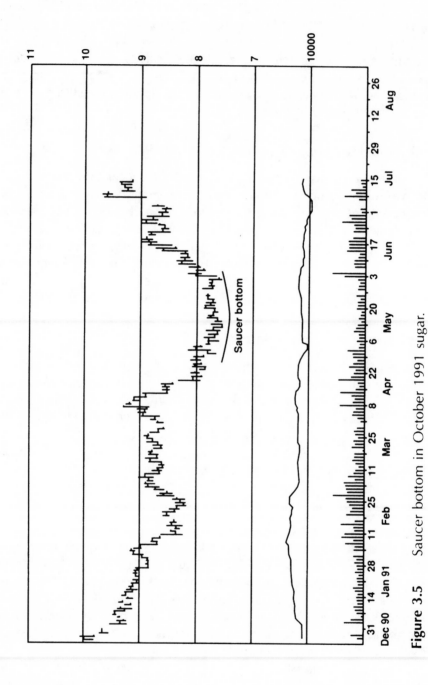

Figure 3.5 Saucer bottom in October 1991 sugar.

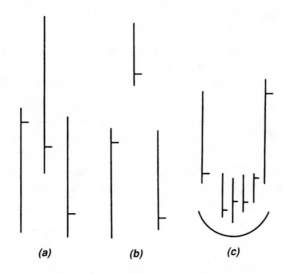

Figure 3.6   Theoretical V-formations and island reversals: (a) spike formation; (b) island reversal; (c) gradual V-formation.

a steep trendline. A reversal day downward is defined as a day when prices reach new highs, only to settle lower than the previous day. Similarly, a reversal day upward is one where prices touch new lows, only to settle higher than the previous day. A key reversal day is one where prices establish new life-of-contract highs (lows), only to settle lower (or higher) than the previous day.

An island reversal, as is evident from Figure 3.6b, is so called because it is flanked by two gaps: an exhaustion gap to its left and a breakaway gap to its right. A gap occurs when there is no overlap in prices from one trading session to the next.

Minimum Measuring Objective

The measuring objective for V-formations may be defined by reference to the previous trend. At a minimum, a V-formation should retrace anywhere between 38 percent and 62 percent of the move preceding the formation, with 50 percent commonly used as a minimum reward target. Once the minimum target is accomplished, it is quite likely that a congestion pattern will develop as traders begin to realize their profits.

Estimated Risk

In the case of a spike or a gradual V-formation, a reasonable place to set a protective stop would be just below the V-formation, for the start of an uptrend, or just above the inverted V-formation, for the start of a downtrend. The logic is that once a peak or trough defined by a V-formation is violated, the pattern no longer serves as a valid reversal signal.

In the case of an island reversal, a reasonable place to set a stop would be just above the low of the island day, in the case of an anticipated downtrend, or just below the high of the island day, in the case of an anticipated uptrend. The rationale is that once prices close the breakaway gap that created the island formation, the pattern is no longer a legitimate island and the trader must look for reversal clues afresh.

Examples of V-formations, Spikes, and Island Reversals

Figure 3.7 gives an example of V-formations in the March 1990 Treasury bond futures contract. A reasonable buy stop would be at 101 for a sell signal triggered by the inverted V-formation in July 1989, labeled A. Similarly, a reasonable sell stop would be just below 95 for the buy signal generated by the gradual V-formation, labeled B. In both cases, the reversal signals given by the V-formations are accurate.

However, if we continue further with the March 1990 Treasury bond chart, we come across another case of a bearish spike at C. A trader who decided to short Treasury bonds at 99-28 on December 15 with a protective buy stop at 100-07 would be stopped out the next day as the market touched 100-10. So much for the infallibility of spike days as reversal patterns! We have yet another bearish spike developing on December 20, denoted by D in the figure. Our trader might want to take yet another stab at shorting Treasury bonds at 100-05 with a buy stop at 100-21. The risk is 16 ticks or $500 a contract—a risk well assumed, as future events would demonstrate.

In Figure 3.8, we have two examples of an island reversal in July 1990 platinum futures. In November 1989, we have an island top. A short position could be initiated on November 27 at $547.1, with a protective stop just above $550.0, the low of the island top. This is denoted by point A in the figure. In January 1990, we have an island bottom, denoted by point B. A trader might want to buy platinum futures

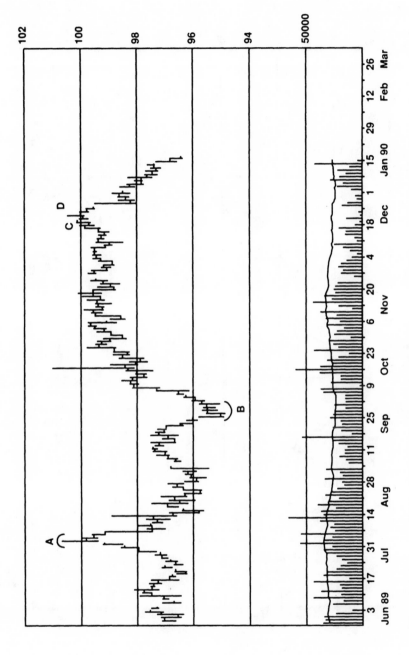

Figure 3.7 V-formation in the March 1990 T-bond futures contract.

39

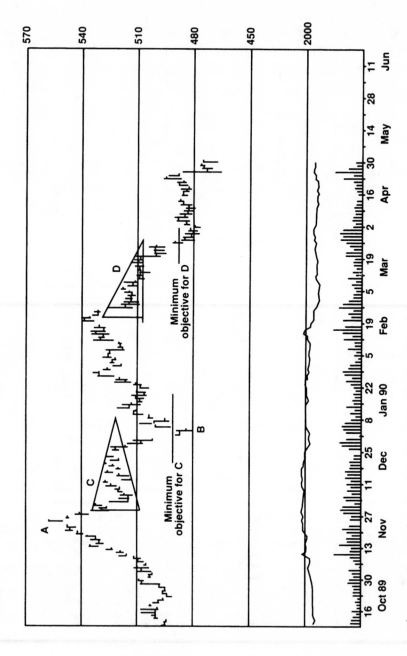

Figure 3.8 Island reversals and triangles in July 1990 platinum.

the following day at $499.9, with a stop just below $489.0, the high of the island reversal day. Notice that the island bottom is formed over a two-day period, disproving the notion that islands must necessarily be formed over a single trading session.

SYMMETRICAL AND RIGHT-ANGLE TRIANGLES

A symmetrical triangle is formed by a series of price reversals, each of which is smaller than its predecessor. For a legitimate symmetrical triangle formation, we need to observe four reversals of the minor trend: two at the top and two at the bottom. Each minor top is lower than the top formed by the preceding rally, and each minor bottom is higher than the preceding bottom. Consequently, we have a downward-sloping trendline connecting the minor tops and an upward-sloping trendline connecting the minor bottoms. The two lines intersect at the apex of the triangle. Owing to its shape, this pattern is also referred to as a "coil." Decreasing volume characterizes the formation of a triangle, as if to affirm that the market is not clear about its future course.

Normally, a triangle represents a continuation pattern. In exceptional circumstances, it could represent a reversal pattern. While a continuation breakout in the direction of the existing trend is most likely, a reversal against the trend is possible. Consequently, avoid outguessing the market by initiating a trade in the direction of the trend until price action confirms a continuation of the trend by penetrating through the boundary line encompassing the triangle. Ideally, such a penetration should occur on heavy volume.

A right-angle triangle is formed when one of the boundary lines connecting the two minor peaks or valleys is flat or almost horizontal, while the other line slants towards it. If the top of the triangle is horizontal and the bottom converges upward to form an apex with the horizontal top, we have an ascending right-angle triangle, suggesting bullishness in the market. If the bottom is horizontal and the top of the triangle slants down to meet it at the apex, the triangle is a descending right-angle triangle, suggesting bearishness in the market.

Right-angle triangles are similar to symmetrical triangles but are simpler to trade, in that they do not keep the trader guessing about their intentions as do symmetrical triangles. Prices can be expected to ascend out of an ascending right-angle triangle, just as they can be expected to descend out of a descending right-angle triangle.

Minimum Measuring Objective

The distance prices may be expected to move once a breakout occurs from a triangle is a function of the size of the triangle pattern. For a symmetrical triangle, the maximum vertical distance between the two converging boundary lines represents the distance prices should move once they break out of the triangle.

The farther out prices drift into the apex of the triangle without bursting through the boundaries, the less powerful the triangle formation. The minimum measuring objective just stated will ensue with the highest probability if prices break out decisively at a point before three-quarters of the horizontal distance from the left-hand corner of the triangle to the apex.

The same measuring rule is applicable in the case of a right-angle triangle. However, an alternative method of arriving at measuring objectives is possible, and perhaps more convenient, in the case of right-angle triangles. Assuming we have an ascending right-angle triangle, draw a line sloping upward parallel to the bottom boundary from the top of the first rally that initiated the pattern. This line slopes upward to the right, forming an upward-sloping parallelogram. At a minimum, prices may be expected to climb until they reach the uppermost corner of the parallelogram.

In the case of a descending right-angle triangle, draw a line parallel to the top boundary from the bottom of the first dip. This line slopes downward to the right, forming a downward-sloping parallelogram. Prices may be expected to drop until they reach the lowermost corner of the parallelogram.

Estimated Risk

A logical place to set a protective stop-loss order would be just above the apex of the triangle for a breakout on the downside. Conversely, for a breakout on the upside, a protective stop-loss order may be set just below the apex of the triangle. The dollar value of the difference between the entry price and the stop price represents the permissible risk per contract.

An Example of a Triangle Formation

In Figure 3.8, we have an example of a symmetrical and a right-angle triangle formation in the July 1990 platinum futures, marked C and D, respectively. In both cases, the breakout is to the downside, and in both cases the minimum measuring objective is attained and surpassed. permissible risk per contract.

WEDGES

A wedge is yet another continuation pattern in which price fluctuations are confined within a pair of converging lines. What distinguishes a wedge from a triangle is that both boundary lines of a wedge slope up or down together, without being strictly parallel. In the case of a triangle, it may be recalled that if one boundary line were upward-sloping, the other would necessarily be flat or downward-sloping.

In the case of a rising wedge, both boundary lines slope upward from left to right, but for the two lines to converge the lower line must necessarily be steeper than the upper line. In the case of a falling wedge, the two boundary lines slant downward from left to right, but the upper boundary line is steeper than the lower line.

A wedge normally takes between two and four weeks to form, during which time volume is gradually diminishing. Typically, a rising wedge is a bearish sign, particularly if it develops in a falling market. Conversely, a falling wedge is bullish, particularly if it develops in a rising market.

Minimum Measuring Objective

Once prices break out of a wedge, the expectation is that, at a minimum, they will retrace the distance to the point that initiated the wedge. In a falling wedge, the up move may be expected to take prices back to at least the uppermost point in the wedge. Similarly, in a rising wedge, the down move may be expected to take out the low point that first started the wedge formation. Care must be taken to ensure that a breakout from a wedge occurs on heavy volume. This is particularly important in the case of a price breakout on the upside out of a falling wedge.

Estimated Risk

In the case of a rising wedge, a logical place to set a stop would be just above the highest point scaled prior to the downside breakout. The rationale is that if prices take out this high point, then the breakout is not genuine. Similarly, in the case of a falling wedge, a logical place to set a stop would be just below the lowest point touched prior to the upside breakout. Once again, if prices take out this point, then the wedge is negated.

An Example of a Wedge

Figure 3.9 gives an example of a rising wedge in a falling September 1991 British pound futures market. The wedge was set off on May 17 when the pound settled at $1.6816. On this date, the pound could have been short-sold with a buy stop just above the high point of the wedge, namely $1.7270, for a risk of $0.0454 per pound. The objective of this move is a retracement to the low of $1.6346 established on April 29. Accordingly, the estimated reward is $0.0470 per pound, representing the difference between the entry price of $1.6816 and the target price of $1.6346. Given a permissible risk of $0.0454 per pound, we have a reward/risk ratio of 1.03.

Notice that the pound did not perform according to script over the next seven trading sessions, coming close to stopping out the trader on May 28, when it touched $1.7230. However, on May 29, the pound resumed its journey downwards, meeting and surpassing the objective of the rising wedge. A trader who had the courage to live through the trying period immediately following the short sale would have been amply rewarded, as the pound went on to make a new low at $1.5896 on June 18.

FLAGS

A flag is a consolidation action whose chart, during an uptrend, has the shape of a flag: a compact parallelogram of price fluctuations, either horizontal or sloping against the trend during the course of an almost vertical move. In a downtrend, the formation is turned upside down. It is almost as though prices are taking a break before resuming their

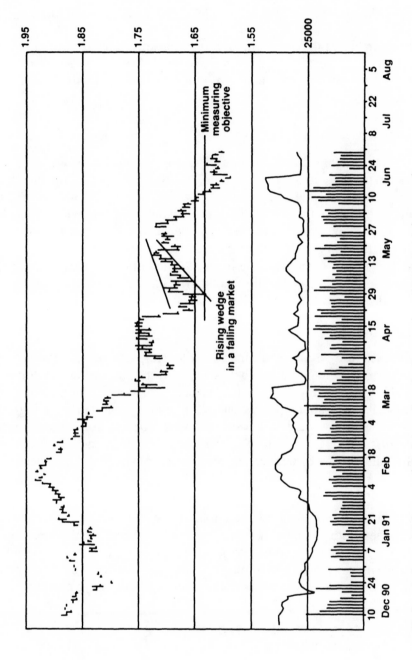

Figure 3.9 Rising wedge formation in September 1991 British pound.

journey. Whereas the flag formation is characterized by low volume, the breakout from the flag is characterized by high volume. Seldom does a flag formation last more than five trading sessions; the trend resumes thereafter.

Minimum Measuring Objective

In order to define the magnitude of the expected move, we need to measure the length of the "flagpole" immediately preceding the flag formation. To do this, we must first go back to the beginning of the immediately preceding move, be it a breakout from a previous consolidation or a reversal pattern. Having measured the distance from this breakout to the point at which the flag started to form, we then measure the same distance from the point at which prices penetrate the flag, moving in the direction of the breakout. This represents the minimum measuring objective for the flag formation.

Estimated Risk

In the case of a flag in a bull market, a logical place to set a protective stop-loss order would be just below the lowest point of the flag formation. If prices were to retrace to this point, then we have a case of a false breakout. Similarly, in the case of a flag in a bear market, a logical place to set a protective stop-loss order would be just above the highest point of the flag formation. The risk for the trade is measured by the dollar value of the difference between the entry and stop-loss prices.

An Example of a Flag Formation

In Figure 3.10, we have two examples of bear flags in the September 1991 wheat futures chart, denoted by A and B. Each of the flags represents a low-risk opportunity to short the market or to add to existing short positions. As is evident, each of the flags was a reliable indicator of the subsequent move, meeting the minimum measuring objective.

REWARD ESTIMATION IN THE ABSENCE OF MEASURING RULES

Determining the maximum permissible risk on a trade is relatively straightforward, inasmuch as chart patterns have a way of signaling

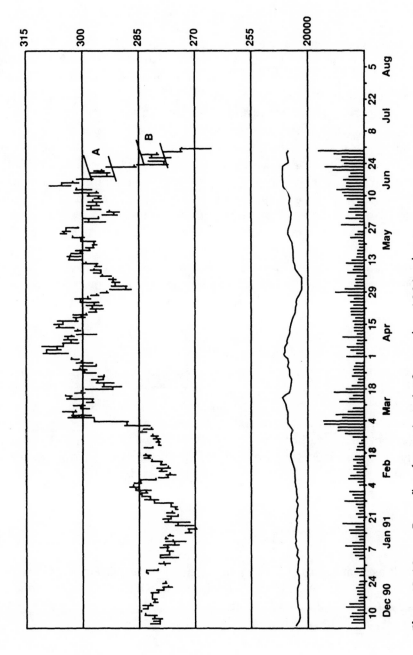

Figure 3.10 Bear flag formations in September 1991 wheat.

47

the most reasonable place to set a stop-loss order. However, we do not always enjoy the same facility in terms of estimating the likely reward on a trade. This is especially true when a commodity is charting virgin territory, making new contract highs or lows. In this case, there is no prior support or resistance level to fall back on as a reference point.

Consider, for example, the February 1990 crude oil futures chart given in Figure 3.11. Notice the resistance around $20 a barrel between October and December 1989. Once prices break through this resistance level and make new contract highs, the trader is left with no means to estimate where prices are headed, primarily because prices are not obeying the dictates of any of the chart patterns discussed above.

One solution is to refer to a longer-term price chart, such as a weekly chart, to study longer-term support or resistance levels. Sometimes even longer-term charts are of little help, as prices touch record highs or record lows. A case in point is cocoa, which in 1991 fell below a 15-year low of $1200 a metric ton, leaving a trader guessing as to how much farther it would fall.

In such a situation, it would be worthwhile to analyze price action in terms of waves and retracements thereof. This information, coupled with Fibonacci ratios, could be used to estimate the magnitude of the subsequent wave. For example, Fibonacci theory says that a 38 percent retracement of an earlier move projects to a continuation wave 1.38 times the magnitude of the earlier move. Similarly, a 62 percent retracement of an earlier wave projects to a new wave 1.62 times the original wave. Prechter[3] provides a more detailed discussion on wave theory.

Revising Risk Estimates

A risk estimate, once established, ought to be respected and never expanded. A trader who expanded the initial stop to accommodate adverse price action would be under no pressure to pull out of a bad trade. This could be a very costly lesson in how not to manage risk!

---

[3] Robert Prechter, *The Elliot Wave Principle*, 5th ed. (Gainesville, GA: New Classics Library, 1985).

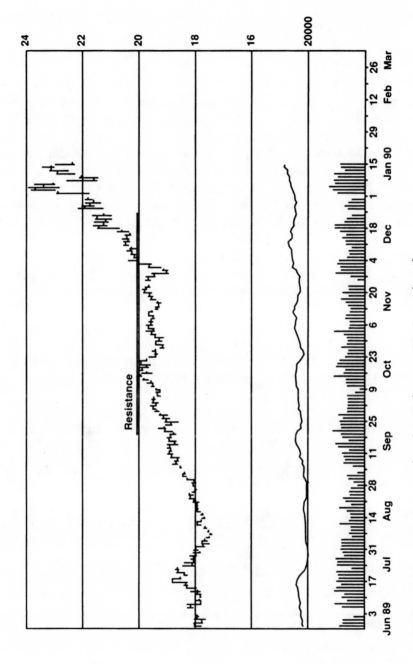

Figure 3.11   Resistance level in February 1990 crude oil.

49

However, the rigidity of the initial risk estimates does not imply that the initial stop-loss price ought never to be moved in response to favorable price movements. On the contrary, if prices move as anticipated, the original stop-loss price should be moved in the direction of the move, locking in all or a part of the unrealized profits. Let us illustrate this with the help of a hypothetical example.

Assume for a moment that gold futures are trading at $400 an ounce. A trader who is bullish on gold anticipates prices will test $415 an ounce in the near future, with a possible correction to $395 on the way up. She figures that she will be wrong if gold futures close below $395 an ounce. Accordingly, she buys a contract of gold futures at $400 an ounce with a sell stop at $395. The estimated reward and risk on this trade are graphically displayed in Figure 3.12.

The estimated reward/risk ratio on the trade works out to be 3:1 to begin with. Assume that subsequent price action confirms the trader's expectations, with a rally to $410. If the earlier stop-loss price of $395 is left untouched, the payoff ratio now works out to be a lopsided 1:3! This is displayed in the adjacent block in Figure 3.12.

Although the initial risk assessment was appropriate when gold was trading at $400 an ounce, it needs updating based on the new price of

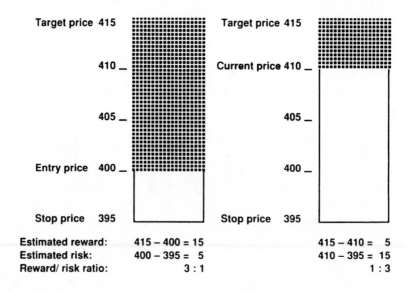

Estimated reward:	415 – 400 = 15	415 – 410 = 5
Estimated risk:	400 – 395 = 5	410 – 395 = 15
Reward/ risk ratio:	3 : 1	1 : 3

Figure 3.12   The dynamic nature of risk and reward.

$410. Regardless of the precise location of the new stop price, it should be higher than the original stop price of $395, locking in a part of the favorable price move. If the scenario of rising gold prices were not to materialize, the trader should have no qualms about liquidating the trade at the predefined stop-loss price of $395. She ought not to move the stop downwards to, say, $390 simply to persist with the trade.

SYNTHESIZING RISK AND REWARD

The objective of estimating reward and risk is to synthesize these two numbers into a ratio of expected reward per unit of risk assumed. The ratio of estimated reward to the permissible loss on a trade is defined as the reward/risk ratio. The higher this ratio, the more attractive the opportunity, disregarding margin considerations.

A reward/risk ratio less than 1 implies that the expected reward is lower than the expected risk, making the risk not worth assuming. Table 3.1 provides a checklist to help a trader assess the desirability of a trade.

Table 3.1   Risk and Reward Estimation Sheet

Commodity/Contract _____ Current Price _____

1.(a) Where is the market headed? What is the probable
　　　price? _____
　(b) Estimated reward:
　　　if long: target price − current price _____
　　　if short: current price − target price _____

2.(a) At what price must I pull out if the market does not go
　　　in the anticipated direction? _____
　(b) Permissible risk:
　　　if long: current price − sell stop price _____
　　　if short: buy stop price − current price _____

3. What is the reward/risk ratio for the trade?
　　　Estimated reward/permissable risk _____

CONCLUSION

Risk and reward estimates are two important ingredients of any trade. As such, it would be shortsighted to neglect either or both of these estimates before plunging into a trade. Risk and reward could be viewed as weights resting on adjacent scales of the same weighing machine. If there is an imbalance and the risk outweighs the reward, the trade is not worth pursuing.

Obsession with the expected reward on a trade to the total exclusion of the permissible risk stems from greed. More often than not this is a road to disaster, as instant riches are more of an exception than the rule. The key to success is to survive, to forge ahead slowly but surely, and to look upon each trade as a small step in a long, at times frustrating, journey.

4

Limiting Risk
through Diversification

In Chapter 2, we observed that reducing exposure, or the proportion of capital risked to trading, was an effective means of reducing the risk of ruin. This chapter stresses diversification as yet another tool for risk reduction.

The concept of diversification is based on the premise that a trader's forecasting skills are fallible. Therefore, it is safer to bet on several dissimilar commodities simultaneously than to bet exclusively on a single commodity. The underlying rationale is that a prudent trader is not interested in maximizing returns per se but in maximizing returns for a given level of risk. This insightful fact was originally pointed out by Harry Markowitz.[1]

The key to trading success is to survive rather than be overwhelmed by the vicissitudes of the markets, even if this entails forgoing the chance of striking it exceedingly rich in a hurry. In addition to providing for dips in equity during the life of a trade, a trader also should be able to withstand a string of losses across a series of successive bad trades. There might be a temptation to shrug this away as a remote possibility. However, a trader who equates a remote possibility with a zero probability is unprepared both financially and emotionally to deal with this contingency should it arise.

[1] Harry Markowitz, *Portfolio Selection: Efficient Diversification of Investments* (New York: John Wiley, 1959).

When a trading system starts generating a series of bad signals, the typical response is to abandon the system in favor of another system. In the extreme case, the trader might want to give up on trading in general, if the losses suffered have cut deeply into available trading capital. It would be much wiser to recognize up front that the best trading systems will generate losing trades from time to time and to provide accordingly for the worst-case scenario. Here is where diversification can help.

Let us, for purposes of illustration, consider the hypothetical trading results for a commodity over a one-year period, shown in Table 4.1. Here we have a reasonably good trading system, given that the dollar

Table 4.1   Results for a Commodity across 20 Trades

Trade #	Change in Equity Profit (+)/Loss (−)	Cum. Value of Losing Trades
1	−500	−500
2	−300	−800
3	−100	−900
4	+200	
5	+300	
6	+1000	
7	−600	−600
8	−500	−1100
9	−300	−1400
10	−400	−1800
11	+200	
12	+2000	
13	−200	−200
14	+500	
15	−500	−500
16	+1000	
17	−700	−700
18	+2500	
19	+500	
20	+800	

Summary of Results

	#	$
Winning trades	10	9000
Losing trades	10	4100

value of winning trades ($9000) more than twice outweighs the dollar value of losing trades ($4100). The total number of profitable trades exactly equals the total number of losing trades, leading to a 50 percent probability of success. Nevertheless, there is no denying the fact that the system does suffer from runs of bad trades, and the cumulative effect of these runs is quite substantial. Unless the trader can withstand losses of this magnitude, he is unlikely to survive long enough to reap profits from the system.

A trader might convince himself that the string of losses will be financed by profits already generated by the system. However, this could turn out to be wishful thinking. There is no guarantee that the system will get off to a good start, helping build the requisite profit cushion. This is why it is essential to trade a diversified portfolio.

Assuming that a trader is simultaneously trading a group of unrelated commodities, it is unlikely that all the commodities will go through their lean spells at the same time. On the contrary, it is likely that the losses incurred on one or more of the commodities traded will be offset by profits earned concurrently on the other commodities. This, in a nutshell, is the rationale behind diversification.

In order to understand the concept of diversification, we must understand the risk of trading commodities (a) individually and (b) jointly as a portfolio. In Chapter 3, the risk on a trade was defined as the maximum dollar loss that a trader was willing to sustain on the trade. In this chapter, we define statistical risk in terms of the volatility of returns on futures trades. A logical starting point for the discussion on risk is a clear understanding of how returns are calculated on futures trades.

MEASURING THE RETURN ON A FUTURES TRADE

Returns could be categorized as either (a) realized returns on completed trades or (b) anticipated returns on trades to be initiated. Realized returns are also termed historical returns, just as anticipated returns are commonly referred to as expected returns. In this section, we discuss the derivation of both historical and expected returns.

Measuring Historical Returns

The historical or realized return on a futures trade is arrived at by summing the present value of all cash flows on a trade and dividing this sum by the initial margin investment. This ratio gives the return over the life of the trade, also known as the holding period return.

Technically, the cash flows on a futures trade would have to be computed on a daily basis, since prices are marked to market each day, and the difference, either positive or negative, is adjusted against the trader's account balance. If the equity on the trade falls below the maintenance margin level, the trader is required to deposit additional monies to bring the equity back to the initial margin level. This is known as a variation margin call. If the trade registers an unrealized profit, the trader is free to withdraw these profits or to use them for another trade.

However, in the interests of simplification, we assume that unrealized profits are inaccessible to the trader until the trade is liquidated. Therefore, the pertinent cash flows are the following:

1. The initial margin investment
2. Variation margin calls, if any, during the life of the trade
3. The profit or loss realized on the trade, given by the difference between the entry and liquidation prices
4. The release of initial and variation margins on trade liquidation

The initial margin represents a cash outflow on inception of the trade. Whereas cash flows (3) and (4) arise on liquidation of the trade, cash flow (2) can occur at any time during the life of the trade.

Since there is a mismatch in the timing of the various cash flows, we need to discount all cash flows back to the trade initiation date. Discounting future cash flows at a prespecified discount rate, i, gives the present value of these cash flows. The discount rate, i, is the opportunity cost of capital and is equal to the trader's cost of borrowing less any interest earned on idle funds in the account.

Care should be taken to align the rate, i, with the length of the trading interval. If the trading interval is measured in days, then i should be expressed as a rate per day. If the trading interval is measured in weeks, then i should be expressed as a rate per week.

The rate of return, r, for a purchase or a long trade initiated at time t and liquidated at time l, with an intervening variation margin call at time v, is calculated as follows:

$$r = \frac{-IM - \dfrac{VM}{(1+i)^{v-t}} + \dfrac{(P_l - P_t)}{(1+i)^{l-t}} + \dfrac{(IM + VM)}{(1+i)^{l-t}}}{IM}$$

where IM = the initial margin requirement per contract

   VM = the variation margin called upon at time v

   P_t = the dollar equivalent of the entry price

   P_l = the dollar equivalent of the liquidation price

All cash flows are calculated on a per-contract basis. Using the foregoing notation, the rate of return, r, for a short sale initiated at time t and liquidated at time l is given as follows:

$$r = \frac{-IM - \dfrac{VM}{(1 + i)^{v-t}} - \dfrac{(P_l - P_t)}{(1 + i)^{l-t}} + \dfrac{(IM + VM)}{(1 + i)^{l-t}}}{IM}$$

For a profitable long trade, the liquidation price, P_l, would be greater than the entry price, P_t. Conversely, for a profitable short trade, the liquidation price, P_l, would be lower than the entry price, P_t. Hence we have a positive sign for the price difference term for a long trade and a negative sign for the same term for a short trade. The variation margin is a cash outflow, hence the negative sign up front. This money reverts back to the trader along with the initial margin when the trade is liquidated, representing a cash inflow.

The rate, r, represents the holding period return for $(l - t)$ days. When this is multiplied by $365/(l - t)$, we have an annualized return for the trade. Therefore, the annualized rate of return, R, is

$$R = r \times \frac{365}{l - t}$$

This facilitates comparison across trades of unequal duration.

Suppose a trader has bought a contract of the Deutsche mark at $0.5500 on August 1. The initial margin is $2500. On August 5, she is required to put up a further $1000 as variation margin as the mark drifts lower to $0.5400. On August 15, she liquidates her long position at $0.5600, for a profit of 100 ticks or $1250. Assuming that the annualized interest rate on Treasury bills is 6 percent, we have a daily interest rate, i, of 0.0164 percent or 0.000164. Using this information, the return, r, and the annualized return, R, on the trade works out to be

$$r = \frac{-2500 - \dfrac{1000}{(1.000164)^5} + \dfrac{1250}{(1.000164)^{15}} + \dfrac{3500}{(1.000164)^{15}}}{2500}$$

$$= \frac{-2500 - 999.18 + 1246.93 + 3491.40}{2500}$$

$$= \frac{+1239.15}{2500}$$

$$= 0.4957 \quad \text{or} \quad 49.57\%$$

$$R = 49.57\% \times \frac{365}{15}$$

$$= 1206.10\%$$

Measuring Expected Returns

The expected return on a trade is defined as the expected profit divided by the initial margin investment required to initiate the trade. The expected profit represents the difference between the entry price and the anticipated price on liquidation of the trade. Since there is no guarantee that a particular price forecast will prevail, it is customary to work with a set of alternative price forecasts, assigning a probability weight to each forecast. The weighted sum of the anticipated profits across all price forecasts gives the expected profit on the trade.

The anticipated profit resulting from each price forecast, divided by the required investment, gives the anticipated return on investment for that price forecast. The overall expected return is the summation across all outcomes of the product of (a) the anticipated return for each outcome and (b) the associated probability of occurrence of each outcome.

Assume that a trader is bullish on gold and is considering buying a contract of gold futures at the current price of $385 an ounce. The trader reckons that there is a 0.50 probability that prices will advance to $390 an ounce; a 0.20 probability of prices touching $395 an ounce; and a 0.30 probability that prices will fall to $380 an ounce. The margin for a contract of gold is $2000 a contract. The expected return is calculated in Table 4.2.

Table 4.2   Expected Return on Long Gold Trade

Probability	Price	Profit ($/contract)	Return	Probability × Return
0.30	380	−500	−0.25	−0.075
0.50	390	+500	+0.25	+0.125
0.20	395	+1000	+0.50	+0.100
	Overall Expected Return =			+0.150
				or 15%

MEASURING RISK ON INDIVIDUAL COMMODITIES

Statistical risk is measured in terms of the variability of either (a) historic returns realized on completed trades or (b) expected returns on trades to be initiated—the profit in respect of which is merely anticipated, not realized. Whereas the risk on completed trades is measured in terms of the volatility of historic returns, the projected risk on a trade not yet initiated is measured in terms of the volatility of expected returns.

Measuring the Volatility of Historic Returns

The volatility or variance of historic returns is given by the sum of the squared deviations of completed trade returns around the arithmetic mean or average return, divided by the total number of trades in the sample less 1. Therefore, the formula for the variance of historic returns is

$$\text{Variance of historic returns} \; = \; \frac{\sum_{i=1}^{n}(\text{Return}_i - \text{Mean return})^2}{n-1}$$

where n is the number of trades in the sample period.

The historic return on a trade is calculated according to the foregoing formula. The mean return is defined as the sum of the returns across all trades over the sample period, divided by the number of trades, n, considered in the sample.

The greater the volatility of returns about the mean or average return, the riskier the trade, as a trader can never be quite sure of the ultimate outcome. The lower the volatility of returns, the smaller the dispersion of returns around the arithmetic mean or average return, reducing the degree of risk.

To illustrate the concept of risk, Table 4.3 gives details of the historic returns earned on 10 completed trades for two commodities, gold (X) and silver (Y).

Whereas the average return for gold is slightly higher than that for silver, there is a much greater dispersion around the mean return in case of gold, leading to a much higher level of variance. Therefore, investing in gold is riskier than investing in silver.

The period over which historical volatility is to be calculated depends upon the number of trades generated by a given trading system. As a general rule, it would be desirable to work with at least 30 returns. The length of the sample period needs to be adjusted accordingly.

Measuring the Volatility of Expected Returns

This measure of risk is used for calculating the dispersion of anticipated returns on trades not yet initiated. The variance of expected returns is defined as the summation across all possible outcomes of the product of the following:

1. The squared deviations of individual anticipated returns around the overall expected return
2. The probability of occurrence of each outcome

The formula for the variance of expected returns is therefore:

$$\text{Variance of expected returns} = \sum_{i=1}^{n} \left(\text{Anticipated return}_i - \text{Overall expected return} \right)^2 \times \text{Prob}_i$$

Continuing with our earlier example of the expected return on gold, the variance of such expected returns may be calculated as shown in Table 4.4.

The variance of expected returns works out to be 7.75%. Since assigning probabilities to forecasts of alternative price outcomes is difficult, calculating the variance of expected returns can be cumbersome. In order to simplify computations, the variance of historic returns is often used as a proxy for the variance of expected returns. The assumption is that expected returns will follow a variance pattern identical to that observed over a sample of historic returns.

Table 4.3   Historic Returns on 10 Trades in Gold (X) and Silver (Y)

X_i	$(X_i - \bar{X})$	$(X_i - \bar{X})^2$	Y_i	$(Y_i - \bar{Y})$	$(Y_i - \bar{Y})^2$	$(X_i - \bar{X}) \times (Y_i - \bar{Y})$
250	222	49,284	125	100	10,000	22,200
50	22	484	75	50	2,500	1,100
-150	-178	31,684	-100	-125	15,625	22,250
-50	-78	6,084	-25	-50	2,500	3,900
100	72	5,184	100	75	5,625	5,400
175	147	21,609	90	65	4,225	9,555
-100	-128	16,384	-50	-75	5,625	9,600
0	-28	784	20	-5	25	140
50	22	484	40	15	225	330
-45	-73	5,329	-25	-50	2,500	3,650
$\sum = 280$		$\sum = 137,310$	$\sum = 250$		$\sum = 48,850$	$\sum = 78,125$
$\bar{X} = 28$		$Var_X = 15256.67$	$\bar{Y} = 25$		$Var_Y = 5247.78$	$Cov_{XY} = 8680.55$

Table 4.4   Variance of Expected Return on Long Gold Trade

Probability	Return	Return − Expected Return	(Return − Expected Return)^2 × Probability
0.30	−0.25	−0.40	0.0480
0.50	+0.25	+0.10	0.0050
0.20	+0.50	+0.35	0.0245

Variance = 0.0775 or 7.75%

MEASURING RISK ACROSS COMMODITIES TRADED JOINTLY: THE CONCEPT OF CORRELATION BETWEEN COMMODITIES

The risk of trading two commodities jointly is given by the covariance of their returns. As the name suggests, the covariance between two variables measures their joint variability. Referring to the example of gold and silver given in Table 4.3, we observe that an increase in the return on gold is matched by an increase in the return on silver and vice versa. This leads to a positive covariance term between these two commodities.

The covariance between returns on gold and silver is measured as the sum of the product of their joint excess returns over their mean returns divided by the number of trades in the sample less 1. The formula for the covariance between the historic returns on X and Y is given as

Covariance between the historic returns X_i and Y_i on commodities X and Y

$$= \frac{\sum_{i=1}^{n}\left(\text{Return } X_i - \frac{\text{Mean return}}{\text{on } X}\right)\left(\text{Return } Y_i - \frac{\text{Mean return}}{\text{on } Y}\right)}{n-1}$$

where n is the number of trades in the sample period.

The formula for the covariance between the expected returns on X and Y is similar to that for the covariance across historic returns. The exception is that each of the i observations is assigned a weight equal to its individual probability of occurrence, P_i. Therefore, the formula for the covariance between the expected returns on X and Y reads as follows:

Covariance between the expected returns X_i and Y_i on commodities X and Y

$$= \sum_{i=1}^{n} \left(\text{Return } X_i - \begin{array}{c} \text{Exp. Return} \\ \text{on } X \end{array} \right) \left(\text{Return } Y_i - \begin{array}{c} \text{Exp. Return} \\ \text{on } Y \end{array} \right) (P_i)$$

If there are two commodities under review, there is one covariance between the returns on them. If there are three commodities, X, Y, and Z, under review, there are three covariances to contend with: one between X and Y, the second between X and Z, and the third between Y and Z. If there are four commodities under review, there are six distinct covariances between the returns on them. In general, if there are K commodities under review, there are $[K(K-1)]/2$ distinct covariance terms between the returns on them.

In the foregoing example, the covariance between the returns on gold and silver works out to be 8680.55, suggesting a high degree of positive correlation between the two commodities. The correlation coefficient between two variables is calculated by dividing the covariance between them by the product of their individual standard deviations. The standard deviation of returns is the square root of the variance. The correlation coefficient assumes a value between $+1$ and -1. In the above example of gold and silver, the correlation works out to be $+0.95$, as shown as follows:

$$\begin{array}{c} \text{Correlation betwen} \\ \text{gold and silver} \end{array} = \frac{\text{Covariance between returns on gold and silver}}{(\text{Std. dev. gold})(\text{Std. dev. silver})}$$

$$= \frac{8680.55}{123.52 \times 73.67}$$

$$= +0.95$$

Two commodities are said to exhibit perfect positive correlation if a change in the return of one is accompanied by an equal and similar change in the return of the other. Two commodities are said to exhibit perfect negative correlation if a change in the return of one is accompanied by an equal and opposite change in the return of the other. Finally, two commodities are said to exhibit zero correlation if the return of one

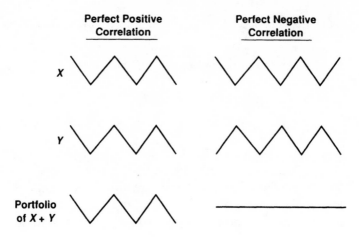

Figure 4.1   Positive and negative correlations.

is unaffected by a change in the other's return. The concept of correlation is graphically illustrated in Figure 4.1.

In actual practice, examples of perfectly positively or negatively correlated commodities are rarely found. Ideally, the degree of association between two commodities is measured in terms of the correlation between their returns. For ease of exposition, however, it is assumed that prices parallel returns and that correlations based on prices serve as a good proxy for correlations based on returns.

WHY DIVERSIFICATION WORKS

Diversification is worthwhile only if (a) the expected returns associated with diversification are comparable to the expected returns associated with the strategy of concentrating resources in one commodity and (b) the total risk of investing in two or more commodities is less than the risk associated with investing in any single commodity. Both these conditions are best satisfied when there is perfect negative correlation between the returns on two commodities. However, diversification will work even if there is less than perfect negative correlation between two commodities.

The returns associated with the strategy of concentrating all resources in a single commodity could be higher than the returns associated with diversification, especially if prices unfold as anticipated. However, the risk or variability of such returns is much greater, given the higher probability of error in forecasting the movement of a single commodity. Given the lower variability of returns of a diversified portfolio, it makes sense to trade a diversified portfolio, especially if the expected return in trading a single commodity is no greater than the expected return from trading a diversified portfolio.

We can illustrate this idea by means of a simple example involving two perfectly negatively correlated commodities, X and Y. The distribution of expected returns is given in Table 4.5. Consider an investor who wishes to trade a futures contract of one or both of these commodities. If he invests his entire capital in either X or Y, he has a 0.50 chance of losing 50 percent and a 0.50 chance of making 100 percent. This results in an expected return of 25 percent and a variance of 5625 for both X and Y individually.

What will our investor earn, should he decide to split his investment equally between both X and Y? The probability of earning any given return jointly on X and Y is the product of the individual probabilities of achieving this return. For example, the joint probability that the return on both X and Y will be −50 percent is the product of the probabilities of achieving this return separately for X and Y. This is the product of 0.50 for X and 0.50 for Y, or 0.25. Similarly, there is a 0.25 chance of making +100 percent on both X and Y simultaneously. Moreover, there

Table 4.5   Expected Returns on Perfectly Negatively Correlated Commodities

	X			Y	
Return	Probability	Prob. × Return	Return	Probability	Prob. × Return
(%)		(%)	(%)		(%)
−50	.50	−25	+100	.50	+50
+25	0	0	25	0	0
+100	.50	+50	−50	.50	−25
Overall Expected Return	for X = 25%			for Y = 25%	
Variance of Exp. Returns	for X = 5625			for Y = 5625	

is a 0.25 chance that X will lose 50 percent and Y will earn 100 percent, and another 0.25 chance that X will make 100 percent and Y will lose 50 percent. In both these cases, the expected return works out to be 25 percent, as

$$.50 \times (-50\%) + .50 \times (+100\%) = 25\%$$

Therefore, the probability of earning 25 percent on the portfolio of X and Y is the sum of the individual probabilities of the two mutually exclusive alternatives resulting in this outcome, namely $0.25 + 0.25$, or 0.50.

Using this information, we come up with the probability distribution of returns for a portfolio which includes X and Y in equal proportions. The results are outlined in Table 4.6. Notice that the expected return of the portfolio of X and Y at 25 percent is the same as the expected return on either X or Y separately. However, the variance of the portfolio at 2812.5 is one-half of the earlier variance. The creation of the portfolio reduces the variability or dispersion of joint returns, primarily by reducing the probability of large losses and large gains. Assuming that our investor is risk-averse, he is happier as the variance of returns is reduced for a given level of expected return.

In the foregoing example, we have shown how diversification can help an investor when the returns on two commodities are perfectly negatively correlated. In practice, it is difficult to find perfectly negatively correlated returns. However, as long as the return distributions on two commodities are even mildly negatively correlated, the trader could stand to gain from the risk reduction properties of diversification. For

Table 4.6   Joint Returns on a
Portfolio of 50% X and 50% Y

Return	Probability	Probability × Return
(%)		(%)
−50	.25	−12.5
+25	.50	+12.5
+100	.25	+25

Overall Expected Return for the Portfolio =   25%
Variance of the portfolio = 2812.5

example, a portfolio comprising a long position in each of the negatively correlated crude oil and U.S. Treasury bonds is less risky than a long position in two contracts of either crude oil or Treasury bonds.

AGGREGATION: THE FLIP SIDE TO DIVERSIFICATION

If a trader were to assume similar positions (either long or short) concurrently in two positively correlated commodities, the resulting portfolio risk would outweigh the risk of trading each commodity separately. Trading the same side of two or more positively correlated commodities concurrently is known as aggregation. Just as diversification helps reduce portfolio risk, aggregation increases it. An example would help to clarify this.

Given the high positive correlation between Deutsche marks and Swiss francs, a portfolio comprising a long position in both the Deutsche mark and the Swiss franc is more risky than investing in either the Deutsche mark or the Swiss franc exclusively. If the trader's forecast is proved wrong, he or she will be wrong on both the mark and the franc, suffering a loss on both long positions.

The first step to limiting the risk associated with concurrent exposure to positively correlated commodities is to categorize commodities according to the degree of correlation between them. This is done in Appendix C. Next, the trader must devise a set of rules which will prevent him or her from trading the same side of two or more positively correlated commodities simultaneously.

CHECKING FOR SIGNIFICANT CORRELATIONS ACROSS COMMODITIES

Appendix C gives information on price correlations between pairs of 24 commodities between July 1983 and June 1988. Correlations have been worked out using the Dunn & Hargitt commodity futures prices database. The correlations are arranged commodity by commodity in descending order, beginning with the highest number and working down to the lowest number. For example, in the case of the S&P 500 stock index futures, correlations begin with a high of 0.999 (with the NYSE index) and gradually work their way down to a low of −0.862 (with corn).

As a rule of thumb, it is recommended that all commodity pairs with correlations that are (a) in excess of +0.80 or less than −0.80 and (b) statistically significant be classified as highly correlated commodities.

Checking the Statistical Significance of Correlations

The most common test of significance checks whether a sample correlation coefficient could have come from a population with a correlation coefficient of 0. The null hypothesis, H_0, posits that the correlation coefficient, C, is 0. The alternative hypothesis, H_1, says that the population correlation coefficient is significantly different from 0. Since H_1 simply says that the correlation is significantly different from 0 without saying anything about the direction of the correlation, we use a two-tailed test of rejection of the null hypothesis. The null hypothesis is tested as a t-test with $(n - 2)$ degrees of freedom, where n is the number of paired observations in the sample. Ideally, we would like to see at least 32 paired observations in our sample to ensure validity of the results. The value of t is defined as follows:

$$t = \frac{C}{\sqrt{(1 - C^2)/(n - 2)}}$$

The value of t thus calculated is compared with the theoretical or tabulated value of t at a prespecified level of significance, typically 1 percent or 5 percent. A 1 percent level of significance implies that the theoretical t value encompasses 99 percent of the distribution under the bell-shaped curve. The theoretical or tabulated t value at a 1 percent level of significance for a two-tailed test with 250 degrees of freedom is ±2.58. Similarly, a 5 percent level of significance implies that the theoretical t value encompasses 95 percent of the distribution under the bell-shaped curve. The corresponding tabulated t value at a 5 percent level of significance for a two-tailed test with 250 degrees of freedom is ±1.96.

If the calculated t value lies beyond the theoretical or tabulated value, there is reason to believe that the correlation is nonzero. Therefore, if the calculated t value exceeds +2.58 (+1.96), or falls below −2.58 (−1.96), the null hypothesis of zero correlation is rejected at the 1 percent (5 percent) level. However, if the calculated value falls between

± 2.58 (± 1.96), the null hypothesis of zero correlation cannot be rejected at the 1 percent (5 percent) level.

Continuing with our gold-silver example, the correlation between the two was found to be +0.95 across 10 sample returns. Is this statistically significant at a 1 percent level of significance? Using the foregoing formula,

$$t = \frac{0.95}{\sqrt{(1 - 0.9025)/(10 - 2)}} = 8.605$$

With eight degrees of freedom, the theoretical or table value of t at a 1 percent level of significance is 3.355. Since the calculated t value is well in excess of 3.355, we can conclude that our sample correlation between gold and silver is significantly different from zero.

In some cases the correlation numbers are meaningful and can be justified. For example, any change in stock prices is likely to have its impact felt equally on both the S&P 500 and the New York Stock Exchange (NYSE) futures index. Similarly, the Deutsche mark and the Swiss franc are likely to be evenly affected by any news influencing the foreign exchange markets.

However, some of the correlations are not meaningful, and too much weight should not be attached to them, notwithstanding the fact that they have a correlation in excess of 0.80 and the correlation is statistically significant. If two seemingly unrelated commodities have been trending in the same direction over any length of time, we would have a case of positively correlated commodities. Similarly, if two unrelated commodities have been trending in opposite directions for a long time, we would have a case of negative correlation. This is where statistics could be misleading. In the following section, we outline a procedure to guard against spurious correlations.

A NONSTATISTICAL TEST OF SIGNIFICANCE OF CORRELATIONS

A good way of judging whether a correlation is genuine or otherwise is to rework the correlations over smaller subsample periods. For example, the period 1983–1988 may be broken down into subperiods, such as 1983–84, 1985–86, and 1987–88, and correlations obtained for each of these subperiods, to check for consistency of the results. Appendix C presents correlations over each of the three subperiods.

If the numbers are fairly consistent over each of the subperiods, we can conclude that the correlations are genuine. Alternatively, if the numbers differ substantially over time, we have reason to doubt the results. This process is likely to filter away any chance relationships, because there is little likelihood of a chance relationship persisting with a high correlation score across time.

Table 4.7 illustrates this by first reporting all positive correlations in excess of +0.80 for the entire 1983–88 period and then reporting the corresponding numbers for the 1983–84, 1985–86, and 1987–88 subperiods.

Table 4.7 reveals the tenuous nature of some of the correlations. For example, the correlation between soybean oil and Kansas wheat is 0.876 between 1987 and 1988, whereas it is only 0.410 between 1983 and 1984. Similarly, the correlation between corn and crude oil ranges from a low of −0.423 in 1987–88 to a high of 0.735 between 1983 and 1984. Perhaps more revealing is the correlation between the S&P 500 and the Japanese yen, ranging from a low of −0.644 to a high of 0.949! Obviously it would not make sense to attach too much significance to high positive or negative correlation numbers in any one period, unless the strength of the correlations persists across time.

If the high correlations do not persist over time, these commodities ought not to be thought of as being interrelated for purposes of diversification. Therefore, a trader should not have any qualms about buying (or selling) corn and crude oil simultaneously. Only those commodities that display a consistently high degree of positive correlation should be treated as being alike and ought not to be bought (or sold) simultaneously.

MATRIX FOR TRADING RELATED COMMODITIES

The matrix in Figure 4.2 summarizes graphically the impact of holding positions concurrently in two or more related commodities. If two commodities are positively correlated and a trader were to hold similar positions (either long or short) in each of them concurrently, the resulting aggregation would result in the creation of a high-risk portfolio.

Table 4.7 Positive Correlations in
Excess of 0.80 during 1983–88 Period

	Correlation between commodities			
Commodity pair	1983–88	1983–84	1985–86	1987–88
S&P 500/NYSE indices	0.999	0.991	1.000	0.997
D. Mark/Swiss Franc	0.998	0.966	0.997	0.991
T-Bonds/T-Notes	0.996	0.996	0.993	0.996
Eurodollar/T-Bills	0.989	0.976	0.995	0.909
D. Mark/Yen	0.983	0.642	0.981	0.933
Swiss Franc/Yen	0.981	0.613	0.983	0.925
Chgo. Wheat/Kans. Wheat	0.964	0.817	0.954	0.950
T-Bills/T-Notes	0.955	0.879	0.953	0.822
Eurodollar/T-Notes	0.953	0.937	0.946	0.945
T-Bills/T-Bonds	0.942	0.876	0.928	0.842
Eurodollar/T-Bonds	0.937	0.933	0.919	0.948
British Pound/Swiss Franc	0.901	0.973	0.809	0.913
Corn/Kansas Wheat	0.891	0.440	0.825	0.803
British Pound/D. Mark	0.889	0.947	0.800	0.928
Corn/Soybean oil	0.886	0.573	0.871	0.848
Soybean oil/Kansas Wheat	0.868	0.410	0.804	0.876
S&P 500/Yen	0.864	−0.363	0.949	−0.644
S&P 500/D. Mark	0.857	−0.195	0.933	−0.766
Gold/Swiss Franc	0.855	0.916	0.879	0.627
NYSE/Yen	0.855	−0.350	0.945	−0.676
British Pound/Yen	0.854	0.479	0.779	0.974
Gold/British Pound	0.853	0.943	0.565	0.596
NYSE/D. Mark	0.846	−0.170	0.928	−0.796
Corn/Chicago Wheat	0.844	0.426	0.769	0.692
Crude oil/Kansas Wheat	0.843	0.423	0.818	−0.671
Gold/D. Mark	0.841	0.893	0.875	0.561
S&P 500/Swiss Franc	0.840	−0.045	0.922	−0.741
Soybean oil/Chicago Wheat	0.837	0.420	0.727	0.838
NYSE/T-Bonds	0.832	0.748	0.976	0.044
NYSE/Swiss Franc	0.828	−0.022	0.917	−0.776
Corn/Soybeans	0.826	0.925	0.875	0.912
NYSE/T-Notes	0.825	0.733	0.970	0.061
S&P 500/T-Bonds	0.818	0.747	0.975	−0.004
NYSE/T-Bills	0.816	0.533	0.892	−0.257
Soybeans/Soymeal	0.811	0.919	−0.443	0.886
S&P 500/T-Notes	0.811	0.731	0.971	0.010
Corn/Crude oil	0.808	0.735	0.645	−0.423
S&P 500/T-Bills	0.804	0.530	0.894	−0.286

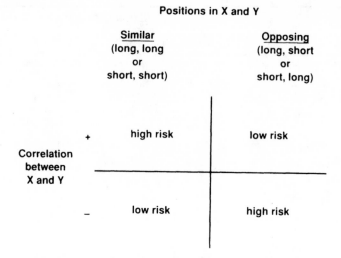

Figure 4.2   Matrix for trading related commodities

Typically, a trend-following system would have us gravitate towards the higher-risk strategies, given the strong correlation between certain commodities. For example, an uptrend in soybeans is likely to be accompanied by an uptrend in soymeal and soybean oil. A trend-following system would recommend the simultaneous purchase of soybeans, soymeal, and soybean oil. This simultaneous purchase ignores the overall riskiness of the portfolio should some bearish news hit the soybean market. It is here that the diversification skills of a trader are tested. He or she must select the most promising commodity out of two or more positively correlated commodities, ignoring all others in the group.

SYNERGISTIC TRADING

Synergistic trading is the practice of assuming positions concurrently in two or more positively or negatively correlated commodities in the hope that a specified scenario will unfold. Often the positions are held in direct violation of diversification theory. For example, the unfolding of a scenario might require that a trader assume similar positions in two or more positively correlated commodities. Alternatively, opposing positions could be assumed in two or more negatively correlated commodities. If the scenario were to materialize as anticipated, each of the trades could result in a profit. However, if the scenario were not to materialize, the domino effect could be devastating, underscoring the inherent danger of this strategy.

For example, believing that lower inflation is likely to lead to lower interest rates and lower silver prices, a trader might want to buy a contract of Eurodollar futures and sell a contract of silver futures. This portfolio could result in profits on both positions if the scenario were to materialize. However, if inflation were to pick up instead of abating, leading to higher silver prices and lower Eurodollar prices, losses would be incurred on both positions, because of the strong negative correlation between silver and Eurodollars.

SPREAD TRADING

One way of reducing risk is to hold opposing positions in two positively correlated commodities. This is commonly termed spread trading. The objective of spread trading is to profit from differences in the relative speeds of adjustment of two positively correlated commodities. For example, a trader who is convinced of an impending upward move in the currencies and who believes that the yen will move up faster than the Deutsche mark, might want to buy one contract of the yen and simultaneously short-sell one contract of the Deutsche mark for the same contract period.

In technical parlance, this is called an intercommodity spread. A spread trade such as this helps to reduce risk inasmuch as it reduces the impact of a forecast error. To continue our example, if our trader is wrong about the strength of the yen relative to the mark, he or she could incur a loss on the long yen position. However, assuming that the mark falls, a portion of the loss on the yen will be cushioned by the profits earned on the short Deutsche mark position. The net profit or loss picture will be determined by the relative speeds of adjustment of the yen against the Deutsche mark.

In the unlikely event that two positively correlated commodities were to move in opposite directions, the trader could be left with a loss on both legs of the spread. To continue with our example, if the yen were to fall as the mark rallied, the trader would be left with a loss on both the long yen and the short mark positions. In this exceptional case, a spread trade could actually turn out to be riskier than an outright position trade, negating the premise that spread trades are theoretically less risky than outright positions. After all, it is this theoretical premise that is responsible for lower margins on spread trades as compared to outright position trades.

LIMITATIONS OF DIVERSIFICATION

Diversification can help to reduce the risk associated with trading, but it cannot eliminate risk completely. Even if a trader were to increase the number of commodities in the portfolio indefinitely, he or she would still have to contend with some risk. This is illustrated graphically in Figure 4.3.

Notice that the gains from diversification in terms of reduced portfolio risk are very apparent as the number of commodities increases from 1 to 5. However, the gains quickly taper off, as portfolio risk can no longer be diversified away. This is represented by the risk line becoming parallel

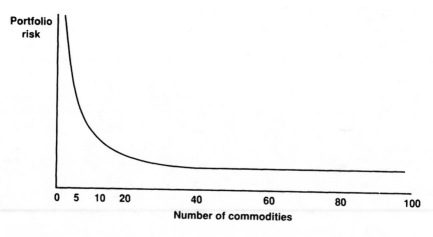

Figure 4.3   Graph illustrating the benefits and limitations of diversification.

to the horizontal axis. There is a certain level of risk inherent in trading commodities, and this minimum level of risk cannot be eliminated even if the number of commodities were to be increased indefinitely.

CONCLUSION

Whereas volatility in the futures markets opens up opportunities for enormous financial gains, it also adds to the dangers of trading. Traders who tend to get carried away by the prospects of large gains sometimes deliberately overlook the fact that leverage is a double-edged sword. This leads to unhealthy trading habits.

Typically, diversification is one of the first casualties, as traders tend to place all their eggs in one basket, hoping to maximize leverage for their investment dollars. If there were such a thing as perfect foresight, it would make sense to bet everything on a given trade. However, in the absence of perfect foresight, concentrating all one's money on a single trade or on the same side of two or more positively correlated commodities could prove to be disastrous.

Diversification helps reduce risk, as measured by the variability of overall trading returns. Ideally, this is accomplished by assuming similar positions across two unrelated or negatively correlated commodities. Diversification could also be accomplished by assuming opposing positions in two positively correlated commodities, a practice known as spread trading.

Finally, a trader might assume that the unfolding of a certain scenario will affect related commodities in a certain fashion. Accordingly, he or she would hold similar positions in two positively correlated commodities and opposing positions in two or more negatively correlated commodities. This is known as synergistic trading. Synergistic trading is a risky strategy, because nonrealization of the forecast scenario could lead to losses on all positions.

5

Commodity Selection

The case for commodity selection is best presented by J. Welles Wilder, Jr.[1] Wilder observes that "most technical systems are trend-following systems; however, most commodities are in a good trending mode (high directional movement) only about 30 percent of the time. If the trader follows the same commodities or stocks all of the time, then his system has to be good enough to make more money 30 percent of the time than it will give back 70 percent of the time. Compare that approach to trading only the top five or six commodities on the CSI [Commodity Selection Index] scale. This is the underlying concept..."[2]

Currently, there are over 50 futures contracts being traded on the exchanges in the United States. The premise behind the selection process is that not all 50 contracts offer trading opportunities that are equally attractive. The goal is to enable the trader to identify the most promising opportunities, allowing him or her to concentrate on these trades instead of chasing every opportunity that presents itself. By ranking commodities on a desirability scale, commodity selection creates a short list of opportunities, thereby helping to allocate limited resources more effectively.

---

[1] J. Welles Wilder, Jr., *New Concepts in Technical Trading Systems* (Greensboro, NC: Trend Research, 1978).

[2] Wilder, *New Concepts*, p. 115.

MUTUALLY EXCLUSIVE VERSUS INDEPENDENT OPPORTUNITIES

Opportunities across commodities can be categorized as being either mutually exclusive or independent. Two opportunities are mutually exclusive if the selection of one precludes the selection of the other. Two opportunities are said to be independent if the selection of one has no impact on the selection of the other.

Accordingly, if two commodities are highly positively correlated, as, for example, the Deutsche mark and the Swiss franc, a trader would want to trade either the mark or the franc. Diversification theory dictates that one should not hold identical positions in both currencies simultaneously. Hence, selection of one currency precludes selection of the other, rendering an objective evaluation of both opportunities that much more important. In the case of mutually exclusive commodities, the aim is to trade the commodity that offers the greatest reward potential for a given level of risk and investment.

In the case of independent opportunities, as, for example, gold and corn, the trader is free to trade both simultaneously, provided they are both short-listed on a desirability scale. However, if resources do not permit trading both commodities concurrently, the trader would select the commodity that ranks higher on his or her desirability scale.

Although selection is especially important when tracking two or more commodities simultaneously, it can also be justified when only one commodity is traded. By comparing the potential of a trade against a prespecified benchmark or cutoff rate, a trader can decide whether he or she wishes to pursue or forgo a given signal.

THE COMMODITY SELECTION PROCESS

Commodity selection is the process of evaluating alternative opportunities that may emerge at any given time. The objective is to rank each of the opportunities in order of desirability. Of primary importance, therefore, is the creation of a yardstick that facilitates objective comparison of competing opportunities across an attribute or attributes of desirability.

Having created the yardstick, the next step is to specify a benchmark measure below which opportunities fail to qualify for consideration. The decision regarding a cutoff level is a subjective one, depending on the trader's attitudes towards risk and the funds available for trading. The more risk-averse the trader, the more selective he or she is, and this is reflected in a higher cutoff level. Similarly, the smaller the size of the account, the more restricted the alternatives available to the trader, leading to a higher cutoff level. In this chapter, we shall restrict ourselves to a discussion of the construction of objective measures of assessing trade desirability.

Typically, the desirability of a trade is measured in terms of (a) its expected profitability, (b) the risk associated with earning those profits, and (c) the investment required to initiate the trade. The higher the expected profit, the more desirable a trade. The lower the investment required to initiate the trade, the higher the expected return on investment, and the greater its desirability. Finally, the lower the risk associated with earning a projected return on investment, the more desirable the trade.

A commodity selection yardstick is designed to synthesize all of these attributes of desirability in order to arrive at an objective measure for comparing opportunities. We now present four plausible approaches to commodity selection:

1. The Sharpe ratio approach, which measures the return on investment per unit risk
2. Wilder's commodity selection index
3. The price movement index
4. The adjusted payoff ratio index

THE SHARPE RATIO

In a study of mutual fund performance, William Sharpe[3] emphasized that risk-adjusted returns, rather than returns per se, were a reliable measure of comparative performance. Accordingly, he studied the returns on individual mutual funds in excess of the risk-free rate as a ratio of the riskiness of such returns, measured by their standard deviation. This

[3] William Sharpe, "Mutual Fund Performance," *Journal of Business* (January 1966), pp. 119–138.

ratio has since come to be known as the Sharpe ratio. The Sharpe ratio is computed as follows:

$$\text{Sharpe ratio} = \frac{\text{Return} - \text{Risk-free Interest Rate}}{\text{Standard Deviation of Return}}$$

The higher the Sharpe ratio, the greater the excess return per unit of risk, enhancing the desirability of the investment under review.

The Sharpe ratio may be defined in terms of the expected return on a trade and the associated standard deviation. Alternatively, a trader who is working with a mechanical system, which is incapable of estimating future returns, might want to use the average historic return as the best estimator of the future expected return. In this case, the relevant measure of risk is the standard deviation of historic returns. The formulas for calculating historic and expected trade returns and their standard deviations are given in Chapter 4.

Care should be taken to annualize trade returns so as to facilitate comparison across trades. This is accomplished by multiplying the raw return by a factor of $365/n$, where n is the estimated or observed life of the trade in question. Deducting the annualized risk-free interest rate from the annualized trade return gives an estimate of the incremental or excess return from futures trading. A negative excess return implies that the trader would be better off not trading. The risk-free rate is given by the prevailing interest rate on Treasury bills. This is the rate the trader could have earned had he or she invested the capital in Treasury bills rather than trading the market.

Assume that a trader is evaluating opportunities in crude oil, Deutsche marks, and world sugar, with the expected trade returns, the risk-free return, and standard deviation of expected returns as given in Table 5.1.

Table 5.1   Calculating Sharpe Ratios across Three Commodities

Commodity	Expected Return (2)	Risk-free Return (3)	Excess Returns (4) = (2)−(3)	Standard Deviation (5)	Sharpe Ratio (6) = (4)/(5)
Crude Oil	0.46	0.06	0.40	0.80	0.50
D. mark	0.36	0.06	0.30	0.50	0.60
Sugar	0.26	0.06	0.20	0.30	0.67

Notice that whereas the expected excess return on crude oil is the highest at 0.40, the corresponding Sharpe ratio is the lowest at 0.50. The converse is true for sugar. This is because the variability of returns on crude oil is more than twice that for sugar, rendering crude oil a much riskier proposition as compared to sugar. Since the Sharpe ratio measures return per unit of risk rather than return per se, sugar outperforms crude oil.

A benchmark Sharpe ratio could be set separately for each commodity, based on past data for the commodity in question. Alternatively, an overall benchmark Sharpe ratio could be set across all commodities. Consequently, comparisons of the Sharpe ratio may be effected across time for a given commodity, or across commodities at a given time.

WILDER'S COMMODITY SELECTION INDEX

Wilder's commodity selection index is particularly suited for use alongside conventional mechanical trading systems, which signal the beginning of a trend but are silent as regards the magnitude of the projected move. Wilder analyzes price action in terms of its (a) directional movement and (b) volatility, observing that "volatility is always accompanied by movement, but movement is not always accompanied by volatility."[4]

The commodity selection index for a given commodity is based on (a) Wilder's average directional movement index rating, (b) volatility as measured by the 14-day average true range, (c) the margin requirement in dollars, and (d) the commission in dollars. The higher the average directional movement index rating for a commodity and the greater its volatility, the higher is its selection index value. Similarly, the lower the margin required for a commodity, the higher the selection index value. Let us begin with a discussion of Wilder's average directional movement index rating.

Directional Movement

Wilder defines directional movement (DM) as the largest portion of the current day's trading range that lies outside the preceding day's range. In

---

[4] Wilder, *New Concepts*, p. 111.

the case of an up move today, this would represent positive directional movement, representing the difference between today's high and yesterday's high. Conversely, for a move downwards, we would have negative directional movement, representing the difference between today's low and yesterday's low.

In the case of an outside range day, where the current day's range includes and surpasses yesterday's range, we have simultaneous occurrence of both positive and negative directional movement. Here, Wilder defines the directional movement to be the greater of positive and negative movements. In the case of an inside day, where the range for the current day is contained within the range for the preceding day, the directional movement is assumed to be zero.

When prices are locked limit-up, the directional movement is positive and represents the difference between the locked-limit price and yesterday's high. Similarly, when prices are locked limit-down, the directional movement is negative, representing the difference between yesterday's low and the locked-limit price. Negative directional movement is simply a description of downward movement: it is not considered as a negative number but rather an absolute value for calculation purposes.

The Directional Indicator

Next, Wilder divides the directional movement number for any given day by the true range for that day to arrive at the directional indicator (DI) for that day. The true range is a positive number and represents the largest of (a) the difference between the current day's high and low, (b) the difference between today's high and yesterday's close, and (c) the difference between yesterday's close and today's low.

Summing the positive directional movement over the past 14 days and dividing by the true range over the same period, we arrive at a positive directional indicator over the past 14 days. Similarly, summing the absolute value of the negative directional movement over the past 14 days and dividing by the true range over the same period, we arrive at a negative directional indicator over the past 14 days.

The Average Directional Movement Index Rating

The net directional movement is the difference between the 14-day positive and negative directional indicators. This difference, when divided by the sum of the 14-day positive and negative directional indicators, gives the directional movement index (DX).

Therefore,

$$DX = \frac{+DI_{14} - -DI_{14}}{+DI_{14} + -DI_{14}}$$

The average directional movement index (ADX) is the 14-day average of the directional movement index. The average directional movement index rating (ADXR) is the average of the ADX value today and the ADX value 14 days ago. Therefore,

$$ADXR = \frac{ADX_{today} + ADX_{14\ days\ ago}}{2}$$

Mathematically, the commodity selection index (CSI) may be defined as:

$$CSI = ADXR \times ATR_{14} \times \left[\frac{V}{\sqrt{M}} \times \frac{1}{150 + C} \right] \times 100$$

where   ADXR = average directional movement index rating

ATR_{14} = 14-day average true range

V = dollar value of a unit move in ATR

$\sqrt{M}$ = square root of the margin requirement in dollars

C = per-trade commission in dollars

An example will help clarify the formula. Assume once again that a trader is evaluating opportunities in crude oil, Deutsche marks, and sugar. Details of the average directional movement index rating (ADXR), the 14-day average true range (ATR), the dollar value (V) of a unit move in the average true range, and the margin investment (M) are given in Table 5.2. Assume further that the commission for each of the three commodities is $50.

Notice that the Deutsche mark has the highest index value, primarily because of its high directional index movement rating and moderate margin requirement. Crude oil, on the other hand, has a low directional index movement rating and a high margin requirement, both of which have an adverse impact upon its selection index. Sugar has a low margin

Table 5.2   Calculating the Commodity
Selection Index across Commodities

Commodity	ADXR	ATR	V	M	CSI
			$/ATR		
Crude Oil	40	1.50	1000	5000	424.26
D. mark	80	75.00	12.50	2500	750.00
Sugar	60	0.50	1120	1000	531.26

requirement but suffers from low volatility, moderating the value of its
selection index.

THE PRICE MOVEMENT INDEX

The price movement index is an adaptation of Wilder's commodity selection index, designed to simplify the arithmetic of the calculations.
Whereas Wilder's index segregates price movement according to its directional and volatility components, the price movement index does not
attempt such a breakdown. The price movement index is based on the
premise that once a price move has begun, it can be expected to continue
for some time to come. The greater the dollar value of a price move for
a given margin investment, the more appealing the trade.

As is the case with Wilder's commodity selection index, the price
movement index is most useful when precise estimation of reward is
infeasible. This is particularly true of mechanical trading systems, which
signal precise entry points without giving a clue as to the potential
magnitude of the move.

As the name suggests, the price movement index measures the dollar
value of price movement for a commodity over a historical time period.
This number is divided by the initial margin investment required for
that commodity, multiplying the answer by 100 percent to express it as
a percentage. Mathematically, the price movement index for commodity
X may be defined as

$$\text{Index for X} = \frac{\text{Dollar value of price move over } n \text{ sessions}}{\text{Margin investment for commodity X}} \times 100$$

where n is a predefined number of trading sessions, expressed in days
or weeks, over which price movement is measured.

Table 5.3   Calculating the Price
Movement Index Across Commodities

Commodity	Price Move (ticks)	$ Value of 1 tick	$ Value of Price Move	Margin Investment	Price Movement Index (%)
Crude oil	250	10	2500	5000	50
D. mark	150	12.5	1875	2500	75
Sugar	60	11.2	672	1000	67.2

Price movement represents the difference between the maximum and minimum prices recorded by the commodity in question over the past n trading sessions. If n were 14, calculate the difference between the maximum (or highest high) and minimum (or lowest low) prices for the commodity over the past 14 days.

For example, if the maximum price registered by the Deutsche mark were $0.5800 and the minimum price were $0.5500, the difference would be 300 ticks. Given that each tick in the Deutsche mark futures is worth $12.50, the dollar value of 300 ticks is $3750. Assuming an initial margin investment of $2500, the price movement index works out to be 150 percent. If this happens to fall short of the trader's cutoff level, he would not pursue the mark trade. Alternatively, if it surpasses his cutoff level, he would be interested in trading the mark.

Assume once again that a trader is evaluating opportunities in crude oil, Deutsche marks, and sugar, with the respective n-day historical price movements and margin investments as given in Table 5.3.

If the trader did not wish to trade any commodity with a price movement index less than 60, he would ignore crude oil. Notice that the rankings given by Wilder's commodity selection index match those given by the price movement index. Although this is coincidental, it could be argued that the similarity in the construction of the two indices could account for a similarity in the two sets of rankings.

THE ADJUSTED PAYOFF RATIO INDEX

The payoff or reward/risk ratio is arrived at by dividing the potential dollar reward by the permissible dollar risk on a trade under consideration.

Therefore, if the potential reward on a trade is $1000 and the permissible risk is $250, the payoff ratio is 4. The higher the payoff ratio, the more promising the trade.

Notice that the payoff ratio says nothing about the investment required for initiating a trade, thereby limiting its usefulness as a yardstick for comparison. Given that investment requirements are dissimilar across commodities, it would be necessary to factor such differences into the payoff ratio.

One way of doing this is to divide the payoff ratio by the relative investment required for a given commodity. This is known as the adjusted payoff ratio. Therefore, the adjusted payoff ratio for commodity X is

$$\frac{\text{Adjusted payoff}}{\text{ratio for X}} = \frac{\text{Payoff ratio for X}}{\text{Relative investment for X}}$$

The relative investment for a given commodity is arrived at by dividing the investment required for that commodity by the maximum investment across all commodities:

$$\frac{\text{Relative investment}}{\text{for X}} = \frac{\text{Investment required for commodity X}}{\text{Maximum investment across all commodities}}$$

Let us assume that the margin for a Standard & Poor's 500 index futures contract, say $25,000, represents the maximum investment across all commodities. If the investment required for a contract of gold futures is $1250, the relative investment in gold represents $1250/$25,000, which is 0.05 or 5 percent of the maximum investment.

The relative investment ratio ranges between 0 and 1; the lower the relative investment, the higher the adjusted payoff ratio. In turn, the higher the adjusted payoff ratio, the more attractive the trade. For example, assuming the payoff ratio for the proposed gold trade is 3, the adjusted payoff ratio works out to be 3/0.05 or 60. If, on the other hand, the investment needed for a contract of gold were $20,000, the relative investment would be $20,000/$25,000 or 0.80. In this case, the adjusted payoff ratio would work out to 3/0.80 or 3.75, significantly lower than the earlier adjusted payoff ratio of 60.

An example would help clarify the process. Assume that a trader is evaluating opportunities in crude oil, Deutsche marks, and sugar with the respective payoff ratios and investments as given in Table 5.4. Assume further that the maximum investment across all commodities is $25,000. Therefore, the relative investment for a given commodity is arrived

Table 5.4   Calculating the Adjusted
Payoff Ratio across Commodities

Commodity	Payoff ratio	Margin Investment	Relative Investment	Adjusted Payoff ratio
Crude oil	5	5000	0.20	25
D. mark	3	2500	0.10	30
Sugar	2	1000	0.04	50

at by dividing the investment required for the commodity by
$25,000.

Notice that the payoff ratio is the highest for crude oil, more than twice
as large the payoff ratio for sugar. However, the investment needed for
a contract of crude oil at $5000 is five times as large as the investment
of $1000 for sugar. Consequently, the adjusted payoff ratio for sugar
is higher than that for crude oil, implying that sugar is relatively more
attractive. If, as a matter of policy, trades with an adjusted payoff ratio
of less than 30 were disregarded, the crude oil trade would not qualify
for consideration.

CONCLUSION

The selection process is based on the premise that all trading opportunities are not equally desirable. Whereas some trades may justifiably
be forgone, others might present a compelling case for a greater than
average allocation. These decisions can only be made if the trader has
an objective yardstick for measuring the desirability of trades.

Four alternative approaches to commodity selection have been sug-
gested. It is conceivable that the trade rankings could vary across different approaches. However, as long as the trader uses a particular approach
consistently to evaluate all opportunities, the differences in rankings are
largely academic.

The selection techniques outlined above allow the trader to sift through
a maze of opportunities, arriving at a short list of those trades that satisfy
his criteria of desirability. Now that the trader has a clear idea of the
commodities he wishes to trade, the next step is to allocate risk capital
across them. This is the subject matter of our discussion in Chapter 8.

6

Managing Unrealized Profits and Losses

The goal of risk management is conservation of capital. This implies getting out of a trade without (a) giving up too much of the unrealized profits earned or (b) incurring too much of an unrealized loss. The purpose of this chapter is to define how much is "too much." An unrealized profit or loss arises during the life of a trade, reflecting the difference between the current price and the entry price. As soon as the trade is liquidated, the unrealized profit or loss is converted into a realized profit or loss.

An equity reduction or "drawdown" results from a reduction in the unrealized profit or an increase in the unrealized loss on a trade. When confronted with an equity drawdown on a trade in progress, a trader must choose between two conflicting courses of action: (a) liquidating the trade with a view to conserving capital or (b) continuing with it in the hope of making good on the drawdown.

Liquidating a profitable trade at the slightest sign of a drawdown will prevent further evaporation of unrealized profits. However, by exiting the trade, the trader is forgoing the opportunity to earn any additional profits on the trade. Similarly, an unrealized loss might possibly be recouped by continuing with the trade, instead of being converted into a realized loss upon liquidation. However, if the trade continues to deteriorate, the unrealized loss could multiply.

The aim is to be mindful of equity drawdowns while simultaneously minimizing the probability of erroneously short-circuiting a trade. Obviously, a trader does not have the luxury of hindsight to help decide whether an exit is timely or premature. While there are no cut-and-dried formulas to resolve the problem, we will present a series of plausible solutions. We begin by discussing the treatment of unrealized losses. Subsequently, we focus on unrealized profits.

DRAWING THE LINE ON UNREALIZED LOSSES

Consider the life cycles of two trades, represented by Figures 6.1a and 6.1b. In Figure 6.1a, the trade starts out with an unrealized loss, only to recover and end on a profitable note. In Figure 6.1b, the trade starts out as a loser and never recovers.

The trader must decide upon an unrealized loss level beyond which it is highly unlikely that a losing trade will turn around. This cutoff price, or stop-loss price, defines the maximum permissible dollar risk per contract. Setting a stop-loss order shows that a trader has thought through the risk on a trade and made a determination of the price at which he wishes to dissociate himself from the trade. Ideally, this determination will be made before the trade is initiated, so as to avoid needless second-guessing when it comes time to act.

If the stop-loss price is too far from the entry price, it is less likely that a trader will be forced out of his position when he would rather continue with it. However, if his stop is hit, the magnitude of the dollar

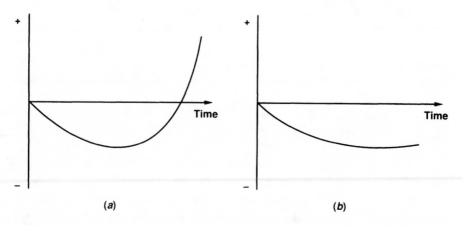

(a)   (b)

Figure 6.1   The profit life cycles of two potentially losing trades.

loss is relatively more painful. A stop-loss price closer to the entry price minimizes the size of the loss, but there is a greater likelihood that random price action will force a trader out of his position needlessly.

In this chapter, we discuss five approaches to setting stop-loss orders:

1. A visual approach to setting stops
2. Volatility stops
3. Time stops
4. Dollar-value stops
5. Probability stops, based on an analysis of the unrealized loss patterns on completed profitable trades

THE VISUAL APPROACH TO SETTING STOPS

One way of deciding on a stop-loss point for a trade is to be mindful of clues offered by the commodity price chart in question. As discussed in Chapter 3, a chart pattern that signals a reversal formation will also let the trader know precisely when the pattern is no longer valid.

Another commonly used technique is to set a buy stop to liquidate a short sale just above an area of price resistance. Similarly, a sell stop to liquidate a long trade could be set below an area of price support. Prices are said to encounter resistance if they cannot overcome a previous high. By the same token, prices are said to find support if they have difficulty falling below a previous low. Support or resistance is that much stronger if prices fail to take out a previous high or low on repeated tries.

Consider, for example, the price chart for the British pound June 1990 futures contract given in Figure 6.2a. Notice the contract high of $1.6826 established on February 19. Subsequently, the pound retreated to a low of $1.5700 in March, before staging a gradual recovery. On May 15, the pound closed sharply lower, after making a higher high. Anticipating a double top formation, a trader might be tempted to short the pound on the close on May 15 at $1.6630, with a buy stop at $1.6830, just above the high of February 19.

As is evident from Figure 6.2b, our trader was stopped out on May 17 when the pound broke past the earlier high. The breakout on the upside negated the double top hypothesis, proving once again that anticipating a pattern before it is set off can be expensive. Be that as it may, liquidating the trade with a small loss saved the trader from a much bigger loss had

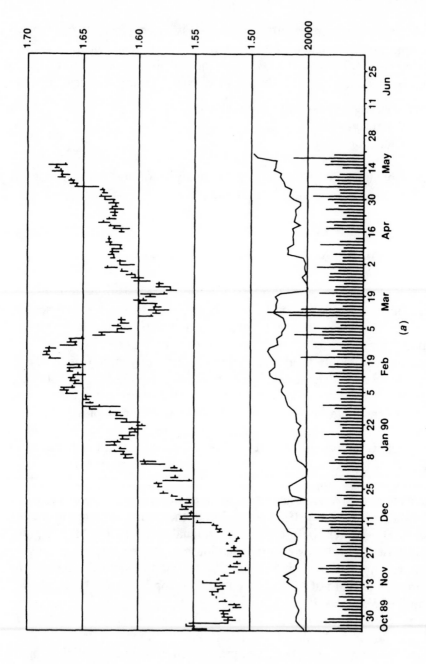

Figure 6.2a   Setting stops: June 1990 British pound.

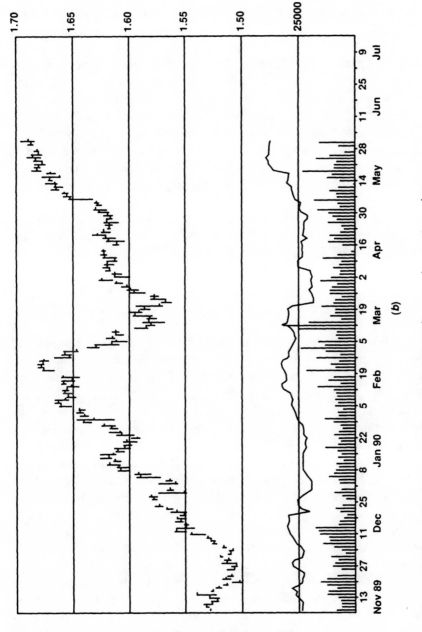

Figure 6.2b Setting stops: June 1990 British pound, continued.

he or she continued with the trade: the June futures rallied to $1.6996 on May 30!

Chart patterns offer a simple yet effective, tool for setting stop-loss orders. However, the reader must be cautioned against placing a stop-loss order exactly at or very close to the support or resistance point. This is because support and resistance prices are quite apparent, and a large number of stop-loss orders could possibly be set off at these levels. Consequently, one might be needlessly stopped out of a good trade.

Critics of this approach discount it as being subjective and open to the chartist's interpretation. However, it is worth noting that speculation entails forecasting, and in principle all forecasting is subjective. Subjectivity can hurt only when it creates a smoke screen around the trader, making an objective assessment of market reality difficult. As long as the trader has the discipline to abide by his stop-loss price, the methodology used for setting stops is of little consequence.

VOLATILITY STOPS

The volatility stop acknowledges the fact that there is a great deal of randomness in price behavior, notwithstanding the fact that the market may be trending in a particular direction. Essentially, volatility stops seek to distinguish between inconsequential or random fluctuations and a fundamental shift in the trend. In this section, we discuss some of the more commonly used techniques that seek to make this distinction.

Ideally, a trader would want to know the future volatility of a commodity so as to distinguish accurately between random and nonrandom price movements. However, since it is impossible to know the future volatility, this number must be estimated. Historic volatility is often used as an estimate of the future, especially when the future is not expected to vary significantly from the past.

However, if significant changes in market conditions are anticipated, the trader might be uncomfortable using historic volatility. One commonly used alternative is to derive the theoretical futures volatility from the price currently quoted on an associated option, assuming that the option is fairly valued. This estimate of volatility is also known as the implied volatility, since it is the value implicit in the current option premium. In this section, we discuss both approaches to computing volatility.

Using Standard Deviations to Measure Historical Volatility

Historical volatility, in a strictly statistical sense, is a one–standard–deviation price change, expressed in percentage terms, over a calendar year. The assumption is that the percent changes in a commodity's prices, as opposed to absolute dollar changes, are normally distributed. The assumption of normality implies that the percentage price change distribution is bell-shaped, with the current price representing the mean of the distribution at the center of the bell. A normal distribution is symmetrical around the mean, enabling us to arrive at probability estimates of the future price of the commodity.

For example, if cocoa is currently trading at $1000 a metric ton and the historic volatility is 25 percent, cocoa could be trading anywhere between $750 and $1250 ($1000 ± 1 × 25 percent × $1000) a year from today approximately 68 percent of the time. More broadly, cocoa could be trading between $250 and $1750 ($1000 ± 3 × 25 percent × $1000) one year from now approximately 99 percent of the time.

In order to compute the historic volatility, the trader must decide on how far back in time he wishes to go. He or she would want to go as far back as is necessary to get an accurate picture of future market conditions. Accordingly, the period might vary from two weeks to, say, 12 months. Typically, daily close price changes are used for computing volatility estimates.

Since a trader's horizon is likely to be shorter than one year, the annualized volatility estimate must be modified to acknowledge this fact. Assume that there are 250 trading days in a year and that a trader wishes to estimate the volatility over the next n days. In order to do this, the trader would divide the annualized volatility estimate by the squareroot of $250/n$.

Continuing with our cocoa example, assume that the trader were interested in estimating the volatility over the next week or five trading days. In this case, n is 5, and the volatility discount factor would be computed as follows:

$$\text{Discount Factor} = \sqrt{\frac{250}{5}} = 7.07$$

$$\text{Volatility over next 5 days} = \frac{0.25}{7.07} = 0.03536 \text{ or } 3.536\%$$

The dollar equivalent of this one–standard–deviation percentage price change over the next five days is simply the product of the current price of cocoa times the percentage. Therefore, the dollar value of the volatility expected over the next five days is

$1000 × 0.03536 = $35.36

Consequently, there is a 68 percent chance that prices could fluctuate between $1035.36 and $964.64 ($1000 ± 1 × $35.36) over the next five days. There is a 99 percent chance that prices could fluctuate between $1106.08 and $893.92 ($1000 ± 3 × $35.36) within the same period.

The definition of price used in the foregoing calculations needs to be clarified for certain interest rate futures, as for example Eurodollars and Treasury bills, which are quoted as a percentage of a base value of 100. The interest rate on Treasury bills is arrived at by deducting the currently quoted price from 100. Therefore, if Treasury bills futures were currently quoted at 94.45, the corresponding interest rate would be 5.55 percent (100 − 94.45). Volatility calculations will be carried out using this value of the interest rate rather than on the futures price of 94.45.

Using The True Range as a Measure of Historical Volatility

A nontechnical measure of historical volatility is given by the range of prices during the course of a trading interval, typically a day or a week. The range of prices represents the difference between the high and the low for a given trading interval. Should the range of the current day lie beyond the range of the previous day (a phenomenon referred to as a "gap day") the current day's range must include the distance between today's range and yesterday's close. This is commonly referred to as the true range. The true range for a gap-down day is the difference between the previous day's settlement price and today's low. Similarly, the true range for a gap-up day is the difference between today's high and the previous day's settlement price.

A percentile distribution of daily and weekly true ranges in ticks is given for 24 commodities in Appendix D. A tick is the smallest increment by which prices can move in a given futures market. Appendix D also translates a tick value stop into the equivalent dollar exposure resulting from trading one through 10 contracts of the commodity. A tick value corresponding to 10 percent signifies that only 10 percent of all observations in our sample had a range equal to or less than this number. In other words, the true range exceeded this number for 90 percent of the observations studied. Similarly, a value corresponding to 90 percent implies that the range exceeded this value only 10 percent of the time. Therefore, a stop equal to the 10 percent range value is far more likely to be hit by random price action than is a stop equal to the 90 percent value.

Reference to Appendix D for British pound data shows that 90 percent of all observations between 1980 and 1988 had a daily true range equal to or less than 117 ticks. Therefore, a trader who was long the pound, might want to set a protective sell stop 117 ticks below the previous day's close. The chances of being incorrectly stopped out of the long trade are 1 in 10. Similarly, a trader who had short-sold the pound might want to set a buy stop 117 ticks above the preceding day's close. The dollar value of this stop is $1462.50, or $1463 as rounded off in Appendix D, per contract.

Instead of concentrating on the true range for a day or a week, a trader might be more comfortable working with the average true range over the past *n* trading sessions, where *n* is any number found to be most effective through back-testing. The belief is that the range for the past *n* periods is a more reliable indicator of volatility as compared to the range for the immediately preceding trading session. An example would be to calculate the average range over the past 15 trading sessions and to use this estimate for setting stop prices.

A slightly modified approach recommends working with a fraction or multiple of the volatility estimate. For example, a trader might want to set his stop equal to 150 percent of the average true range for the past *n* trading sessions. The supposition is that the fraction or multiple enhances the effectiveness of the stop.

Implied Volatility

The implied volatility of a futures contract is the volatility derived from the price of an associated option. Implied volatility estimates are particularly useful in turbulent markets, when historical volatility measures are inaccurate reflectors of the future. The theoretical price of an option is given by an options pricing model, as, for example, the Black-Scholes model. The theoretical price of an option on a futures contract is determined by the following five data items:

1. The current futures price
2. The strike or exercise price of the option
3. The time to expiration

4. The prevailing risk-free interest rate, and
5. The volatility of the underlying futures contract.

Assuming that options are fairly valued, we can say that the current option price matches its theoretical value given by the options pricing model. Using the current price of the option as a given and plugging in values for items 1 to 4 in the theoretical options pricing model, we can solve backwards for item 5, the volatility of the futures contract. This is the implied volatility, or the volatility implicit in the current price of the option.

The implied volatility estimate is expressed as a percentage and represents a one–standard–deviation price change over a calendar year. The trader can use the procedure just outlined for historical volatility computations, to derive the likely variability in prices over an interval of time shorter than a year.

TIME STOPS

Instead of working with a volatility stop, a trader might want to base stops on price action over a fixed interval of time. A trader who has bought a commodity would want to set a sell stop below the low of the past n trading sessions, where n is the number found most effective in back-testing over a historical time period. A trader who has short-sold the commodity would set a buy stop above the high of the past n trading sessions. For example, a 10–day rule would specify that a sell-stop be set just under the low of the preceding 10 days and that a buy stop would be set just above the high of the preceding 10 days. The logic is that if a commodity has not traded beyond a certain price over the past n days, there is little likelihood it will do so now, barring a change in the trend. The value of n may be determined by a visual examination of price charts or through back-testing of data.

Bruce Babcock, Jr. presents a slight variation for setting time stops, which he terms a "prove-it-or-lose-it" stop.[1] This stop recommends liquidation of a trade that is not profitable after a certain number of days, n, to be prespecified by the trader. The idea is that if a trade is going to be profitable, it should "prove" itself over the first n days. If

[1] Bruce Babcock, Jr., *The Dow Jones-Irwin Guide to Trading Systems* (Homewood, IL: Dow Jones-Irwin, 1989).

it stagnates within this time frame, the trader would be well advised to look for alternative opportunities.

Clearly, there should be a mechanism to safeguard against undue losses in the interim period while the trade is left to prove itself. The "prove-it-or-lose-it" stop, therefore, is best used in conjunction with another stop designed to prevent losses from getting out of control.

DOLLAR-VALUE MONEY MANAGEMENT STOPS

Some traders prefer to set stops in terms of the dollar amount they are willing to risk on a trade. Often, this dollar risk is arrived at as a percentage of available trading capital or the initial margin required for the commodity. If the permissible risk is expressed as a percentage of capital, this would entail using the same money management stop across all commodities. This may not be appropriate if the volatility of the markets traded is vastly different. For example, a $500 stop would allow for an adverse move of 10 cents in corn, whereas it would only allow for a 1-index-point adverse move in the S&P 500 index futures. The stop for corn is reasonable, inasmuch as it allows for normally expected random fluctuations. However, the stop for the S&P 500 is simply too tight. This is the problem with money management stops fixed as a percentage of capital. In order to overcome this problem, the money management stop is often set as a percentage of the initial margin for the commodity. The logic is that the higher the volatility, the greater the required margin for the commodity. This translates into a larger dollar stop for the more volatile commodities.

The dollar amount of the money management stop is translated into a stop-loss price using the following formula:

Stop-loss price =
Entry price ± Tick value of permissible dollar loss

where

$$\text{Tick value of permissible dollar loss} = \frac{\text{Permissible dollar loss}}{\$ \text{ value of a tick}}$$

Assume that the margin for soybeans is $1000 and that the trader wishes to risk a maximum of 50 percent of the initial margin, or $500 per contract. This translates into a stop-loss price 40 ticks or 10 cents from the entry price, given that each soybean tick is worth $\frac{1}{4}$ cent per bushel. For two contracts, the dollar risk under this rule translates into $1000; for five contracts, the risk is $2500; for 10 contracts, the risk escalates to $5000.

Appendix D defines the dollar equivalent of a specified risk exposure in ticks for up to 10 contracts of each of 24 commodities. A percentile distribution of daily and weekly true ranges in ticks helps the trader place the money management stop in perspective. For example, the daily analysis for soybeans reveals that 60 percent of the days had a true range less than or equal to 42 ticks. Therefore, there is approximately a 40 percent chance of the daily true range exceeding a 40-tick money management stop.

ANALYZING UNREALIZED LOSS PATTERNS ON PROFITABLE TRADES

A trader could undertake an analysis of the maximum unrealized loss or equity drawdown suffered during the course of each profitable trade completed over a historical time period, with a view to identifying distinctive patterns. If a pattern does exist, it could be used to formulate appropriate drawdown cutoff rules for future trades. This approach assumes that the larger the unrealized loss, the lower the likelihood of the trade ending on a profitable note. A hypothetical analysis of unrealized losses incurred on all profitable trades over a given time period may look as shown in Table 6.1.

Armed with this information, the trader can estimate a cutoff value, beyond which it is highly unlikely that the unrealized loss will be recouped and the trade will end profitably. In the example given in Table 6.1, it is a good idea to pull out of a trade when unrealized losses equal or

Table 6.1   Unrealized Loss Patterns on Profitable Trades

$ Value of Unrealized Loss	# of Profitable Trades	Cumulative # of Profitable Trades	Cumulative %
100	4	4	40%
200	3	7	70%
500	2	9	90%
1000	0	9	90%
1500	1	10	100%

exceed $501. This is because only 10 percent of all profitable trades suffer an unrealized loss of greater than $500, mitigating the odds of prematurely pulling out of a profitable trade.

Instead of discussing the hypothetical, let us evaluate the unrealized loss patterns for Swiss francs, the Standard & Poor's (S&P) 500 Index futures, and Eurodollars, using a dual-moving-average crossover rule. A buy signal is generated when the shorter of two moving averages exceeds the longer one; a sell signal is generated when the shorter moving average falls below the longer moving average. Four sets of daily moving average crossover rules have been selected randomly for the analysis.

The time period considered is January 1983 to December 1986, divided into two equal subperiods: January 1983 to December 1984 and January 1985 to December 1986. Optimal drawdown cutoff rules have been arrived at by analyzing drawdown patterns over the 1983–84 subperiod. These drawdown cutoff rules are then applied to data for 1985–86, and a comparison effected against the conventional no-stop moving-average rule for the same period.

The optimal unrealized loss cutoff levels for each of the three commodities, across all four crossover rules, using daily data for January 1983 to December 1984, are summarized in Table 6.2. The optimal loss drawdown cutoff is set at a level equal to the maximum unrealized loss registered on 90 percent of all winning trades.

Once stopped out of a trade, the system stays neutral until a reversal signal is generated. Therefore, the total number of trades generated for each commodity remains unaffected by the stop rule, although the split between winners and losers does change.

The results are summarized in Tables 6.3 to 6.5. Notice from the tables that in the no-stop case, as the unrealized loss drawdown increases, the

Table 6.2 Optimal Unrealized Loss Stop on Winning Trades

Crossover rule	Eurodollars		S&P 500		Swiss francs	
	ticks	$	ticks	$	ticks	$
6- & 27-day	15	375	19	475	81	1013
9- & 33-day	24	600	52	1300	63	788
12- & 39-day	30	750	51	1275	80	1000
15- & 45-day	40	1000	46	1150	72	900

Table 6.3 Analysis of Unrealized Loss Drawdowns on Eurodollars during 1985–86 using stops based on 1983–84 data

	Without Stops		Using Drawdown Stops	
	Winners	Losers	Winners	Losers
6- & 27-day Crossover				
0–8	5	0	4	0
9–16	2	3	2	20
17–24	1	5	0	1
>24	1	11	0	1
Total Trades	9	19	6	22
Profit/(Loss) without stops:	($2,600)			
Profit/(Loss) using 15-tick stop:	($3,600)			
9- & 33-day Crossover				
0–7	2	0	2	0
8–21	3	5	3	5
22–28	1	2	0	11
>28	0	9	0	1
Total Trades	6	16	5	17
Profit/(Loss) without stops:	($900)			
Profit/(Loss) using 24-tick stop:	($175)			
12- & 39-day Crossover				
0–8	6	0	6	0
9–24	3	2	3	2
25–40	0	4	0	9
>40	0	5	0	0
Total Trades	9	11	9	11
Profit/(Loss) without stops:	$2,250			
Profit/(Loss) using 30-tick stop:	$4,025			
15- & 45-day Crossover				
0–8	5	0	5	0
9–24	1	2	1	8
25–40	0	1	0	0
>40	0	5	0	0
Total Trades	6	8	6	8
Profit/(Loss) without stops:	($1,300)			
Profit/(Loss) using 40 tick stop:	$1,575			

Table 6.4 Analysis of Unrealized Loss Drawdowns on Swiss Francs during 1985–86 using stops based on 1983–84 data

	Without Stops		Using Drawdown Stops	
	Winners	Losers	Winners	Losers
6- & 27-day Crossover				
0–30	4	0	4	0
31–60	2	0	2	0
61–120	1	5	0	13
> 121	1	7	0	1
Total Trades	8	12	6	14
Profit/(Loss) without stops:		$1,188		
Profit/(Loss) using 81-tick stop:		($1,613)		
9- & 33-day Crossover				
0–46	3	0	3	0
47–92	2	1	0	14
93–184	1	4	0	1
> 185	0	7	0	0
Total Trades	6	12	3	15
Profit/(Loss) without stops:		($10,713)		
Profit/(Loss) using 63-tick stop:		($ 8,987)		
12- & 39-day Crossover				
0–48	5	0	5	0
49–144	5	2	2	9
145–240	0	0	0	0
> 241	0	4	0	0
Total Trades	10	6	7	9
Profit/(Loss) without stops:		$5,012		
Profit/(Loss) using 80-tick stop:		$6,700		
15- & 45-day Crossover				
0–43	5	2	5	2
44–129	2	1	2	7
130–258	1	1	0	0
> 259	0	4	0	0
Total Trades	8	8	7	9
Profit/(Loss) without stops:		$ 7,863		
Profit/(Loss) using 72-tick stop:		$13,838		

Table 6.5 Analysis of Unrealized Loss Drawdowns on S&P 500 Index Futures during 1985-86 using stops based on 1983–84 data

	Without Stops		Using Drawdown Stops	
	Winners	Losers	Winners	Losers
6- & 27-day Crossover				
0–35	7	0	3	19
36–105	2	5	0	0
106–175	0	6	0	0
>175	0	2	0	0
Total Trades	9	13	3	19
Profit/(Loss) without stops:			$ 800	
Profit/(Loss) using 19-tick (0.95 index point) stop:			$ 4,500	
9- & 33-day Crossover				
0–40	8	0	8	0
41–82	0	1	0	8
83–165	0	2	0	0
> 165	0	5	0	0
Total Trades	8	8	8	8
Profit/(Loss) without stops:			$ 6,400	
Profit/(Loss) using 52-tick (2.60 index points) stop:			$30,525	
12- & 39-day Crossover				
0–40	9	0	9	0
41–81	1	1	0	9
82–161	0	1	0	0
> 161	0	6	0	0
Total Trades	10	8	9	9
Profit/(Loss) without stops:			($7,800)	
Profit/(Loss) using 51-tick (2.55 index points) stop:			$21,225	
15- & 45-day Crossover				
0–46	4	0	4	11
47–94	1	1	0	0
95–188	0	3	0	0
> 188	0	6	0	0
Total Trades	5	10	4	11
Profit/(Loss) without stops:			($18,250)	
Profit/(Loss) using 46-tick (2.30 index points) stop:			$16,600	

number of profitable trades declines sharply, both in absolute numbers and as a percentage of total trades. In other words, the larger the loss drawdown, the smaller is the probability of the trade ending up a winner. Consequently, as the unrealized loss increases, losing trades outnumber winning trades. Significantly, this conclusion holds consistently across each of the three commodities and four crossover rules, supporting the belief that unrealized loss cutoff rules could help short-circuit losing trades without prematurely liquidating profitable trades.

In general, using drawdown stops based on 1983–84 data tends to stem the drawdown on losing trades. This is true for all commodities and crossover rules. Gap openings through the stipulated stop price at times result in unrealized losses exceeding the level stipulated by our optimal drawdown cutoff rule. This is particularly true of the Swiss franc.

There is a significant increase in profits in case of the S&P 500 Index futures as a result of using stops. In the case of the Swiss franc and Eurodollars, the increase in profits is most noticeable in case of the slow-reacting, longer-term moving-average crossover rules.

As a note of caution, it must be pointed out that optimal drawdown cutoff rules are likely to be sensitive to changes in market conditions. A significant shift in market conditions could result in a dramatic change in the unrealized loss pattern on both winning and losing trades. In view of this, the optimal drawdown cutoff rule for a given period should be based on the results of a drawdown analysis for profitable trades effected in the immediately preceding period.

BULL AND BEAR TRAPS

We now digress into a discussion of bull and bear traps and how not to fall prey to them. Bull and bear traps typically result from chasing a market that is perceived to be extremely bullish or bearish, as the case may be. Bullish expectations are reinforced by a sharply higher or "gap-up" opening, just as bearish expectations are supported by a sharply lower or "gap-down" opening. The trader enters the market at the opening price, hoping that the market will continue to move in the direction signaled by the opening price.

A bull trap occurs as a result of prices retreating from a sharply higher or gap-up opening. The pullback occurs during the same trading session that witnessed the strong opening, belying hints of a major rally.

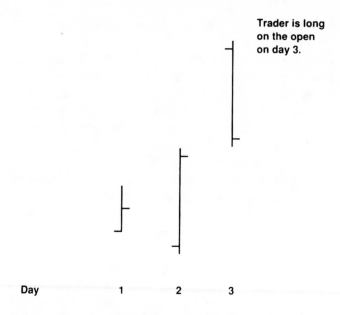

Day   1   2   3

Note: Notch to the left is opening price.
Notch to the right is settlement price.

Figure 6.3   A hypothetical example of a bull trap.

Consequently, an unsuspecting bull who bought the commodity at the opening price is left with an unrealized loss. The fact that prices might actually settle marginally higher than the preceding session offers little consolation to our harried trader, who has already fallen victim to a bull trap. Figure 6.3 illustrates the working of a bull trap.

A bear trap occurs as a result of prices recovering from a sharply lower or gap-down opening. The retracement occurs during the same trading session that witnessed the depressed opening, confounding expectations of an outright collapse. The retracement results in an unrealized loss for a gullible bear who sold the commodity at the gap-down opening price or shortly thereafter. Figure 6.4 illustrates a bear trap.

AVOIDING BULL AND BEAR TRAPS

The trauma arising out of bull and bear traps is not inevitable and should be avoided by means of an appropriate stop-loss order. Since a bull or

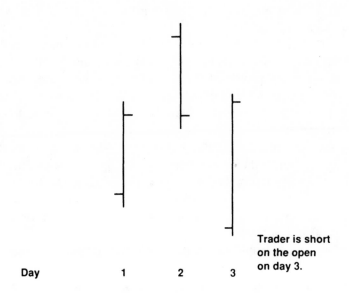

Day   1   2   3
                                           Trader is short
                                           on the open
                                           on day 3.

Note: Notch to the left is opening price.
Notch to the right is settlement price.

Figure 6.4   A hypothetical example of a bear trap.

bear trap develops as a result of entering the market at or soon after the
opening on any given day, a stop-loss order should be set with reference
to the opening price. In the following section, we analyze the location
of the opening price in relation to the high and low ends of the daily (or
weekly) trading range over a historical time period.

Analyzing Historical Opening Price Behavior

It is common knowledge that when prices are trending upwards, the
opening price for any given period lies near the low end of the day's
range and the settlement price lies above the opening price. Similarly,
when prices are trending downwards, the opening price for any given
period lies near the high end of the day's range and the settlement
price lies below the opening price. As a result, we observe a narrow
spread between the opening price and the day's low when prices are
trending upwards. Conversely, we observe a narrow spread between the

daily high and the opening price when prices are trending downwards. In some cases, we find the opening price to be exactly equal to the high of a down day or the low of an up day, leading to a zero spread.

For purposes of this analysis, an "up" period, either day or week, is defined as a trading period at the end of which the settlement price is higher than the opening price. Similarly, a "down" period is defined as a trading period at the end of which the settlement price is lower than the opening price.

Using this definition of up and down periods, we analyze the percentile distribution of the spread between the opening price and the high (low) for down (up) periods. Appendix E tabulates the findings separately for both up and down periods for 24 commodities and gives a percentage distribution of the spread. The results are based on data from January 1980 through June 1988.

Consider, for example, the 10 percent value of 2 ticks for up days in the British pound. This suggests that 10 percent of all up days in our sample have an opening price within 2 ticks of the day's low. Similarly, the 90 percent value of 32 ticks for down days implies that in 90 percent of the down days surveyed in our sample, the opening price is within 32 ticks of the day's high.

USING OPENING PRICE BEHAVIOR INFORMATION TO SET PROTECTIVE STOPS

The information given in Appendix E can be used by a trader who (a) has a definite opinion about the future direction of the market, (b) observes a gap opening in the direction he believes the market is headed, and (c) wishes to participate in the move without getting snared in a costly bull or bear trap. A bullish trader who enters a long position at a gap-up opening on a given day would want to set a stop-loss order n ticks below the opening price of that day. A bearish trader who enters a short position at a gap-down opening on a given day, would want to set a stop-loss order n ticks above the opening price of that day.

The value of n is based on the information given in Appendix E and corresponds to the percentile value of the spread between the open and the high (or the low) the trader is most comfortable with. A conservative approach would be to set the stop-loss order based on the 90 percent value of the distance in ticks between the open and the high price for an anticipated move downwards, or between the open and the low price, for an anticipated move upwards.

Suppose a trader is bearish on the Deutsche mark futures. Assume further that the Deutsche mark futures contract has a gap-down opening at $0.5980 just as our trader wishes to initiate a short position. In order to avoid falling into a bear trap, he would be advised to set a protective buy stop 17 ticks above the opening price, or at $0.5997. This is because our analysis reveals that the opening price lies within 17 ticks of the day's high in 90 percent of the down days for the Deutsche mark. The likelihood of getting stopped out of the trade erroneously is 10 percent. This implies that there is a 1 in 10 chance of the daily high being farther than 17 ticks from the opening price, with the day still ending up as a down day.

SURVIVING LOCKED-LIMIT MARKETS

A market is said to be "locked-limit" when trading is suspended consequent upon prices moving the exchange–stipulated daily limit. This section discusses strategies aimed at surviving a market that is "locked-limit" against the trader. Prices have moved against the trader, perhaps even through the stop-loss price. However, since trading is suspended, the position cannot be liquidated. What is particularly worrisome is the uncertainty surrounding the exit price, since there is no telling when normal trading will resume.

When caught in a market that is trading locked-limit, the primary concern is to contain the loss as best as is possible. In this section, we examine some of the alternatives available to help a trader cope with a locked-limit market.

Using Options to Create Synthetic Futures

In certain futures markets, options on futures are not affected by limit moves in the underlying futures. In such a case, the trader is free to use options to create a synthetic futures position that neutralizes the trader's existing futures position. For example, if she is long pork belly futures and the market is locked-limit against her, she might want to create a synthetic short futures position by simultaneously buying a put option and selling a call option for the same strike or exercise price on pork belly futures. Similarly, if she is short pork belly futures, and is caught in a limit-up market, she might create a synthetic long futures position by buying a call option and selling a put option for the same strike or exercise price on pork belly futures.

Since the synthetic futures position offsets the original futures position, the trader need not fret over her inability to exit the futures market. She has locked in a loss, as any loss suffered in subsequent locked-limit sessions in the futures market will be offset by an equal profit in the options market.

Using Options to Create a Hedge Against the Underlying Futures

If the trader is of the opinion that the locked-limit move represents a temporary aberration rather than a shift in the underlying trend, he might want to use options to protect or hedge rather than to liquidate his futures position. For example, if a trader is short pork belly futures, he might want to hedge himself by buying call options. Alternatively, if he is long pork belly futures, and believes that the limit move against him is a temporary setback, he might want to hedge himself by buying put options. When the market resumes its journey upwards after the temporary detour, the hedge may be liquidated by selling the option in question.

The protection offered by the hedge depends on the nature of the hedge. An in-the-money option has intrinsic value, which makes it a better hedge than an at-the-money option. In turn, an at-the-money option, with a strike or exercise price exactly equal to the current futures price, provides a better hedge than an out-of-the-money option with no intrinsic value. This is because an in-the-money option replicates the underlying futures contract more closely than an at-the-money option and much more so than an out-of-the-money option.

Whereas hedging a futures position with options does help ease the pain of loss, the magnitude of relief depends on the nature of the hedge. If the hedge is not perfect, or "delta neutral" in options parlance, the trader is still exposed to adverse futures price action and his loss might continue to grow.

Switching Out of a Locked-Limit Market

A switch is a two-step strategy that is available when at least one contract month in a given commodity has no trading limit. The rules as to when a switch is available vary from commodity to commodity and from exchange to exchange.

For example, during the month of July, July soybeans have no limit, whereas all other contract months have price limits. Accordingly, if a trader is long January 1992 soybeans and the market for January soybeans opens locked-limit down sometime in July 1991, the trader might wish to exit the January position through the following set of orders:

1. A spread order to buy a contract of July soybeans at the market, simultaneously selling a contract of January soybeans
2. A second order to sell a contract of July soybeans at the market, entered when order 1 is filled

Whereas the first order switches the trader from long January soybeans to long July soybeans, the second order offsets the July position. This is a circuitous but effective way of liquidating the January position. It may be noted that as long as one contract month is trading, the spread is usually available. However, owing to the extreme volatility of a market that is trading at locked-limit levels, the spreads tend to be extremely volatile. Care must be taken to ensure that the switch is carried out in the order here described.

Exchange for the Physical Commodity

As the name suggests, this strategy involves liquidating a locked-limit futures position by initiating an offsetting trade in the cash market. The cash market is not affected by the suspension of trading in the futures market, making the exchange a viable strategy. Notice that this strategy involves a single transaction and is therefore easier to implement than some of the multistep strategies just outlined.

MANAGING UNREALIZED PROFITS

Since losing trades typically outnumber winning trades, a trader has ample opportunity to master the art of controlling losses. As profitable trades are fewer in number, expertise in managing unrealized profits is that much harder to develop. The objective is to continue with a profitable trade as long as it promises even greater profits, while at the same time not exposing all the profits already earned on the trade.

When a trade is initiated, a protective stop-loss order should be placed to prevent unrealized losses from getting out of control. If prices move as anticipated, the protective stop-loss price should be updated so as to reflect the favorable price action, reducing exposure on the trade. At some stage, this process of updating stop-loss prices will result in a break-even trade. It is only after a break-even trade is assured that a profit conservation stop will take effect. In this section, we discuss strategies for setting profit conservation stops.

Limit Orders to Exit a Position

Often, an exit price is set so as to achieve a given profit target. For example, if a trader is long a commodity, he would set his exit price somewhere above the current market price. Similarly, if he were short, he would set his exit price somewhere below the current market price. These orders are termed limit orders. Once a limit order based on a profit target is hit, a trader ends up observing the rally, as a helpless spectator, instead of participating in it! Alternatively, if the profit target is not hit, the trader might feel pressured to continue with the trade, hoping to achieve his elusive profit target. This could be dangerous, especially if the trader is adamant about his view of the market and decides to wait it out to prove himself right.

Instead of using profit targets to exit the market, it would be more advisable to use stops as a means of protecting unrealized profits. This section offers two different approaches for setting unrealized profit conservation stops using

1. Chart-based support and resistance levels
2. Volatility-based trailing stops

Using Price Charts to Manage Unrealized Profits

Price charts provide a simple but effective means of setting profit conservation stops. A trader who anticipates a continuation of the current trend must decide how much of a retracement the market is capable of making without in any way disturbing the current trend. An example will help clarify this approach.

Consider the Deutsche mark futures price chart for the March 1990 contract given in Figure 6.5. Notice the 100-tick gap between the high of $0.5172 on September 22 and the low of $0.5272 on September 25.

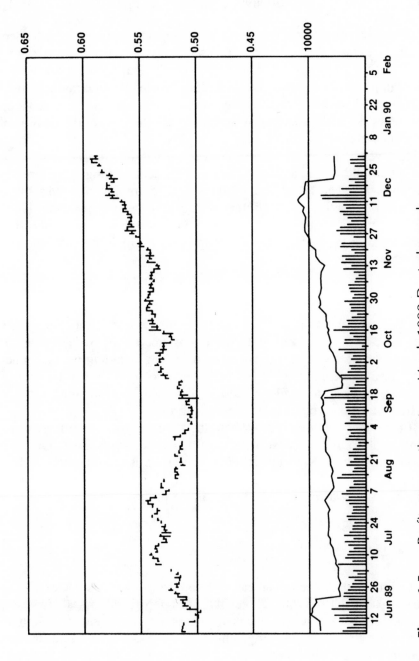

Figure 6.5   Profit conservation stops: March 1990 Deutsche mark.

111

This was the market's response to the weekend meeting of the leaders of seven industrialized nations. Consequently, a trader who was long the Deutsche mark coming into September 25 started the week with a windfall profit of over 100 ticks or $1250. Fearing that the market would fill the gap it had just created, he or she might want to set a sell stop just below $0.5272, the low of September 25, locking in the additional windfall profit of 100 ticks.

However, if the trader were not keen on getting stopped out, he or she would allow for a greater price retracement, setting a looser stop anywhere between $0.5172 and $0.5272. The unfolding of subsequent price action confirms that a trader would have been stopped out if the sell stop were set just below $0.5272. On the other hand, if the stop were set at or below $0.5200, the long position would be untouched by the retracement.

Using Volatility-Based Trailing Stops

The trader might want to set his or her profit conservation stop n ticks below the peak unrealized profit level registered on the trade. The number n could be based on the volatility for a single trading period, either a day or a week, or it could be the average volatility over a number of trading periods. If the trader so desires, he could work off some multiple or fraction of the volatility he proposes to use.

If the trader is not confident about the future course of the market, he might wish to lock in most of his profits. Consequently, he might want to set a tight volatility stop. Alternatively, if he is reasonably confident about the future trend, he might wish to work with a loose trailing stop, locking in only a fraction of his unrealized profits.

CONCLUSION

Setting no stops, although an easy way out, is not a viable alternative to setting reasonable stops to safeguard against unrealized losses. However, the definition of a reasonable stop is not etched in stone, and it is very much dependent on prevailing market conditions and the trading technique adopted by the trader.

A stop-loss order is designed to control the maximum amount that can be lost on a trade. Stop-loss orders may be set by reference to price charts or by reference to historical price action, typified by time and volatility stops. Alternatively, the trader might wish to set dollar value stops based on a predetermined amount he is willing to lose on a trade. Finally, the trader might analyze the unrealized loss pattern on completed profitable trades, using a given system to arrive at probability stops.

As and when the market moves in favor of the trader's position, the initial stop-loss price should be moved to lock in a part of the unrealized profits. A profit conservation stop replaces the initial stop-loss price. The amount of profits to be locked in depends upon an analysis of price charts or an analysis of historical price volatility of the commodity in question.

7

Managing the Bankroll: Controlling Exposure

The fraction of available funds exposed to potential trading loss is termed "risk capital." The higher this fraction, the higher the exposure and the greater the risk of loss. This chapter presents several approaches to determining the dollar amount to be risked to trading. Although the magnitude of this fraction depends upon the approach adopted, the following factors are relevant regardless of approach: (a) the size of the bankroll, (b) the probability of success, and (c) the payoff ratio—the ratio of the average win to the average loss.

Each approach is judged against the following yardsticks: (a) its reward potential, both in dollar terms and in terms of the time it takes to achieve a given target; (b) the associated risk of ruin; and (c) the practicality of the strategy. The optimal strategy is one that offers the greatest reward potential for a given level of risk and lends itself to easy implementation.

EQUAL DOLLAR EXPOSURE PER TRADE

True to its name, the equal-dollar-exposure approach recommends that a fixed dollar amount be risked per trade. The greatest appeal of this system is its simplicity. The dollar amount is independent of changes in

114

the original bankroll, thus necessitating no further calculations. However, the equal-dollar-exposure strategy is surpassed by other strategies that offer greater potential for growth of the bankroll for the same level of risk.

FIXED FRACTION EXPOSURE

A fixed-proportional-exposure system recommends that a trader always risk a fixed proportion of the current bankroll. Should the trader's bankroll decrease, the bet size decreases proportionately; as the bankroll increases, the trader bets more. The fixed-fraction system in its most simplistic sense is based strictly on the probability of trading success. The implicit assumption is that the average win is exactly equal to the average loss, leading to a payoff ratio of 1.

The probability of success is given by the ratio of the number of profitable trades to the total number of trades signaled by a trading system over a given time period. For example, if a system has generated 10 trades over the past year and six of these trades were profitable, the probability of success of that system is 0.60. The fixed fraction, f, of the current bankroll is given by the formula

$$f = [p - (1 - p)]$$

where p is the probability of winning using a given trading system, and $1 - p$ is the complementary probability of losing. If, for example, the trading system is found historically to generate 55 percent winners on average, then the formula would recommend risking $[0.55 - (1 - 0.55)]$ or 10 percent of available capital.

With a slightly higher success rate of 60 percent, the formula would suggest an allocation of $[0.60 - (1 - 0.60)]$ or 20 percent. Intuitively, it makes sense to risk a larger fraction of trading capital when confidence in signals generated by a given trading system runs high. If a system is not very reliable, it is only prudent to be wary about risking money on the basis of such a system.

This method of allocation presupposes that the probability of success for any given trading system is at least 51 percent. If a system cannot satisfy this benchmark criterion, then a trader ought not to rely on it in trading the futures markets. With a success rate of 50 percent, the probability of winning is exactly offset by the probability of losing, reducing the proportion of capital to be risked to $[0.50 - (1 - 0.50)]$ or 0.

Assume that the initial capital is equal to $20,000, and our trader uses a system which has a 55 percent probability of success. Hence, the trader decides to risk 10 percent of $20,000, or $2000, toward active trading. Assume further that every successful trade results in a profit exactly equal to the initial amount invested. For ease of illustration, let us also assume that every unsuccessful trade results in a loss equal to the initial amount invested.

Therefore, an investment of $2000 could result in a profit of $2000 or a loss of $2000. If the first trade turns out to be successful, the total trading capital will grow to 110 percent of the initial amount, or $22,000 ($20,000 × 1.10). The next time around, therefore, the trader should consider risking 10 percent of $22,000, or $2200, toward active trading. If the second trade happens to be a winner as well and results in a 100 percent return on investment, the balance will now grow to $24,200 ($22,000 × 1.10). The trader now can risk $2420 toward the third trade. However, if the first trade results in a loss, the trader now has only $18,000 ($20,000 × .90) available, and the amount that can be allocated toward the second trade will now shrink to 10 percent of $18,000, or $1800. If the second trade again results in a loss, the trader is now left with $16,200 ($18,000 × .90), or $1620, toward the third trade.

Notice that this system gradually increases or decreases the amount applied to active trading, depending on the results of prior trades. The system is particularly good at controlling the risk of ruin. Even if a trader continues to suffer a series of consecutive losses, the fixed-fraction system ensures that there is something left over for yet another trade.

Introducing Payoffs into the Formula

The implicit assumption in the discussion so far is that the dollar value of a profitable trade on average equals the dollar value of a losing trade. However, this is hardly ever true in futures trading. The principle of cutting losses in a hurry and letting profits ride, if faithfully followed, should result in the average profitable trade outweighing the average losing trade.

In other words, the payoff ratio, which compares the average dollar profit to the average dollar loss, is likely to be greater than 1. A payoff ratio of 2, for example, would mean that the dollar value of an average winning trade is twice as large as the dollar value of an average losing trade. The greater the payoff ratio, the more desirable the trading system. A successful trader could have just under 50 percent of trades as winners and come out ahead simply because the average winner is more than twice the average loser. Clearly, a method of exposure determination with no regard to the payoff ratio would be inaccurate at best.

In order to rectify this anomaly, Thorp[1] modified the fixed-fraction formula to account for the average payoff ratio, A, in addition to the average probability of success, p. The formula was originally developed by Kelly and is therefore sometimes referred to as the Kelly system.[2] Thorp also refers to the formula as the "optimal geometric growth portfolio" strategy, because it maximizes the long-term rate of growth of one's bankroll. The optimal fraction, f, of capital to be risked to trading may be defined as

$$f = \frac{[(A + 1)p] - 1}{A}$$

The numerator of this fraction is the expected profit on a one-dollar trade that is anticipated to yield either of two outcomes: (a) a profit of A with a probability p, or (b) a loss of \$1 with a probability of $(1 - p)$. The expected profit on this trade is the net amount likely to be earned, arrived at as follows:

$$A(p) - (1(1 - p)) = A(p) + p - 1$$
$$= [(A + 1)p] - 1$$

The probability-based fixed-fraction allocation formula, discussed earlier, is a special case of the current formula where the payoff ratio is assumed to be 1. To verify this, let us substitute a value of 1 for the payoff ratio, A, in the Kelly formula. Then

$$f = \frac{[(1 + 1)p] - 1}{1} = \frac{2p - 1}{1} = [p - (1 - p)]$$

Recall that in terms of the strict probability-based approach discussed previously, we had advised against trading a system that has a probability of success less than 0.51. However, with the introduction of the payoff

[1] Edward O. Thorp, *The Mathematics of Gambling* (Van Nuys, CA: Gambling Times Press, 1984).

[2] J. L. Kelly, "A New Interpretation of Information Rate," *Bell System Technical Journal*, Vol. 35, July 1956, pp. 917–926.

ratio into the equation, this is no longer true. The more generalized approach is not only more accurate but also more representative of reality. For example, if the probability of success is 0.33, and the payoff ratio is 5, the trader should risk 20 percent of trading capital toward a given trade, as given by

$$f = \frac{[(5 + 1)0.33] - 1}{5} = \frac{2 - 1}{5} = \frac{1}{5} = 0.20$$

The above discussion is based on the probability of success and the payoff ratio over a historical time period. The average probability of success is simply the ratio of the number of winning trades to the total number of trades over a historical time period. Similarly, the average payoff ratio is the ratio of the dollars earned on average across all winning trades to the dollars lost on average across all losing trades over a historical time period.

The major shortcoming of the Kelly approach just discussed is that it assumes that performance measures based on historical results are reliable predictors of the future. In real-life trading it is unlikely that the payoff ratio on a trade or its probability of success will coincide with the historical average. Chapter 9 provides empirical evidence in support of the instability of performance measures across time. In view of this, we need an approach that recognizes that each trade is unique. Average performance measures derived from a historical analysis of completed trades will not yield the optimal exposure fraction.

THE OPTIMAL FIXED FRACTION
USING THE MODIFIED KELLY SYSTEM

The modified approach relies on the original Kelly formula but uses trade-specific performance measures instead of historical averages to arrive at the optimal f. The modified Kelly system assumes that the probability of success and the payoff ratio are likely to vary across trades. Consequently, it reckons the optimal f for a trade based on the performance measures unique to that trade.

Ziemba simulates the performance of several betting systems and finds the modified Kelly system has the highest growth for a given level of risk. Ziemba concludes that "the other strategies either bet too little, and hence have too little growth, or bet too much and have high risk including many tapouts."[3]

ARRIVING AT TRADE-SPECIFIC OPTIMAL EXPOSURE

Trade-specific optimal exposure may be calculated using either (a) projected risk and reward estimates or (b) historic return data. The projected-risk-and-reward approach arrives at the optimal fraction, f, by calculating the payoff ratio and estimating the probability of success associated with a trade. The historic-return approach uses an iterative technique to arrive at the optimal value of f.

The Projected-Risk-and-Reward Approach

The projected-risk-and-reward approach assumes that the trader knows the likely reward and the permissible risk on a trade before its initiation. Based on past experience, the trader can estimate the probability of success. Assume, for example, that a trader is considering buying a contract of soybeans and is willing to risk 8 cents in the hope of earning 20 cents on the trade. Based on past performance, the probability of success is expected to be 0.45. Using this information, we calculate the payoff ratio, A, on the trade as follows:

$$\text{Payoff ratio, A} = \frac{\text{Expected win}}{\text{Permissible loss}}$$

$$= \frac{20}{8}$$

$$= 2.50$$

Next, calculate the expected value of the payoff ratio as under:

$$\begin{matrix} \text{Expected Value} \\ \text{of Payoff ratio} \end{matrix} = \begin{pmatrix} \text{Probability*Payoff} \\ \text{of winning ratio} \end{pmatrix} - \begin{pmatrix} \text{Probability * 1} \\ \text{of losing} \end{pmatrix}$$

$$= (0.45 * 2.50) - (0.55 * 1)$$

$$= 1.125 - 0.550$$

$$= 0.575$$

[3] William T. Ziemba, "A Betting Simulation: The Mathematics of Gambling and Investment," *Gambling Times*, June 1987.

Using this information, the optimal exposure fraction, f, for the soybean trade in question works out to be

$$f = \frac{[(2.50 + 1)0.45 - 1]}{2.50} = \frac{0.575}{2.500} = 0.23 \text{ or } 23\%$$

Hence the trader could risk 23 percent of the current bankroll on the soybean trade.

The Historic-Returns Approach

The historic-returns approach uses an iterative approach to arrive at a value of f that would have maximized the terminal wealth of a trader for a given set of historical trade returns. This is the optimal fraction of funds to be risked. As is true of all historical analyses, this approach makes the assumption that the fraction that was optimal over the recent past will continue to be optimal for the next trade. In the absence of precise risk and reward estimates, we have to live with this assumption.

This method has been developed by Vince[4]. Consider a sample of completed trades that includes at least one losing trade. The raw historical returns for each trade within the sample are divided by the return on the biggest losing trade. Next, the negative of this ratio is multiplied by a factor, f, and added to 1 to arrive at a weighted holding-period return. As a result, the weighted holding-period return (HPR) is defined as

$$\text{HPR on trade } i = 1 + \left[f \times \left(\frac{(-\text{Return on trade } i)}{\text{Return on worst losing trade}} \right) \right]$$

The terminal wealth relative (TWR) is the product of the weighted holding-period returns generated for a commodity across all trades over the sample period. Therefore, the terminal wealth relative (TWR) across n returns is

$$\text{TWR} = [(\text{HPR}_1) \times (\text{HPR}_2) \times (\text{HPR}_3) \times \cdots \times (\text{HPR}_n)]$$

By testing a number of values of f between 0.01 and 1, we arrive at the value of f that maximizes the TWR. This value represents the optimal fraction of funds to be allocated to the commodity in the next round of trading.

---

[4] Ralph Vince, *Portfolio Management Formulas* (New York: John Wiley and Sons, 1990).

Table 7.1   Calculating the Weighted
Holding-Period Return on Five Trades of X

Trade	Holding-Period Return
1	$1 + f\left(-\dfrac{+0.25}{-0.35}\right) = 1 + f(+0.71428)$
2	$1 + f\left(-\dfrac{-0.35}{-0.35}\right) = 1 + f(-1.00000)$
3	$1 + f\left(-\dfrac{+0.40}{-0.35}\right) = 1 + f(+1.14286)$
4	$1 + f\left(-\dfrac{-0.10}{-0.35}\right) = 1 + f(-0.28571)$
5	$1 + f\left(-\dfrac{+0.30}{-0.35}\right) = 1 + f(+0.85714)$

For example, let us consider the following sequence of trade returns for a commodity X:

$$+0.25 \quad -0.35 \quad +0.40 \quad -0.10 \quad +0.30$$

The worst losing trade yields a return of -0.35. Each return is divided by this value, and the resulting holding period returns are given in Table 7.1. Using the information in that table, we calculate the TWR for f values equal to 0.10, 0.25, 0.35, 0.40, and 0.45, as shown in Table 7.2. Since the TWR is maximized when $f = 0.40$, this is the optimal fraction, f^*, of funds to be allocated to the next trade in X.

Table 7.2   Calculating the TWR for X for Different Values of f

	Holding-Period Return (HPR)				
Trade	$f = 0.10$	$f = 0.25$	$f = 0.35$	$f = 0.40$	$f = 0.45$
1	1.07143	1.17857	1.25000	1.28571	1.32143
2	0.90000	0.75000	0.65000	0.60000	0.55000
3	1.11428	1.28571	1.40000	1.45714	1.51429
4	0.97143	0.92857	0.90000	0.88572	0.87143
5	1.08571	1.21429	1.30000	1.34286	1.38571
TWR =	1.13325	1.28144	1.33087	1.33697	1.32899

MARTINGALE VERSUS ANTI-MARTINGALE BETTING STRATEGIES

The discussion so far has concentrated exclusively on the projected performance of a trade in determining the optimal exposure fraction. Changes in available capital are considered, but only indirectly. For example, a 10 percent optimal exposure fraction on available capital of $10,000 would entail risking $1000. If the capital in the account grew to $12,000, a 10 percent exposure would now amount to $1200, an increase of $200. However, if the capital were to shrink to $7500, a 10 percent exposure would amount to $750, a decrease of $250.

Critics of performance-based approaches would like to see a more direct linkage between the exposure fraction and changes in available capital. An aggressive trader, it is argued, might use adversity as a spur to even greater risks. After all, such a trader is interested in recouping losses in the shortest possible time. A risk-averse trader, when faced with similar misfortune, might be inclined to scale down the exposure. Assuming a trader were interested in a more direct linkage between the exposure fraction and changes in available capital, what are the options available and what are their relative merits?

This section examines two strategies that incorporate the outcome of closed-out trades and consequential changes in the bankroll into the calculation of the exposure fraction. The exposure fraction either increases or decreases, depending on the trader's risk threshold. A strategy that doubles the size of the bet after a loss is termed a Martingale strategy. The word Martingale is derived from a village named Martigues in the Provence district of southern France, whose residents were noted for their bizarre behavior. An example of such behavior was doubling up on losing bets. Consequently, the doubling up system was dubbed as gambling "à la Martigals," or "in the Martigues manner." Conversely, a strategy that doubles bet size after each win is referred to as an anti-Martingale strategy.

The Martingale Strategy

The Martingale strategy proposes that a trader bet one unit to begin with, double the bet on each loss, and revert to one unit after each win. The attraction of this technique is that when the trader finally does win, it allows him or her to recover all prior losses. In fact, a win always sets the trader ahead by one betting unit.

However, because the bet size increases rapidly during a sequence of losses, it is quite likely that the trader will run out of capital before recovering the losses! More importantly, in order to prevent heavily capitalized gamblers from implementing this strategy successfully, most casinos impose limits on the size of permissible bets. Similar restrictions are imposed by exchanges on the size of positions that may be assumed by speculators.

The Anti-Martingale Strategy

As the name suggests, the anti-Martingale strategy recommends a starting bet of one unit; the bet doubles after each win and reverts to one unit after each loss. Since the increased bet size is financed by winnings in the market, the trader's capital is secure. The shortcoming of this approach is that since there is no way of predicting the outcome of a trade, the largest bet might well be placed on a losing trade immediately following a successful trade.

Evaluation of the Alternative Strategies

Bruce Babcock[5] provides a comparative study of the two strategies, using a neutral strategy as a benchmark for comparison. The neutral strategy recommends trading an equal number of contracts at all times regardless of wins or losses. The Martingale strategy turns in the largest percentage of winning streaks, regardless of trading system used. However, the high risk of the strategy, given by the magnitude of the worst loss, makes it unsuitable for commodities trading. Moreover, the capital required to carry a trader through periods of adversity makes the strategy impractical.

The anti-Martingale strategy incurs lower risk while affording the highest profit potential. The average profits under the neutral strategy are the lowest, with the worst loss being no greater than under the anti-Martingale strategy. Clearly, the strategy of working with a constant number of contracts was overshadowed by the anti-Martingale strategy.

[5] Bruce Babcock, Jr., *The Dow Jones-Irwin Guide to Trading Systems* (Homewood, IL: Dow Jones-Irwin, 1989).

In Babcock's study the anti-Martingale strategy increased performance appreciably, without any appreciable increase in total risk. This should inspire small, one-contract traders to build steadily on their wins. Babcock's findings confirm that a trader may double exposure after a win, but doubling up after a loss in the hope of recouping the loss could prove to be a risky and financially draining strategy.

As a word of caution, it should be pointed out that the advantage of the anti-Martingale strategy is contingent upon using a winning system — that is, a system with a positive mathematical expectation of reward. As Babcock rightly concludes, "In the long run, no trade management strategy can turn a losing system into a winner."[6]

TRADE-SPECIFIC VERSUS AGGREGATE EXPOSURE

The discussion so far has revolved around the optimal exposure fraction for a trade. Assuming that multiple commodities are traded simultaneously, what should the optimal exposure, F, be across all trades? An obvious answer is to sum the optimal exposure fractions, f, across the individual commodities traded. However, the simple aggregation approach suffers on two counts.

First, it assumes zero correlation between commodity returns. This may not always be true and could lead to inaccurate answers. For example, if the returns on two commodities are positively correlated, the aggregate optimal exposure across both commodities would be lower than the optimal exposure on the commodities individually. Conversely, if the returns are negatively correlated, the aggregate optimal exposure would be higher than the sum of the optimal exposure on the individual commodities.

For ease of analysis, we could assume that (a) positively correlated commodities will not be traded concurrently and (b) negative correlations between commodities may be ignored. Since strong negative correlations between commodities are uncommon, the theoretical invalidity of assumption (b) is not as worrisome as it appears.

The more serious problem with the simple aggregation technique is that it does not guard against an aggregate exposure fraction greater

---

[6] Babcock, *Guide to Trading Systems*, p. 25.

than 1. This is clearly unacceptable, since risking an amount in excess of one's bankroll is practically infeasible! Here is where the simple aggregation technique breaks down, necessitating an alternative approach to defining F.

The approach presented here is an iterative procedure similar to the Vince technique previously discussed for the one-commodity case. This approach assumes that the mix of traded commodities analyzed will be identical to the mix to be traded in the next period. It further assumes stability of the correlations between returns. Finally, it assumes that the sample of joint returns will include at least one losing trade with a negative return.

Calculating Joint Returns across Commodities

The joint return for trade, i, across a set of commodities is the geometric average of the individual commodity returns for that trade. The geometric average gives equal weight to each trade, regardless of the magnitude of the trade return. Therefore, it is not unduly affected by extreme values. The geometric average return, R_i, for trade i across n commodities is worked out as follows:

$$R_i = [(1 + R_{i1}) \times (1 + R_{i2}) \times (1 + R_{i3}) \times \cdots \times (1 + R_{in})]^{1/n} - 1$$

where R_{ij} = realized return on trade i for commodity j.

Assume that a trader has traded three commodities, A, B, and C, over the past year. Assume further that over this period seven trades were executed for A, four for B, and two for C. The returns on the individual trades and the joint returns across commodities were as shown in Table 7.3. Notice that the number of joint returns equals the maximum number of trades for any single commodity in the portfolio. In our example, we have seven joint returns to accommodate the maximum number of trades for commodity A. For trades 5, 6, and 7, the joint returns are essentially the returns on commodity A, since there are no matching trades for B and C.

The negative return on the worst losing trade is -0.25. Each joint return is divided by this value. The negative of this ratio is multiplied by a factor, F, and added to 1 to arrive at an aggregate weighted holding-period return (HPR) for a trade i. Therefore,

$$\text{HPR}_i = 1 + \left[F \times \left(\frac{-\text{Return on trade } i}{\text{Return on worst losing trade}} \right) \right]$$

Table 7.3   Computing Joint Returns
across a Portfolio of Commodities

Trade #	Return Realized on			Geometric Joint Return on A, B and C
	A	B	C	
1	−0.20	−0.35	0.50	$[(0.80)(0.65)(1.50)]^{1/3} - 1 = -0.079$
2	0.25	0.15	−0.25	$[(1.25)(1.15)(0.75)]^{1/3} - 1 = 0.025$
3	−0.50	0.75		$[(0.50)(1.75)]^{1/2} - 1 = -0.065$
4	0.75	−0.10		$[(1.75)(0.90)]^{1/2} - 1 = 0.255$
5	0.35			$= 0.350$
6	−0.25			$= -0.250$
7	0.10			$= 0.100$

In the foregoing example, the weighted holding-period return for each of the 7 trades may be calculated as shown in Table 7.4.

The terminal wealth relative (TWR) is the product of the weighted joint holding-period returns generated across trades over a given time period, using a predefined F value. Therefore, the TWR across n trades

Table 7.4   Calculating the Aggregate
Weighted Holding-Period Return

Trade	Holding-Period Return
1	$1 + F\left(-\dfrac{-0.079}{-0.250}\right) = 1 + F(-0.316)$
2	$1 + F\left(-\dfrac{+0.025}{-0.250}\right) = 1 + F(+0.100)$
3	$1 + F\left(-\dfrac{-0.065}{-0.250}\right) = 1 + F(-0.260)$
4	$1 + F\left(-\dfrac{+0.255}{-0.250}\right) = 1 + F(+1.020)$
5	$1 + F\left(-\dfrac{+0.350}{-0.250}\right) = 1 + F(+1.400)$
6	$1 + F\left(-\dfrac{-0.250}{-0.250}\right) = 1 + F(-1.000)$
7	$1 + F\left(-\dfrac{+0.100}{-0.250}\right) = 1 + F(+0.400)$

Table 7.5   Calculating the Aggregate TWR for Different Values of F

	Holding-Period Return (HPR)				
Trade	$F = 0.25$	$F = 0.30$	$F = 0.35$	$F = 0.40$	$F = 0.45$
1	0.921	0.905	0.889	0.874	0.858
2	1.025	1.030	1.035	1.040	1.045
3	0.935	0.922	0.909	0.896	0.883
4	1.255	1.306	1.357	1.408	1.459
5	1.350	1.420	1.490	1.560	1.630
6	0.750	0.700	0.650	0.600	0.550
7	1.100	1.120	1.140	1.160	1.180
TWR =	1.2337	1.2496	1.2531	1.2450	1.2219

is defined as

$$TWR = [(HPR_1) \times (HPR_2) \times (HPR_3) \times \ldots \times (HPR_n)]$$

where HPR_i represents the joint return for trade i.

By testing a number of values of F between 0.01 and 1, we can arrive at the value of F that maximizes TWR. This value, F^*, represents the optimal fraction of funds to be risked across all commodities during the next round of trading. Continuing with our example, we calculate the TWR for F values equal to 0.25, 0.30, 0.35, 0.40, and 0.45, as shown in Table 7.5. Since the TWR is maximized when $F = 0.35$, this is the optimal fraction, F^*, of funds to be allocated to the next round of trading. More accurately, the TWR is maximized at 1.2539 when $F = 0.34$, suggesting that 34 percent of the available capital should be risked to trading.

CONCLUSION

The allocation of capital across commodities is at the heart of any trading program. If a trader were to risk the entire bankroll to active trading, chances are that all the trades could go against the trader, who could end up losing everything in the account. In view of this, it is recommended that a trader risk only a fraction of his or her total capital to active trading. This fraction is a function of the probability of trading success and the payoff ratio. The fraction of available capital exposed to active trading is termed "risk capital."

The exposure fraction could be a fixed proportion of the trader's current bankroll, or it could vary as a function of changes in the bankroll. A loss results in a depletion of capital, and a trader might want to recoup this loss by increasing exposure. This is referred to as the Martingale strategy. The converse strategy of reducing the size of the bet consequent upon a loss is referred to as the anti-Martingale strategy. The anti-Martingale strategy is a more practical and conservative approach to trading than the Martingale strategy.

8

Managing the Bankroll: Allocating Capital

The previous chapter concentrated on exposure determination for a single commodity as well as across multiple commodities. In this chapter, we present various approaches to risk capital allocation across commodities. Following this discussion, we turn to strategies designed to increase the risk capital allocated to a trade during its life. This is commonly referred to as pyramiding.

ALLOCATING RISK CAPITAL ACROSS COMMODITIES

If all opportunities are assumed to be equally attractive in terms of both their risk and their reward potential, a trader would be best off trading an equal number of contracts of each of the commodities under consideration. For example, a trader might want to trade one contract or, if he or she is better capitalized or more of a risk seeker, more than one contract of each commodity, always keeping the number constant across all commodities traded.

The equal-number-of-contracts technique is particularly easy to implement when a trader is unclear about both the risk and the reward potential associated with a trade. Whereas the simplicity of this technique is its chief virtue, it does not necessarily result in optimal performance. The allocation techniques discussed here assume that (a) some opportunities are more promising than others in terms of higher reward potential or lower risk and (b) there exists a mechanism to identify these differences.

We begin with a discussion of risk capital allocation within the context of a single-commodity portfolio. In subsequent sections, we discuss allocation techniques when more than one commodity is traded simultaneously.

ALLOCATION WITHIN THE CONTEXT OF A SINGLE-COMMODITY PORTFOLIO

When a portfolio is comprised of a single commodity, the optimal exposure fraction, f, for that commodity may be used as the basis for the risk capital allocated to it. Multiplying the optimal fraction, f, by the current bankroll gives the risk capital allocation for the commodity in question. Therefore,

$$\text{Risk capital allocation for a commodity} = f \times \text{Current bankroll}$$

For example, if the current bankroll were \$10,000, and the optimal f for a commodity were 14 percent, the risk capital allocation would be \$1400. However, if the trader wished to set a cap on the maximum amount he or she were willing to risk to a particular trade, such a cap would override the percentage recommended by the optimal f. For example, if the maximum exposure on a single commodity were restricted to 5 percent, this restriction would override the optimal f allocation of 14 percent.

ALLOCATION WITHIN THE CONTEXT OF A MULTI-COMMODITY PORTFOLIO

Risk capital allocation is especially important when more than one commodity is traded simultaneously. This section discusses three alternative techniques for allocating risk capital across a portfolio of commodities:

1. Equal-dollar risk capital allocation
2. Optimal allocation following modern portfolio theory
3. Individual trade allocation based on the optimal f for each commodity.

EQUAL-DOLLAR RISK CAPITAL ALLOCATION

Once the aggregate exposure fraction, F, has been determined, the equal-dollar approach recommends an equal allocation of risk capital across each commodity traded. The exact allocation is a function of (a) the aggregrate exposure and (b) the number of commodities realistically expected to be traded concurrently. This technique is based on the assumption that a trader can quantify the dollar risk for a given trade but is unsure about the associated reward potential. The approach also assumes the existence of negligible correlation between commodity returns.

The dollar allocation for each commodity is arrived at by dividing the total risk capital allocation by the number of commodities expected to be traded concurrently. Assume, for example, that the aggregate risk capital fraction, F, is 20 percent of $25,000, or $5000, and the trader expects to trade a maximum of five commodities concurrently. The risk capital allocation for each commodity would be $1000. However, if the trader expects to trade only two commodities simultaneously, the risk capital allocation works out to be $2500 for each commodity. Therefore,

$$\frac{\text{Risk capital}}{\text{per commodity}} = \frac{\text{Aggregrate exposure across commodities}}{\text{number of commodities traded}}$$

Like the equal-number-of-contracts approach, the equal-dollar risk capital allocation approach is easy to implement. However, it would be naïve to expect it to yield optimal allocations, because reward potentials and correlations between commodity returns are disregarded.

OPTIMAL CAPITAL ALLOCATION:
ENTER MODERN PORTFOLIO THEORY

The optimal-allocation strategy recommends differential capital allocation and is based on the premise that no two opportunities share the same risk and reward characteristics. Modern portfolio theory is based on the premise that there is a definite relationship between reward and risk. The higher the risk, the greater the reward required to induce an investor to assume such risk.

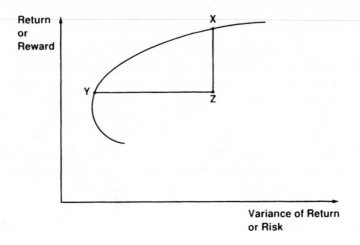

Figure 8.1   Relationship between reward and risk: tracing the efficient frontier.

Harry Markowitz was the first to formalize the relationship between risk and reward.[1] Markowitz argued that investors, given a choice, would like to invest in a portfolio of stocks that offered a return higher than that yielded by their current portfolio but was no more risky. Alternatively, they would like to invest in a portfolio of stocks that would lower the overall risk of investing while holding reward constant. Risk is measured in terms of the variability of portfolio returns. The higher the variability, the greater the risk associated with investing.

The theoretical relationship between reward and risk is graphically demonstrated in Figure 8.1. The curve connecting the various reward and risk coordinates is termed the "efficient frontier." A portfolio that lies below the efficient frontier is an inefficient portfolio inasmuch as it is outperformed by corresponding portfolios on the efficient frontier.

For example, consider the case of portfolio Z in Figure 8.1, which lies vertically below portfolio X and laterally to the right of Y. Portfolio Z is outperformed by both X and Y, insofar as X offers a higher return for the same risk and Y offers a lower risk for the same return. Therefore, the investor would be better off investing in either X or Y, depending on whether he or she wishes to improve portfolio return or to reduce portfolio risk. This, in turn, is a function of the investor's risk preference.

[1] Harry Markowitz: *Portfolio Selection: Efficient Diversification of Investments* (New York: John Wiley and Sons, 1959).

In this section, we construct an optimal futures portfolio that lies on the efficient frontier. This is a portfolio that minimizes the variance of portfolio returns while achieving the target return specified by the trader. The problem seeks to minimize overall portfolio variance while satisfying the following constraints:

1. The expected return on the portfolio must be equal to a prespecified target.
2. The portfolio weights across all trades must sum to 1, signifying that the sum of the allocations across trades cannot exceed the overall risk capital allocation.
3. The individual portfolio weights must equal or exceed 0.

Appendix F defines this as a problem in constrained optimization, to be solved using standard quadratic programming techniques. The solution to the optimization problem is defined in terms of a set of optimal weights, w_i, representing the fraction of risk capital to be exposed to trading commodity i.

Inputs for the Optimization Technique

The inputs for the optimization technique are (a) the expected returns on individual trades, (b) the variance of individual trade returns and the covariances between returns on all possible pairs of commodities in the opportunity set, and (c) the overall portfolio return target. Each of these inputs is discussed in detail here.

The Rate of Return on Individual Trades and the Portfolio

As discussed in Chapter 4, the rate of return, r, on a futures trade is measured as the sum of the present values of all cash flows generated during the life of the trade, divided by the initial margin investment.

Ideally, the portfolio selection model requires that we work with the expected returns on trades under consideration. In order to implement the model, therefore, the trader would need to know the estimated reward on the trade. This could be computed using the reward estimation techniques discussed in Chapter 3. Additionally, the trader would need to estimate the approximate time it would take to reach the target price. Since every trade is expected to be profitable at the outset, the variation margin term could be ignored in the return calculations.

If the trader uses a mechanical system that is silent as regards the estimated reward on a trade, the return cannot be forecast. In such a case, the trader could use the historical average realized return on completed trades for a commodity as a proxy for expected returns on future trades. The historic average is the arithmetic average of returns on completed trades.

The arithmetic average return, $\overline{X}$, on n trades with a return X_i on trade i is the sum of the n returns divided by n and is given by the following formula:

$$\overline{X} = (X_1 + X_2 + X_3 + \cdots + X_n)/n$$

The greater the number of trades in the sample, the more robust the average. Ideally, the arithmetic average should be computed based on a sample of at least 30 realized returns.

The weighted portfolio expected return is calculated by multiplying each commodity's expected return by the corresponding fraction of risk capital allocated to that trade. The overall portfolio return is fixed at a prespecified target, T, to be decided by the trader. The overall portfolio target should be realistic and be in line with the returns expected on the individual commodities. If the return target is set at an unrealistically high level, the optimization program will yield an infeasible solution.

Variance and Covariance of Returns

The riskiness of commodity returns is measured by the variance of such returns about their mean. The covariance between returns seeks to capture interdependencies between pairs of commodity returns. The existence of negative covariances between commodity returns could lead to an overall portfolio variance lower than the sum of the variances on the individual commodities. Similarly, the existence of positive covariances between commodity returns could lead to an overall portfolio variance higher than the sum of the variances on the individual commodities.

To recapitulate, the variance, s_X^2, of n historical returns for commodity X, with an arithmetic average return $\overline{X}$, is calculated as follows:

$$s_X^2 = \frac{\sum_i (X_i - \overline{X})^2}{n - 1}$$

The covariance, s_{XY}, between n historical returns for X and Y, with arithmetic average returns $\overline{X}$ and $\overline{Y}$, respectively, is

$$s_{XY} = \frac{\sum_i (X_i - \overline{X})(Y_i - \overline{Y})}{n - 1}$$

If there are K commodities under consideration, there will be K variance terms and $[K(K - 1)]/2$ covariance terms to be estimated. For example, if there are 3 commodities under review, X, Y, and Z, we need the covariance between returns for (a) X and Y, (b) X and Z, and (c) Y and Z. Typically, the variance-covariance matrix is estimated using historical data on a pair of commodities. The assumption is that the past is a good reflector of the future. Given the disparate nature of trade lives, we could well observe an unequal number of trades for two or more commodities over a fixed historical time period, making it impossible to calculate the resulting covariances between their returns. To remedy this problem, historical price data is often used as a proxy for trade returns.

Assuming portfolio returns are normally distributed, a distance of ± 1.96 standard deviations around the mean portfolio return captures approximately 95 percent of the fluctuations in returns. The lower the specified portfolio variance, the tighter the spread around the mean portfolio return. The assumption of normality of portfolio returns has been empirically validated by Lukac and Brorsen.[2] Their study revealed that whereas portfolio returns are normally distributed, returns on individual commodities tend to be positively skewed, underscoring the fact that most trading systems are designed to cut losses quickly and let profits ride.

Limitations of the Optimal-Allocation Approach

The optimal-allocation approach discussed above is based on a comparison of competing opportunities and is reminiscent of stock portfolio construction. Implicit in this approach is the assumption that there will be no addition to or deletion from the opportunities currently under review. This is well suited to stock investing, where the investment horizon is fairly long-term and the opportunity set is not subject to frequent changes.

Changes in the opportunity set would result in corresponding changes in the relative weights assigned to individual opportunities. Such changes

[2] Louis P. Lukac and R. Wade Brorsen, "A Comprehensive Test of Futures Market Disequilibrium," *The Financial Review*, Vol. 25, No. 4 (November 1990), pp. 593–622.

could result in premature liquidation of trades and would detract from the efficacy of the optimal-allocation exercise. As a result, the optimal-allocation approach would be useful to a position trader with a longer-term perspective. However, it could prove inconvenient for a trader with an extremely short-term view of the markets, who sees the menu of opportunities changing almost every trading day.

A more serious handicap is that the optimal fraction of risk capital allocated to a trade could lie anywhere between 0 and 1. A fraction of 0 implies no position in the commodity, whereas a fraction of 1 implies that the the entire risk capital is allocated to a single trade. If such a concentration of resources were unacceptable, the trader might want to set a cap on the funds to be allocated to a single commodity. However, such a cap would have to be imposed by the trader as a sequel to the results obtained from the optimization program, as the program does not allow for caps to be superimposed on the individual weights.

An Illustration of Optimal Portfolio Construction

Consider Table 8.1, which presents the historical returns on two commodities, A and B. Using historical average returns as estimators of

Table 8.1   Historical Returns on A and B

Trade	% Return on A	% Return on B
1	100	50
2	−45	−20
3	40	−10
4	−25	55
5	−35	100
6	50	−60
7	−10	50
8	50	−45
9	75	−50
10	50	130
Arithmetic Average Return:	25	20
Variance of Returns:	2494	4394
Standard Deviation:	49.94	66.29
Covariance of Returns:		−819.44
Correlation between A and B:		−0.2475

Table 8.2   Tracing the Efficient Frontier for Portfolios of A and B

Portfolio Number	% weight in A	% weight in B	Portfolio Return	Portfolio Variance
1	61.20	38.80	23.06	1206.67
2	78.60	21.40	23.93	1466.64
3	81.00	19.00	24.05	1543.02
4	84.20	15.80	24.21	1660.14
5	88.80	11.20	24.44	1859.11
6	95.60	4.40	24.78	2219.33

future expected returns, we could construct an optimal portfolio of A and B that would minimize variance for a specified target level of portfolio returns. To illustrate the dynamics of this process, Table 8.2 traces the efficient frontier for portfolios of A and B, giving the optimal weights for different levels of portfolio variance and the return associated with each variance level.

Notice that a rise in the portfolio return is accompanied by a corresponding rise in portfolio variance. The trader must specify the portfolio return he or she seeks to achieve. For example, if the trader wishes to earn an overall portfolio return of 23 percent, the optimal portfolio is 1, with weights of 61.20 percent and 38.80 percent for A and B respectively. The variance for this optimal portfolio is 1206.67. If the target return is set slightly higher, at 24 percent, the optimal portfolio is 3, with weights of 81.00 percent and 19.00 percent for A and B respectively. The variance for this portfolio is higher at 1543.02. If the target return were set greater than 25 percent, the optimization program would yield an infeasible solution. This is because the highest return that could be earned by allocating 100 percent of risk capital to the higher return asset, A, would be just 25 percent.

USING THE OPTIMAL *f* AS A BASIS FOR ALLOCATION

This approach uses the optimal exposure fraction, *f*, for a commodity as the basis for the capital allocated to it. For simplicity, the approach assumes that (a) the trader will not trade positively correlated commodities concurrently and (b) negative correlations between commodities may be ignored. Consequently, each opportunity is judged independently rather than as part of a portfolio of concurrently traded commodities.

Multiplying the optimal fraction, f, for a commodity by the current bankroll gives the risk capital allocation for that commodity. The trader might want to set a cap on the maximum percentage of total capital he or she is willing to risk on any given trade. If such a cap were in existence, it would override the percentage recommended by the optimal f. If, for example, the maximum exposure on a single commodity were restricted to 5 percent, this restriction would override an optimal f allocation greater than 5 percent.

The trader must ensure that the total exposure across all commodities at any time does not exceed the overall optimal exposure fraction, F. The problem of overshooting is most likely to arise (a) when positions are assumed in all or a majority of the commodities traded or (b) if one commodity receives a disproportionately large allocation. Complying with the aggregate exposure fraction on an overall basis might necessitate forgoing some opportunities. This is a judgment call the trader must make, not merely to contain the risk of ruin but also to ensure that he or she stays within the confines of the available capital. This brings us to the related issue of the relationship between risk capital and funds available for trading. The following section discusses the linkage.

LINKAGE BETWEEN RISK CAPITAL AND AVAILABLE CAPITAL

Assume that the aggregate exposure fraction across all commodities is given by F. The reciprocal of F, given by $1/F$, represents the multiple of funds available for each dollar at risk. For example, if F is 10 percent or 0.10, we have $1/0.10$, or $10, backing every $1 of capital risked to a trade.

Although this multiple is based on the overall relationship between risk capital and the current bankroll, it could be used to determine the proportion of the bankroll to be set aside for individual trades. Assume that the aggregate risk exposure fraction, F, is 10 percent across all commodities. Assume further that the trader wishes to allocate 4 percent of the risk capital to commodity A, and 2 percent to commodity B. The trader does not wish to pursue any other opportunities at the moment. Given a multiple of $1/0.10$ or 10, commodity A qualifies for an allocation of 4 percent × 10, or 40 percent, of the funds in the account. Commodity B qualifies for a capital allocation of 2 percent × 10, or 20 percent. This will result in a 60 percent utilization of available capital, leaving 40 percent available for future opportunities.

DETERMINING THE NUMBER OF CONTRACTS TO BE TRADED

The number of contracts of a commodity to be traded is a function of (a) the risk capital allocation, in relation to the permissible risk per contract, and (b) the funds allocated to a commodity, in relation to the initial margin required per contract.

The available capital allocated to the commodity, divided by the initial margin requirement per contract, gives a margin-based estimate of the number of contracts to be traded. Similarly, the risk capital allocated to a commodity, divided by the permissible risk per contract, gives a risk-based estimate of the number of contracts to be traded. Therefore,

$$\text{Margin-based estimate of the number of contracts to be traded} = \frac{\text{Available capital allocation}}{\text{Initial margin per contract}}$$

$$\text{Risk-based estimate of the number of contracts to be traded} = \frac{\text{Risk capital allocation}}{\text{Permissible risk per contract}}$$

When the risk-based estimate differs from the margin-based estimate, the trader has a conflict. To resolve this conflict, select the approach that yields the lower of the two estimates, so as to comply with both risk and margin constraints. An example will help illustrate the potential conflict between the two approaches, and its resolution. Assume that the aggregate exposure fraction, F, recommends a risk capital allocation of 10 percent of total capital of $100,000, or $10,000. Assume further that a trader wishes to trade three commodities $A, B,$ and C concurrently, with risk capital allocations of 6 percent, 3 percent, and 1 percent, respectively.

Table 8.3 defines the permissible risk per contract of each of the three commodities along with their initial margin requirements. It also calculates the number of contracts to be traded, based on both the risk and margin criteria.

Table 8.3   Determining the Number of Contracts to be Traded

Commodity	Capital Allocation		Per Contract		Risk/ Margin	Number of Contracts by	
	Risk	Total	Risk	Margin		Risk	Margin
A	6,000	60,000	1,000	20,000	0.05	6	3
B	3,000	30,000	500	2,500	0.20	6	12
C	1,000	10,000	2,000	20,000	0.10	0.5	0.5

Notice that in the case of commodity A, the margin constraint prescribes three contracts, whereas the risk constraint recommends six contracts. The margin constraint prevails over the risk constraint, since the trader simply does not have the margin needed to trade six contracts. In the case of commodity B, the risk constraint recommends six contracts, whereas the margin constraint recommends 12 contracts. In this case the capital allocation is adequate to meet the margin required for 12 contracts; however, the risk capital allocation falls short. Therefore, the risk constraint prevails over the margin constraint. Finally, in the case of commodity C, both risk and margin approaches are unanimous in recommending 0.5 contracts, avoiding the choice problems which arose in cases A and B.

A closer look at the data in Table 8.3 reveals an interesting relationship between the aggregate exposure fraction, F, and the ratio of permissible risk to the initial margin required for each of the three commodities. The aggregate exposure fraction, 10 percent in our example, represents a ratio of overall risk exposure to total capital available for trading. Whereas the ratio of permissible risk/margin is lower, at 5 percent, than the aggregate exposure fraction for A, it is higher for B at 20 percent, and is exactly equal for C.

Consequently, if the permissible risk/margin ratio for a given commodity is greater than the aggregate exposure fraction, F, the permissible risk rather than the margin requirement determines the number of contracts to be traded. Similarly, if the permissible risk/margin ratio for a commodity is lower than the aggregate exposure fraction, F, it is the margin requirement rather than the permissible risk, that determines the number of contracts traded. If the permissible risk/margin ratio for a commodity is exactly equal to the aggregate exposure fraction, F, then both risk and margin constraints yield identical results.

THE ROLE OF OPTIONS IN DEALING WITH FRACTIONAL CONTRACTS

If the allocation strategy just outlined recommends fractional contracts, a conservative rule would be to ignore fractions and to work with the smallest whole number of contracts. For example, if 2.4 contracts of a commodity were recommended, the conservative trader would initiate a position in two rather than three contracts of the commodity. By doing so, the trader ensures that he or she stays within the risk and total capital allocation constraints.

However, this strategy fails when the recommended optimal solution recommends less than one contract, as, for example, commodity C (0.5 contracts) in the preceding illustration. Since the trader is advised against rounding off to the next higher whole number, he or she would have to forgo the trade. This problem is likely to arise in the case of commodities with large margin requirements, as, for example, the Standard & Poor's (S&P) 500 Index futures. A trader who is keen on pursuing opportunities in the S&P 500 futures without compromising on risk control must look for alternatives to outright futures positions. Options on futures contracts offer one such alternative.

A trader would buy a call option if the underlying futures price were expected to increase. Conversely, the trader would buy a put option if he or she expected the underlying futures price to decrease. Buying an options contract enables the options buyer to replicate futures price action while limiting the risk of loss to the initial premium payment.

The extent to which the options premium mirrors movement in the underlying futures price depends on the proximity of the strike or exercise price of the option to the current futures price. The delta of an option measures its responsiveness to shifts in futures prices. A delta close to 1 suggests high responsiveness of the option premium to changes in the underlying futures price, whereas a delta close to 0 suggests minimal responsiveness.

The intrinsic value inherent in an in-the-money option makes it mirror futures price changes more closely, giving it a delta closer to 1. An out-of-the-money option with no intrinsic value has a delta closer to 0, whereas an at-the-money option with a strike price approximately equal to the current futures price has a delta close to 0.50.

The delta of a futures contract is, by definition, 1, leading to the following delta equivalence relationship between futures and options.

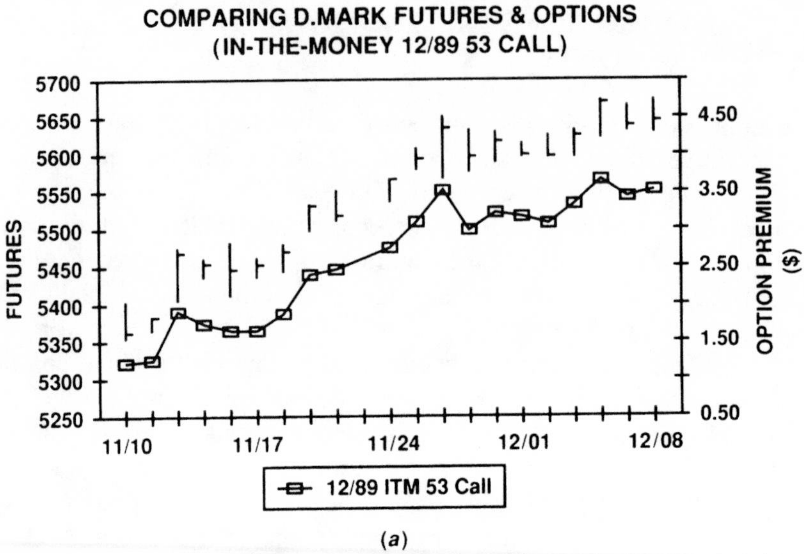

COMPARING D.MARK FUTURES & OPTIONS
(IN-THE-MONEY 12/89 53 CALL)

(a)

FIGURE 8.2a   Comparing Deutschemark futures and options: (a) in-the-money December 1989, 53 call.

Number of futures contracts	×	Delta of each contract	=	Number of options contracts	×	Delta of each option

or

Number of futures contracts	× 1	=	Number of options contracts	×	Delta of each option

An allocation of 0.50 futures contracts is equivalent to one option with a delta of 0.50. Therefore, a trader who wishes to trade 0.50 futures contracts might want to buy one at-the-money option with a delta of 0.50 or two out-of-the-money options with a delta of 0.25 each. The trader who uses options to replicate futures must realize that the replication is largely a function of the option strike price and the associated delta value.

Figures 8.2a through 8.2d outline the relationship between futures prices and options premiums for in-, at-, out-, and deep-out-of-the-money calls on the Deutsche mark futures expiring in December 1989.

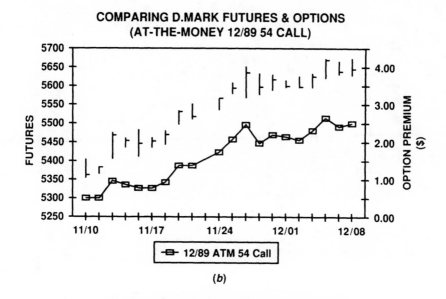

(b)

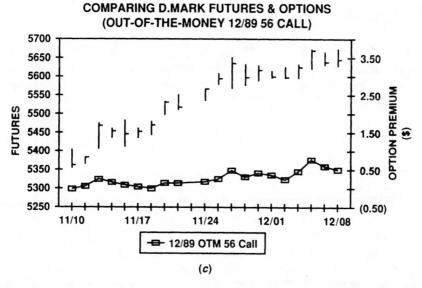

(c)

FIGURE 8.2b & c   Comparing Deutschemark futures and options: (b) at-the-money December 1989, 54 call; (c) out-of-the-money December 1989, 56 call.

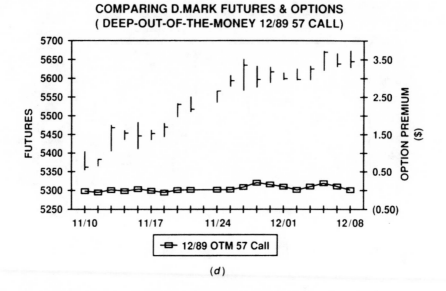

FIGURE 8.2d Comparing Deutschemark futures and options: (d) deep-out-of-the-money December 1989, 57 call.

Notice that the strong rally in the mark is best mirrored by the sharp rise in premiums on the in-the-money 53 calls (Figure 8.2a); it has hardly any impact on the deep-out-of-the-money 57 calls (Figure 8.2d).

PYRAMIDING

Pyramiding is the act of increasing exposure by adding to the number of contracts during the life of a trade. It needs to be distinguished from the strategy of adjusting trade exposure consequent upon the outcome of closed-out trades. Pyramiding is typically undertaken with a view to concentrating resources on a winning position. However, pyramids are also used at times to "average out" or dilute the entry price on a losing trade.

This practice of averaging prices has a parallel in stock investing, where it is referred to as "scaled down buying." A notable example of averaging down is when a commodity is trading at or near its historic lows. A trader might buy the commodity, only to discover that a new low is emerging. Convinced that the bottom cannot be much farther away, the trader might be tempted to buy more at the lower price.

The practice of adding to a losing position is essentially a case of good money chasing after bad. Since that practice cannot be condoned no matter how compelling the reasons, this section will confine itself strictly to a discussion of adding to profitable positions. Critical to successful pyramiding is an appreciation of the concept of the effective exposure on a trade.

The Concept of Effective Exposure

The effective exposure on a trade measures the dollar amount at risk during the life of a trade. It is a function of (a) the entry price, (b) the current stop price, and (c) the number of contracts traded of the commodity in question. The effective exposure on a trade depends on whether or not the trade has registered an assured or locked-in unrealized profit.

As long as a trade has not generated an unrealized profit, the effective exposure is positive and represents the difference between the entry price and the protective stop price. A trade protected by a break-even stop has zero effective exposure. Once the stop is moved beyond the break-even level, the trade has a locked-in, or assured, unrealized profit. This is when the effective trade exposure turns negative, implying that the trader's funds are no longer at risk.

For example, if gold has been purchased at $400 an ounce and the current price is $420 an ounce, the unrealized profit on the trade is $20. A trader who now sets a sell stop at $415 is effectively assured of a $15 profit on the trade, assuming that prices do not gap through the stop price.

Effective Exposure in the Absence of Assured Unrealized Profits

A negative assured unrealized profit, or an assured unrealized loss, represents the maximum permissible loss on the trade. For simplicity, we shall assume that prices do not gap through our stop price. Consequently, the maximum possible loss on the trade is equal to the maximum permissible loss. For example, continuing with our example of the gold trade, if gold were purchased at $400 per ounce and the initial stop were set at $380, this would imply a maximum permissible loss of $20 per ounce.

Once again, assuming that prices will not gap below the stop price of $380 an ounce, this is also the maximum possible loss on the trade.

As long as the assured unrealized profit on a trade is negative, the effective exposure on the trade measures the maximum amount that can be lost on the trade. On a short position, until such time as the stop price exceeds or is exactly equal to the entry price, the exposure per contract is given by the difference between the current stop price and the entry price. Similarly, on a long position, until such time as the stop price is less than or equal to the entry price, the exposure per contract is given by the difference between the entry price and the current stop price. The effective exposure is the product of the exposure per contract and the number of contracts traded.

To recapitulate, when assured unrealized profits are negative, the effective exposure on a trade is defined as follows:

$$\text{Effective exposure on short trade} = \left(\text{Current stop price} - \text{Entry price}\right) \times \text{Number of contracts}$$

$$\text{Effective exposure on long trade} = \left(\text{Entry price} - \text{Current stop price}\right) \times \text{Number of contracts}$$

The effective exposure is a positive number, signifying that this amount of capital is in danger of being lost.

Net Exposure with Positive Assured Unrealized Profits

When the current stop price is moved past the entry price, the assured unrealized profit on the trade turns positive, leading to a negative effective exposure on the trade. Now the trader is playing with the market's money. The negative exposure measures the locked-in profit on the trade.

The trader might now wish to expose a part or all of the locked-in profits by adding to the number of contracts traded. The fraction p, ranging between 0 and 1, determines the proportion of assured unrealized profits to be reinvested into the trade. A value of $p = 1$ implies that 100 percent of the value of assured unrealized profits is to be reinvested into the trade. A value of $p = 0$ implies that the assured unrealized profits are not to be reinvested into the trade.

The formula for the additional dollar exposure on a trade with positive assured unrealized profits may therefore be written as

$$\text{Additional exposure} = \left[p \times \text{Assured profits} \right] \times \text{Number of contracts}$$

where p is the fraction of assured profits reinvested, ranging between 0 and 1.

The net exposure on a trade with positive assured unrealized profits is the sum of (a) the effective exposure on the trade and (b) the additional exposure resulting from a reinvestment of all or a part of assured unrealized profits. Whereas (a) is a negative quantity, (b) could be either zero or positive. Hence,

Net exposure = Effective exposure + Additional exposure

The net exposure on a trade with positive assured unrealized profits could be either zero or negative.

When $p = 0$, the trader does not wish to allocate any further amount from assured unrealized profits toward the trade. Consequently, there is no change in the number of contracts traded, leading to a negative net exposure exactly equal to the value of assured unrealized profits. When $p = 1$, the net exposure on the trade is 0 because the trader has chosen to increase exposure by an amount exactly equal to the value of assured unrealized profits, leading to a possible loss that could completely wipe out the assured profits earned on the trade. When p is somewhere between 0 and 1, the net exposure on the trade is negative, suggesting that the assured unrealized profits on a trade exceed the proposed supplementary allocation to the trade from such profits.

Should p exceed 1, the initial risk capital allocation is supplemented by an amount exceeding the assured unrealized profit on the trade. Since there is no compelling logic supporting an increase in risk capital allocation in excess of the level of assured unrealized profits earned, we shall not pursue this alternative further.

Table 8.4 illustrates the concept of net exposure. Assume that one contract of soybeans futures has been sold at 600 cents a bushel, with a protective buy stop at 610 cents. Assume further that prices rise to 605 cents before retreating gradually to 565 cents. The net exposure is positive until such time as the protective buy stop price exceeds the sale price of 600 cents. Once the protective buy stop falls below the entry price of 600 cents, the assured unrealized profits turn positive, leading to a negative net exposure.

Note that the unrealized trade profits are consistently higher than the assured unrealized profits on the trade. Assuming that the fraction of assured profits plowed back into the trade is 0, 0.50, or 1 respectively, the effective exposure in each case is as shown in the table.

Table 8.4   The Net Exposure on
a Short Trade with Differing p Values

Current Price	Buy Stop Price	Unrealized Profits	Assured Profits	Net Exposure when:		
				$p = 0$	$p = 0.50$	$p = 1.00$
605	610	− 5	−10	+10	+10	+10
600	610	0	−10	+10	+10	+10
595	605	+ 5	− 5	+ 5	+ 5	+ 5
590	600	+10	0	0	0	0
580	587	+20	+13	−13	−6.5	0
575	580	+25	+20	−20	−10	0
565	570	+35	+30	−30	−15	0

Note: All figures are in cents/bushel on a one-contract basis.

Incremental Contract Determination

In practice, the trader must decide the value of p he or she is most comfortable with, risking assured unrealized profits accordingly. The value of p could vary from trade to trade. The fraction, p, when multiplied by the assured unrealized profits, gives the incremental exposure on the trade. This incremental exposure, when divided by the permissible risk per contract, gives the number of additional contracts to be traded, margin requirements permitting. The formula for determining the additional number of contracts to be traded consequent upon plowing back a fraction of assured unrealized profits is given as follows:

$$\text{Increase in number of contracts} = \frac{(p \times \text{Assured unrealized profits}) \times \text{Number of contracts}}{\text{Permissible loss per contract}}$$

To continue with our soybeans example, let us assume that prices have fallen to 575 cents, and our trader, who has sold 1 contract at 600 cents, now moves the stop to 580 cents, locking in an assured profit of 20 cents. Assume further that the trader decides to risk 50% of assured profits, or 10 cents, by selling an additional number, x, of futures contracts at 575 cents, with a protective stop at 580 on the entire position. Using the formula just obtained, the value of x works out to be 2, as follows:

$$x = \frac{0.50 \times 20}{5} = 2$$

Table 8.5   Effects of Price Fluctuations on Incremental Exposure

(a) At the current price of 575 cents

Position	Stop Price	Unrealized Profit (Loss)	Whereof Assured Profit (Loss)
Short 1 @ 600	580	1 × 25 = 25	1 × 20 = 20
Short 2 more @ 575	580	2 × 0 = 0	2 × (5) = (10)
	Net Profit	25	10

(b) At the current price of 580 cents

Action	Entry Price	Realized Profit
Liquidate 1 original short	600	1 × 20 = 20
Liquidate 2 new shorts	575	2 × (5) = (10)
	Net profit	10

(c) At the current price of 565 cents

Position	Stop Price	Unrealized Profit (Loss)	Whereof Assured Profit (Loss)
Short 1 @ 600	570	1 × 35 = 35	1 × 30 = 30
Short 2 more @ 575	570	2 × 10 = 20	2 × 5 = 10
	Net Profit	55	40

Adding two short positions at 575 cents with a stop at 580 cents ensures a worst-case profit of 10 cents on the overall position, which is equal to 50 percent of the assured profits earned on the trade thus far. The positions are tabulated in Table 8.5a for ease of comprehension. If prices were to move up to the protective stop level of 580 cents, our trader would be left with a realized profit of 10 cents as explained in Table 8.5b. However, if prices were to slide to, say, 565 cents, and our stop were lowered to 570 cents, the assured profit on the trade would amount to 40 cents, as shown in Table 8.5c.

Shape of the Pyramid

The number of contracts to be added to a position and the consequential shape of the pyramid is a function of (a) the assured profits on the trade and (b) the proportion, p, of profits to be reinvested into additional contracts. A conventional pyramid is formed by adding a decreasing number of contracts to an existing position. Adding an increasing number of contracts to an existing position creates an inverted pyramid.

The profit-compounding effects of an inverted pyramid are greater than those of the conventional pyramid. However, the leveraging cuts both ways, inasmuch as the impact of an adverse price move will be more severe in case of an inverted pyramid, given the preponderance of recently acquired contracts as a proportion of total exposure.

CONCLUSION

The most straightforward approach to allocation is the equal-number-of-contracts approach, wherein an equal number of contracts of each commodity is traded. This approach makes eminent sense when a trader is not clear about both the risk and reward potential on a trade. A trader who is unclear about the reward potential of competing trades might want to allocate risk capital equally across all commodities traded. Finally, if the trader is clear as regards both the estimated risk and the estimated reward on a trade, he or she might want to allocate risk capital unequally, allowing for risk and return differences between commodities. This could be done using a portfolio optimization routine or using the optimal allocation fraction, f, for a given trade.

The initial risk exposure on a trade is subject to change during the life of the trade, depending on price movement and changes, if any, in the number of contracts traded. Such an increase in the number of contracts during the life of a trade is known as pyramiding. The number of contracts to be added is a function of (a) the assured profits on the trade and (b) the proportion, p, of assured profits to be reinvested into the trade.

9

The Role of Mechanical Trading Systems

A mechanical trading system is a set of rules defining entry into and exit out of a trade. There are two kinds of mechanical systems: (a) predictive and (b) reactive.

Predictive systems use historical data to predict future price action. For example, a system that analyzes the cyclical nature of markets might try to predict the timing and magnitude of the next major price cycle.

A reactive system uses historical data to react to price trend shifts. Instead of predicting a trend change, a reactive system would wait for a change to develop, generating a signal to initiate a trade shortly thereafter. The success of any reactive system is gauged by the speed and accuracy with which it reacts to a reversal in the underlying trend.

In this chapter, we will restrict ourselves to a study of the more commonly used mechanical trading systems of the reactive kind. We discuss the design of mechanical trading systems and the implications of such design for trading and money management. Finally, we offer recommendations for improving the effectiveness of fixed-parameter mechanical trading systems.

THE DESIGN OF MECHANICAL TRADING SYSTEMS

As a rule, mechanical systems are based on fixed parameters defined in terms of either time or price fluctuations. For example, a system may use historical price data over a fixed time period to generate its signals. Alternatively, it may use price breakout by a fixed dollar amount or percentage to generate signals. In this section, we briefly review the logic behind three commonly used mechanical systems: (a) a moving-average crossover system, which is a trend-following system; (b) Lane's stochastics oscillator, which measures overbought/oversold market conditions; and (c) a price reversal or breakout system.

The Moving-Average Crossover System

A moving-average crossover system is designed to capture trends soon after they develop. It is based on the crossover of two or more historical moving averages. The underlying logic is that one of the moving averages is more responsive to price changes than the others, signaling a shift in the trend when it crosses the longer-term, less responsive moving average(s).

For purposes of illustration, consider a dual moving-average crossover system, where moving averages are calculated over the immediately preceding four days and nine days. The four-day moving average is more responsive to price changes than the nine-day moving average, because it is based on prices over the immediately preceding four days. Therefore, in an uptrend, the four-day average exceeds the nine-day average. As soon as the four-day moving average exceeds or crosses above the nine-day moving average, the system generates a buy signal. Conversely, should the four-day moving average fall below the nine-day moving average, suggesting a pullback in prices, the system generates a sell signal. Therefore, the system always recommends a position, alternating between a buy and a sell.

The Stochastics Oscillator

Oscillator-based systems acknowledge the fact that markets are often in a sideways, trendless mode, bouncing within a trading range. Accordingly, the oscillator is designed to signal a purchase in an oversold market and a sale in an overbought market. The stochastics oscillator, developed by George C. Lane,[1] is one of the more popular oscillators. It is based

[1] George C. Lane, *Using Stochastics, Cycles, and R.S.I. to the Moment of Decision* (Watseka, IL: Investment Educators, 1986).

on the premise that as prices trend upward, the closing price tends to lie closer to the high end of the trading range for the period. Conversely, as prices trend downward, the closing price tends to be near the lower end of the trading range for the period.

Once again, the stochastics oscillator is based on price history over a fixed time period, n, as, for example, the past nine trading sessions. The highest high of the preceding n periods defines the upper limit, or ceiling, of the trading range, just as the lowest low over the same period defines the lower limit, or floor. The difference between the highest high and the lowest low of the preceding n sessions defines the trading range within which prices are expected to move. A close near the ceiling is indicative of an overbought market, just as a close near the floor is indicative of an oversold market.

The stochastics oscillator generates sell signals based on a crossover of two indicators, K and D. To arrive at the raw K value for a nine-day stochastic requires the following steps:

1. Subtract the lowest low of the past nine days from the most recent closing price.
2. Subtract the lowest low of the past nine days from the highest high of the past nine days.
3. Divide the result from step 1 by the result from step 2 and multiply by 100 percent to arrive at the raw K value.

Prices are considered to be overbought if the raw K value is above 75 percent, and are oversold if the value is below 25 percent. A three-day average of the raw K value gives a raw D value.

One commonly used approach to safeguard against choppy signals arising from the raw scores is to smooth the K and D values, using a three-day average as follows:

Smoothed $K = \frac{2}{3}$ previous smoothed $K + \frac{1}{3}$ new raw K

Smoothed $D = \frac{2}{3}$ previous smoothed $D + \frac{1}{3}$ new smoothed K

The K line is a faster moving average than the D line. Consequently, a buy signal is generated when K crosses D to the upside, provided the crossover occurs when K is less than 25 percent. A sell signal is generated when K crosses and falls below D, provided the crossover occurs when K is greater than 75 percent. Since not all crossovers are equally valid as signal generators, the stochastics oscillator, unlike the moving-average crossover system, does not automatically reverse from a buy to a sell or vice versa.

Fixed Price Reversal or Breakout Systems

Instead of studying historical prices over a fixed interval of time, some systems choose to generate signals based on a fixed, predetermined reversal in prices. The logic is that once prices break out of a trading range, they are apt to continue in the direction of the breakout. The desired price reversal target could be an absolute amount or a percentage of current prices.

For example, in the case of gold futures, a reversal point could be set a fixed dollar amount, say $5 per ounce, from the most recent close price. Alternatively, the reversal point could be a fixed percentage retracement, say 1.50 percent, from the most recent close price. The belief is that we have a reversal of trend if prices reverse by an amount equal to or greater than a prespecified value. Accordingly, the system generates a signal to liquidate an existing trade and reverse positions.

THE ROLE OF MECHANICAL TRADING SYSTEMS

The primary function of mechanical trading systems is to help a trader with precise entry and exit points. In doing so, mechanical trading systems facilitate the setting of stops, enabling a trader to predefine the dollar risk per contract traded. Additionally, a mechanical trading system facilitates back-testing of data, allowing a trader to gain invaluable insight into the system's efficacy. This information can help the trader allocate capital more effectively. Both these functions are addressed in this section.

Setting Predefined Stop-Loss Orders

Using a mechanical system allows a trader to know the dollar amount at risk going into a trade, since it can make the trader aware of the stop price at which the trade must be liquidated. The lack of fuzziness regarding the exit point gives mechanical systems a definite edge over judgmental systems. Consider a two- and four-day dual moving-average crossover system that recommends buying gold based on the price history in Table 9.1. Since the two-day average is greater than the four-day average, the system

Table 9.1   Price History for Gold

Day	Close Price	Two-Day Moving Average	Four-Day Moving Average
1	350		
2	352	351.0	
3	353	352.5	
4	354	353.5	352.25
5	Stop Price, x		

recommends holding a long position in the commodity. The reversal stop price, x, for the upcoming fifth day may be calculated as the price where the two moving averages will cross over to give a sell signal. This is the price at which the two-day moving average equals the four-day moving average. Therefore,

$$\frac{x + 354}{2} = \frac{x + 354 + 353 + 352}{4}$$

$$0.50x + 177 = 0.25x + 264.75$$

$$0.25x = 87.75$$

$$x = 351$$

The trader could place an open order to sell two contracts of gold at $351 on a close-only basis: one contract to cover the existing long position and the second to initiate a new short sale. The trader's risk on the trade is given by the difference between the current price, $354, and the sell stop price, $351, namely $3 per ounce or $300 a contract. The open order is valid until such time it is executed or is canceled or replaced by the trader. The "close-only" stop signifies that the order will be executed only if gold trades at or below $351 during the final minutes of trading on any day.

Calculating the stop price may be tedious for the more advanced trading systems, especially where there is more than one unknown variable in the formula. However, it should be possible to compute reversal stops with the help of suitable simplifying assumptions.

Generating Performance Measures Based on Back-Testing

Mechanical trading systems are amenable to back-testing, permitting an objective assessment of historical performance. Simulation permits a trader to observe the effects of a change in one or more system parameters. The underlying rules themselves might be modified and the effects of such modifications back-tested. These "what-if" questions would most likely be unanswered in the absence of mechanization. Back-testing over a historical time period yields performance measures that greatly help in making a determination of the proportion of capital to be risked to trading.

The most useful performance measures are (a) the probability of success of a system and (b) its payoff ratio. The probability of success is the ratio of the number of winning trades to the total number of trades over a given time period. The payoff ratio measures the average dollar profit on winning trades to the average dollar loss on losing trades over the same period. The higher the probability of success and the higher the payoff ratio, the more effective the trading system. Both these measures are synthesized into one aggregate measure, known as the profitability index of a system.

The Profitability Index

The profitability index of a system is defined as the product of the odds of success and the payoff ratio. Therefore,

$$\text{Profitability index} = \frac{p}{(1-p)} \times \text{Payoff ratio}$$

where p = probability of success

$(1 - p)$ = the complementary probability of failure

When $p = 0.50$, the ratio $p/(1 - p)$ is 1. Therefore, the profitability index of such a system is determined exclusively by its payoff ratio. The higher the payoff ratio, the higher the profitability index. When the probability of success, p, is greater than 0.50, the ratio $p/(1 - p)$ is greater than 1. The higher the probability of success, the higher the odds of success and the resulting profitability index for a given payoff ratio. A profitability index of 2 signals a good system. An index greater than 3 would be exceptional.

The implicit assumption in our discussion thus far is that the profitability index of a system based on back-testing of historical data is indicative of future performance. This may not always be true, especially if the mechanical system is based on constant or fixed parameters. In the ensuing discussion, we discuss (a) the problems associated with fixed parameter systems, (b) the implications of these problems for trading and money management, and (c) possible solutions.

FIXED-PARAMETER MECHANICAL SYSTEMS

Fixed-parameter mechanical systems hold one of two key parameters constant: (a) the time period over which historical data is analyzed, in the case of trend-following or oscillator-based systems, or (b) the magnitude of the price reversal, in the case of price breakout systems. The implicit assumption is that prices will continue to conform to a fixed set of rules that have best captured market behavior over a historical time period.

While prices do have a tendency to trend every so often, these trends do not seem to recur with definite regularity. Moreover, the magnitude of the price move in a trend varies over time, and no two trends are exact replications. Although the existence of trends cannot be denied, there is an annoying randomness as regards their magnitude and periodicity. This randomness is the Achilles heel of mechanical systems based on fixed, market-invariant parameters, since it is virtually impossible for such systems to capture trends in a timely fashion consistently.

Therefore, the much-touted virtue of consistency in the use of a mechanical rule need not necessarily lead to consistent results. What is needed is a system that responds quickly to changes in market conditions, and this is where a fixed-parameter system falls short. Instead of modifying its parameters to adapt to changes in market conditions, a fixed-parameter system implicitly expects market conditions to adapt to its invariant logic. This could be a cause for concern.

Analyzing the Performance of a Fixed-Parameter System

Instead of speculating on the consequences of fixed-parameter systems, it would be instructive to analyze the historical performance of one such system. We select for our study the ubiquitous dual moving-average crossover system. A total of 31 dual moving-average crossover rules are analyzed over four equal two-year periods from 1979 to 1987, across four commodities: gold, Japanese yen, Treasury bonds, and soybeans.

The shorter moving average is based on historical data for the past 3 to 15 days in increments of 3 days. The longer moving average is based on historical data for the past 9 to 45 days in increments of 6 days. A total of 31 combinations has been studied. An amount of $50 has been deducted from the profits of each trade to allow for brokerage fees and unfavorable order executions, commonly known as slippage.

Table 9.2 summarizes the average profit and standard deviation of profits across all 31 rules for each of four two-year subperiods. Table 9.3

Table 9.2   Summary of Performance of 31 Moving-Average
Crossover Rules by Time Period and Commodity

	1979–81	1981–83	1983–85	1985–87	Average 1979–87
Gold:					
Aver Profit	$58,283	−$2,798	−$7,421	−$1,207	$11,714
Std Dev	$19,595	$11,606	$6,557	$3,904	$29,576
Min $ Profit	−$10,430	−$23,410	−$16,230	−$11,050	−$23,410
Max $ Profit	$93,150	$28,070	$7,150	$7,550	$93,150
Max $ Rule					
(days)	12 & 27	9 & 15	9 & 15	12 & 27	
Coeff of Var	0.34	−4.15	−0.88	−3.23	2.52
Treasury bonds:					
Aver Profit	$9,897	$1,553	$7,949	$9,783	$7,295
Std Dev	$10,117	$6,930	$4,473	$8,769	$8,485
Min $ Profit	−$12,912	−$18,694	−$4,125	−$5,775	−$18,694
Max $ Profit	$30,087	$11,581	$15,875	$37,025	$37,025
Max $ Rule					
(days)	3 & 9	12 & 15	6 & 33	3 & 15	
Coeff of Var	1.02	4.46	0.56	0.89	1.16
Japanese yen:					
Aver Profit	$12,816	$10,044	$3,937	$15,961	$10,690
Std Dev	$5,509	$2,872	$3,905	$6,675	$6,614
Min $ Profit	−$5,050	$2,800	−$4,650	$2,212	−$5,050
Max $ Profit	$22,425	$16,400	$12,950	$28,787	$28,787
Max $ Rule					
(days)	9 & 27	6 & 9	9 & 27	3 & 27	
Coeff of Var	0.43	0.28	0.99	0.42	0.62
Soybeans:					
Aver Profit	$9,800	$11,009	−$568	−$5,836	$3,601
Std Dev	$8,297	$9,029	$7,146	$2,513	$10,050
Min $ Profit	−$4,662	−$7,475	−$9,750	−$9,762	−$9,762
Max $ Profit	$28,512	$25,275	$14,250	$862	$28,512
Max $ Rule					
(days)	3 & 45	15 & 21	6 & 15	12 & 15	
Coeff of Var	0.85	0.82	−12.58	−0.43	2.79

summarizes the average profit and standard deviation of profits for each of the 31 rules across the entire period, 1979–87.

Variability of profits across the different rules is measured by the coefficient of variation. The coefficient of variation is arrived at by dividing the standard deviation of profits across different rules by the average profit. A low positive coefficient of variation is desirable, inasmuch as it suggests low variability of average profits.

The Japanese yen has the lowest average coefficient of variation, followed by Treasury bonds, suggesting a healthy consistency of performance. Gold and soybeans have average coefficients of variation in excess of 2, indicating wide swings in the performance of the dual moving-average crossover rules.

The optimal profit and the rule generating it for each commodity are summarized in Table 9.4 for each of the four time periods. The optimal profit for a commodity represents the maximum profit earned in each time period across the 31 rules studied. Notice that none of the rules consistently excels across all commodities. Moreover, a rule that is optimal in one period for a given commodity is not necessarily optimal across other time periods. For example, in the case of gold the 12- and 27-day average crossover rule was optimal during 1979–81. However, the rule came close to being the worst performer in 1981–83 and 1983–85 before becoming a star performer once again during 1985–87! Similar findings, albeit not as dramatic, hold for each of the other three commodities surveyed.

A Statistical Test of Performance Differences

To examine more closely the differences in performance of a trading rule across time periods, we employ a two-way analysis of variance (ANOVA) test. The model states that differences in performance could be a function of either (a) differences across trading rules or (b) inherent differences in market conditions across time periods. Differences in performance not explained by either trading rule or time period are attributed to a random error term.

The statistic used to check for significant differences across a test variable X is the F statistic, computed as follows:

$$F(\text{DF}_1, \text{DF}_2) = \frac{\text{Sums of squares for } X \ / \ \text{DF}_1}{\text{Sums of squares for error term} \ / \ \text{DF}_2}$$

Table 9.3 Summary of 31 Moving-Average Crossover Rules by Commodity: Average Performance between 1979 and 1987

Parameters	Gold			T. bonds			Yen			Soybeans		
	Aver $	sd	Coeff of Var	Aver $	sd	Coeff of Var	Aver $	sd	Coeff of Var	Aver $	sd	Coeff of Var
3 & 9 days	-$4,405	$5,539	-1.26	$9,930	$17,571	1.77	$12,603	$4,051	0.32	-$3,894	$5,732	-1.47
3 & 15 days	$10,208	$13,128	1.28	$14,352	$15,775	1.10	$14,191	$10,541	0.74	-$1,481	$9,899	-6.28
3 & 21 days	$17,155	$38,201	2.22	$8,379	$9,864	1.18	$13,091	$10,278	0.78	$3,200	$6,450	2.01
3 & 27 days	$15,495	$43,864	2.83	$9,283	$3,727	0.40	$14,328	$10,135	0.71	$3,144	$9,145	2.91
3 & 33 days	$12,648	$32,800	2.59	$12,714	$8,682	0.68	$13,328	$6,550	0.49	$5,363	$12,226	2.28
3 & 39 days	$8,773	$30,101	3.43	$9,505	$7,192	0.75	$9,153	$3,698	0.40	$5,869	$15,452	2.63
3 & 45 days	$6,663	$25,528	3.83	$10,027	$11,440	1.14	$10,666	$3,533	0.33	$9,469	$17,160	1.81
6 & 9 days	$7,955	$18,752	2.36	$6,936	$18,597	2.68	$7,422	$9,010	1.21	-$444	$6,267	-14.11
6 & 15 days	$16,370	$28,197	1.72	$4,461	$7,934	1.78	$9,691	$8,189	0.84	$3,131	$8,494	2.71
6 & 21 days	$15,520	$36,644	2.36	$5,042	$2,288	0.45	$12,909	$6,936	0.54	$5,256	$5,345	1.02
6 & 27 days	$16,860	$41,428	2.46	$9,770	$8,496	0.87	$13,653	$4,487	0.33	$6,700	$9,664	1.44
6 & 33 days	$9,613	$29,547	3.07	$13,139	$6,811	0.52	$14,047	$5,507	0.39	$4,956	$12,104	2.44
6 & 39 days	$10,253	$28,545	2.78	$13,524	$10,055	0.74	$10,897	$5,630	0.52	$3,425	$8,006	2.34
6 & 45 days	$9,708	$27,905	2.87	$9,830	$7,277	0.74	$8,166	$2,613	0.32	$5,406	$12,218	2.26

9 & 15 days	$19,740	$24,742	1.25	$3,886	$4,097	1.05	$9,053	$5,457	0.60	$7,569	$10,272	1.36
9 & 21 days	$12,145	$28,508	2.35	$6,989	$3,858	0.55	$12,766	$6,907	0.54	$4,400	$7,670	1.74
9 & 27 days	$14,245	$46,946	3.29	$6,930	$6,532	0.94	$14,728	$5,202	0.35	$2,706	$10,454	3.86
9 & 33 days	$11,198	$36,883	3.29	$7,926	$3,590	0.45	$10,959	$8,081	0.74	$2,419	$9,922	4.10
9 & 39 days	$4,208	$34,380	8.17	$8,698	$7,907	0.91	$9,741	$6,694	0.69	$4,119	$9,185	2.23
9 & 45 days	$9,053	$25,118	2.77	$6,130	$3,219	0.52	$9,747	$5,785	0.59	$5,813	$11,898	2.05
12 & 15 days	$15,020	$22,958	1.53	$3,370	$7,940	2.35	$10,228	$4,391	0.43	$6,394	$4,324	0.67
12 & 21 days	$13,910	$43,270	3.11	$4,098	$4,844	1.18	$13,097	$9,191	0.70	-$444	$10,060	-22.66
12 & 27 days	$18,075	$51,105	2.83	$1,033	$11,838	11.46	$11,047	$7,004	0.63	$1,419	$14,005	9.87
12 & 33 days	$9,380	$36,280	3.87	$8,883	$3,161	0.35	$10,453	$5,604	0.53	$3,163	$12,111	3.83
12 & 39 days	$9,368	$30,546	3.26	$8,426	$6,435	0.76	$6,941	$6,036	0.87	$3,956	$11,296	2.85
12 & 45 days	$12,088	$28,482	2.35	$4,926	$4,783	0.97	$9,191	$9,069	0.99	$7,488	$14,290	1.91
15 & 21 days	$9,540	$39,114	4.10	-$5,714	$11,042	-1.93	$10,134	$10,820	1.07	$557	$16,617	29.83
15 & 27 days	$15,998	$48,695	3.04	$3,961	$5,617	1.42	$11,066	$7,836	0.71	$4,113	$15,598	3.79
15 & 33 days	$8,918	$40,501	4.54	$8,939	$5,513	0.62	$6,684	$6,074	0.91	$3,450	$11,665	3.38
15 & 39 days	$13,368	$30,577	2.29	$6,348	$5,298	0.83	$4,828	$4,835	1.00	$2,313	$10,799	4.67
15 & 45 days	$14,103	$27,039	1.92	$4,448	$4,443	1.00	$6,578	$6,573	1.00	$2,106	$11,148	5.29

Table 9.4   Optimal Profit ($) and Optimal Rule Analysis

	1979–81	1981–83	1983–85	1985–87
Gold:				
Optimal Profit	93150	28070	7150	7550
Optimal Rule	12 & 27	9 & 15	9 & 15	12 & 27
Treasury bonds:				
Optimal Profit	30087	11581	15875	37025
Optimal Rule	3 & 9	12 & 15	6 & 33	3 & 15
Japanese yen:				
Optimal Profit	22425	16400	12950	28787
Optimal Rule	9 & 27	6 & 9	9 & 27	3 & 27
Soybeans:				
Optimal Profit	28512	25275	14250	862
Optimal Rule	3 & 45	15 & 21	6 & 15	12 & 15

or,

$$F(DF_1, DF_2) = \frac{\text{Mean square across } X}{\text{Mean square of error term}}$$

where DF_1 represents the degrees of freedom for X, the numerator, and DF_2 represents the degrees of freedom for the unexplained error term, the denominator. The degrees of freedom are equal to the number of parameters estimated in the analysis less 1.

In our study, we have a matrix of 31×4 observations, with a row for each of the 31 rules studied and a column for each of the 4 time periods surveyed. Each cell of the 31×4 matrix represents the profit earned by a trading rule for a given time period. Since we have a total of 124 data cells, there are 123 degrees ($124 - 1$) of freedom. There are 3 degrees of freedom for the 4 time periods, and 30 degrees of freedom for the 31 moving-average crossover rules analyzed, leaving 90 degrees of freedom ($123 - 30 - 3$) for the unexplained error term.

Table 9.5 checks for differences in average profits generated by each of the 31 trading rules across four time periods. The calculated F value for the observed data is compared with the corresponding theoretical F value derived from the F tables at a level of significance of 1 percent.

If the calculated F value exceeds the tabulated F value, the hypothesis of equality of profits over the different subperiods is rejected. A 1 percent

Table 9.5 Testing for Differences Across Time in Average Profits for a Moving-Average Crossover Rule

| Commodity | Mean Square Value Across | | | F Value: Rules | | F Value: Time | | Degrees of Freedom | |
	Rules	Time	Error	Calculated	Table	Calculated	Table	Rule	Time
Soybeans	32.08	2064.21	58.56	0.55	1.94	35.25	4.04	30	3
Gold	89.34	30095.45	162.53	0.55	1.94	185.17	4.04	30	3
Yen	27.03	809.35	23.80	1.14	1.94	34.01	4.04	30	3
Bonds	64.56	479.01	60.92	1.06	1.94	7.86	4.04	30	3

Note: The table values correspond to a 1% level of significance for a 1-tail F test. There are 90 degrees of freedom for the denominator, the Error term.

F calculated value: Rules $= \dfrac{\text{Mean square value across rules}}{\text{Mean square value across error}}$

F calculated value: Time $= \dfrac{\text{Mean square value across time}}{\text{Mean square value across error}}$

level of significance implies that the theoretical value of F is likely to lead to an erroneous rejection of the null hypothesis in 1 percent of the cases, a highly remote possibility.

Interestingly, the calculated F value across time is greater than the tabulated value at the 1 percent level of significance for all four commodities. The calculated F value across rules is less than the tabulated value at a 1 percent level of significance across all four commodities. Therefore, we can conclude that differences in profits are significantly affected by changes in market conditions across time, rather than by parameter differences in the construction of the rules themselves.

Table 9.6 extends the above analysis of variance to check for differences in the average probability of success across time for each of the 31 trading rules. Again, we have a 31×4 data matrix, with each cell now representing the probability of success for a trading rule during a given time period. Once again, we find the difference in the probability of success across all four commodities to be significantly affected by changes in market conditions across time. This is in line with the results of the analysis of profit differences given in Table 9.5. Rule differences account for significant changes in the probability of success only in case of the Japanese yen.

Table 9.7 checks for differences in the average payoff ratio across time for each of the 31 rules. Each cell of the 31×4 matrix now represents the payoff ratio for a trading rule during a given time period. The results of the analysis reveal that differences in the payoff ratio are influenced primarily by changes in market conditions across time, except for the yen. Rule differences account for significant changes in the payoff ratio in the case of the yen and Treasury bonds.

Implications for Trading and Money Management

To the extent the dual moving-average crossover system is a typical example of conventional fixed-parameter systems, the results are fairly representative of what could be expected of similar fixed-parameter systems. The implications for trading and money management are discussed here.

Swings in performance could result in corresponding swings in the probability of success and the payoff ratio for a given mechanical rule across different time periods. As a result, the profitability index of a system is suspect. Further, risk capital allocations based on historic performance measures are likely to be inaccurate. Most significantly, wide swings in performance could also have a deleterious effect on the

Table 9.6 Testing for Differences Across Time in the
Probability of Success for a Moving-Average Crossover Rule

| Commodity | Mean Square Value Across | | | F Value: Rules | | F Value: Time | | Degrees of Freedom | |
	Rules	Time	Error	Calculated	Table	Calculated	Table	Rule	Time
Soybeans	0.007	0.163	0.010	0.70	1.94	16.30	4.04	30	3
Gold	0.009	0.431	0.010	0.90	1.94	43.10	4.04	30	3
Yen	0.011	0.062	0.005	2.20	1.94	12.40	4.04	30	3
Bonds	0.005	0.070	0.006	0.83	1.94	11.67	4.04	30	3

Note: The table values correspond to a 1% level of significance for a 1-tail F test.
There are 90 degrees of freedom for the denominator, the Error term.

$$F \text{ calculated value: Rules} = \frac{\text{Mean square value across rules}}{\text{Mean square value across error}}$$

$$F \text{ calculated value: Time} = \frac{\text{Mean square value across time}}{\text{Mean square value across error}}$$

Table 9.7 Testing for Differences Across Time in the Payoff Ratio for a Moving-Average Crossover Rule

Commodity	Mean Square Value Across			F Value: Rules		F Value: Time		Degrees of Freedom	
	Rules	Time	Error	Calculated	Table	Calculated	Table	Rule	Time
Soybeans	3.065	32.069	1.745	1.76	1.94	18.37	4.04	30	3
Gold	1.331	44.573	0.894	1.49	1.94	49.86	4.04	30	3
Yen	1.997	2.767	0.850	2.35	1.94	3.26	4.04	30	3
Bonds	1.724	10.144	0.822	2.10	1.94	12.34	4.04	30	3

Note: The table values correspond to a 1% level of significance for a 1-tail F test. There are 90 degrees of freedom for the denominator, the Error term.

F calculated value: Rules $= \dfrac{\text{Mean square value across rules}}{\text{Mean square value across error}}$

F calculated value: Time $= \dfrac{\text{Mean square value across time}}{\text{Mean square value across error}}$

precision of system-generated entry signals or exit stops. These are genuine difficulties, which merit attention and suitable resolution. In the following section, we offer possible solutions.

POSSIBLE SOLUTIONS TO THE PROBLEMS OF MECHANICAL SYSTEMS

The most obvious solution to the problems raised in the preceding section would be to rid a mechanical system of its inflexibility. A good starting point would be to think of more effective alternatives to rules that have been defined in terms of fixed parameters such as a prespecified number, n, of completed trading sessions to evaluate market behavior or a fixed dollar or percentage price value for assessing a valid breakout.

Toward Flexible-Parameter Systems

A flexible-parameter system, as the name suggests, would adjust its parameters in line with market action. For example, in a choppy market devoid of direction, the system would call for a loosening of trigger points to enter into or exit out of a position. Conversely, in a directional market, such triggers would be tightened.

Unlike a fixed-parameter system, a flexible-parameter system does not expect the market to abide by the logic of its rules; instead, it adapts its rules to accommodate shifts in market conditions. Efforts to develop such systems would be extremely helpful from the standpoint of both trading and money management. Although the construction flexible-parameter systems is beyond the purview of this book, it would suffice to note that such systems can be designed. Neural networks are one such example. They learn by example and adapt to changing market conditions rather than expecting the market to adapt to a set of predefined, unalterable rules.

Using Most Recent Results as Predictors of the Future

Assuming a trader is unable to inject flexibility into a mechanical system, he or she would have to make the most of it as a fixed-parameter system.

One possible solution is to use the performance parameters generated by a fixed-parameter system over the most recent past. The definition of "recent past" depends on the trading horizon of the trader. A trader using a system based on weekly data would consider a longer history in defining the recent past than would a trader using a system based on daily data. Similarly, a trader who relies on a system that generates multiple signals per day would have a different understanding of the term "recent past" from that of a trader using a system based on daily data.

The assumption here is that the most recent past is the best estimator of the future. This is true as long as there is no reason to suspect a fundamental shift in market behavior. However, if recent market action belies the assumption of stability, past performance can no longer be used as a reflector of the future. In such a case, it would be necessary to determine and use those parameters that are optimal in an environment after the change occurred. This is accomplished through a procedure known as curve fitting or optimizing.

The Role of Curve Fitting or Optimizing a System

The process of curve fitting or finding the optimal parameters for a system entails back-testing the system over a historical time period using a variety of different parameters. Ideally, the time period selected for analysis should be representative of current market conditions. This is to ensure that the optimality of parameters is not unique to the period under review. One way of checking that this is indeed so is to retest the mechanical rule over yet another sample period. If the parameters originally found to be optimal are truly optimal, they should continue to turn in superior results over the new sample period.

For example, a trader might want to back-test a dual moving-average crossover system using all feasible combinations of short and long moving averages. The trader would then scan the results to select the combination that yields the highest profitability index. Next, he or she would rerun the test over yet another sample period to check for consistency of the results. If a certain combination does yield superior performance over the two sample periods, the trader can be reasonably sure of its optimality. The following subsection summarizes the rules for optimization.

Rules for Optimization

The greater the number of variables in a system, the more complex the system is from an optimization standpoint. If even one of the optimized parameters were to malfunction, this would hurt the overall performance of the system. Consequently, the fewer the number of system parameters to be optimized, the more robust the results of the optimization are likely to be. This is a compelling argument in favor of simplifying the logic of a mechanical system.

The implicit assumption in any curve fitting exercise is that a set of parameters found to be optimal over a given time period will continue to perform optimally in the future. However, if conditions are fundamentally different from those considered in the sample period, this would render invalid the results from an earlier back-testing. In this case, it would be incumbent upon the analyst to repeat the optimization exercise, using price history after the change as a basis for the new analysis.

One way around the problem of changing market conditions is to use as long a historical database as possible. This allows the analyst to examine the performance of the system over varying market conditions. For example, a moving-average crossover system might work wonderfully in trending markets only to get whipsawed in sideways markets. Ideally, therefore, the optimization study should be carried out over a sample period that covers both trending and sideways markets. Generally, the sample period should be no less than five years. In terms of completed trades, the back-testing should cover at least 30 trades.

Once the optimal parameters have been established, the next step would be to conduct an out-of-sample or forward test of these parameters. An out-of-sample or forward test is conducted using a period of time that is beyond the original sample period. For example, if the optimal parameters were arrived at by analyzing data over the 1980 to 1985 time period, a forward test would check the efficacy of these optimal parameters over a subsequent period, say 1986 to 1990. This process enables the analyst to judge the robustness, or lack thereof, of the optimal parameters. If the optimal parameters are found to be equally effective over the periods 1980 to 1985 and over 1986 to 1990, there is reason to be confident about the future effectiveness of these parameters.

CONCLUSION

Mechanical trading systems are objective inasmuch as they are not swayed by emotions when they recommend entry into or exit out of a market. However, a mechanical system may also introduce a certain amount of rigidity, especially if the system expects the market to adjust to a given set of rules instead of adapting its rules to adjust to current market conditions.

This could lead to imprecision in the timing of signals generated by the system. Consequently, fixed-parameter systems are subject to major shifts in trading performance; what is optimal in one time period need not necessarily be optimal in another period. Accompanying the shifts in trading performance are related shifts in performance measures, such as the probability of success and the payoff ratio. These measures are useful for determining the proportion of capital to be risked to trading.

One solution would be to rid the system of its inflexibility by adapting the rules to adjust quickly and effectively to changes in market conditions. In the absence of a flexible system, it would be appropriate to use the most recent past performance as being indicative of the future. The assumption is that market conditions that prevailed in the recent past will not change dramatically in the immediate future. If such a change is evident, do not regard past performance as being reflective of the future. Instead, find out what parameters perform best for a given rule under the new environment, using data for the period since the change occurred.

10

Back to the Basics

Judicious market selection and capital allocation separate the outstanding trader from the marginally successful trader. However, it is failure to control losses, coupled with a knack for letting emotions overrule logic, that often makes the difference between success and failure at futures trading. Although these issues are hard to quantify, they cannot be ignored or taken for granted. This chapter outlines the key issues responsible for poor performance, in the hope that reiterating them will help keep the reader from falling prey to them.

AVOIDING FOUR-STAR BLUNDERS

Success in the futures markets is measured in terms of the growth of one's account balance. A trader is not expected to play God and call market turns correctly at all times. Therefore, she should not berate herself for errors of judgment. Even the most successful traders commit errors of judgment every so often. What distinguishes them from their less successful colleagues is their ability (a) to recognize an error promptly and (b) to take necessary corrective action to prevent the error from becoming a financial disaster. Therefore, the key to avoiding ruin is simply to make sure that one can live with the financial consequences of one's errors.

An error of judgment results from inaction or incorrect action on the trader's part. Such an error could either (a) stymie growth of a trader's account balance or (b) lead to a reduction in the account balance.

Let us assume for a moment that errors could be ranked on a scale, with one star being awarded to the least significant of errors and four stars reserved for the most serious blunders.

One-Star Errors

There is a commonly held misconception that a profitable trade precludes the possibility of an error of judgment. The truth is that a trader can get out of a profitable trade prematurely, just as he or she can exit the trade after giving back most of the profits earned. As the final profit figure is a mere fraction of what could have been earned, there is cause for concern. This error of judgment is termed a one-star error. A one-star error is the least damaging of errors, because there is some growth in the trader's account balance notwithstanding the error.

Two-Star Errors

A two-star error results from completely ignoring what turns out to be a highly profitable trade. A two-star error tops a one-star error inasmuch as there is absolutely no growth in the account balance. A major move has just whizzed by, and the trader has missed the move. In a period when major rallies are few and far between, the missed opportunity might prove to be quite expensive.

Three-Star Errors

When a trader observes a gradual shrinking of equity, but refuses to liquidate a losing trade, he or she commits a three-star error. Clearly, this error is more serious than the earlier errors, given the reduction in the account balance. A three-star error of judgment typically arises as a result of not using stop-loss orders, or setting such loose stops as to negate their very purpose.

For example, if a trader were to short-sell a contract of gold at $370 an ounce, omit to enter a buy stop order, and finally pull out of the trade when gold touched $400, the resulting loss of $3000 per contract would qualify as a three-star error.

Four-Star Blunders

A four-star blunder is simply a magnified version of a three-star error, caused by overexposure to a single commodity. In the preceding example, short-selling 10 contracts of gold at $370 an ounce would result in a $30,000 loss instead of the $3000 alluded to above. The magnitude of such a loss might well snuff out a promising trading career. Four-star blunders can and must be avoided at all costs.

Consequences of Four-Star Blunders

A four-star blunder must be avoided simply because it is difficult, if not impossible, to redress the financial consequences of such errors. This is because the percentage profit needed to recoup the loss increases as a geometric function of the loss. For example, a trader who sustained a loss equal to 33 percent of the account balance would need a 50 percent gain to recoup the loss. If the loss were to increase to 50 percent of the account value, the gain needed to offset this loss would jump to 100 percent of the account balance after the loss. In this example, as the loss sustained increases 50 percent, the profits needed to recoup the loss increase 100 percent. In general, the percentage profits needed to recoup a percentage loss, L, are given by the following formula:

$$\text{Percentage profit needed to recoup a loss} = \frac{1}{1 - L} - 1$$

In the limit case, when losses equal 90 percent of the value of the account, the profit needed to recoup this loss equals 900 percent of the balance in the account!

Although four-star blunders are serious, their seriousness is magnified when the market is moving in a narrow trading range, devoid of major trends. If there are strong trends in one or more markets in any given period and the trader has caught the trend, four-star errors of judgment seem to pale in the shadow of the profits generated by the strong trends. However, in nontrending markets, when lucrative opportunities are few and far between, even a two-star error of judgment suddenly seems very significant.

THE EMOTIONAL AFTERMATH OF LOSS

Losses are always painful, but the emotional repercussions are often more difficult to redress than the financial consequences. By focusing all his attention on an errant trade, the trader is quite possibly overlooking other emerging opportunities. When this cost of forgone opportunities is factored in, the total cost of unexpected adversity can be very substantial indeed.

When confronted with unexpected adversity, a trader is likely to be gripped by a mix of emotions: panic, hopelessness, or a dogged determination to get even. The consequences of each of these reactions are discussed below.

Trading More Frequently

First, the trading horizon may shrink drastically. If a trader were a position trader trading off daily price charts, he may now convince himself that the daily charts are not responsive enough to market fluctuations. Accordingly, he might step down to the intraday charts. In so doing, the trader hopes that he can react more quickly to market turns, increasing his probability of success.

Trading More Extensively

Looking for instant gratification, the trader may also decide to trade a greater number of commodities in order to recoup his earlier losses. He figures that if he trades more extensively, the number of profitable trades will increase, enabling him to recoup his losses faster.

Taking Riskier Positions

When in trouble, a trader might decide to trade the most volatile commodities, hoping to score big profits in a hurry, rationalizing that there is, after all, a positive correlation between risk and reward: the higher the risk, the higher the expected reward. For example, a trader who has hitherto shunned the highly volatile Standard & Poor's 500 Index futures might be tempted to jump into that market to recoup earlier losses in a hurry.

Despair-Induced Paralysis

Instead of trading more fervently or assuming positions in more volatile commodities, a trader might swing to the other extreme of not trading at all. Although a string of losses hurts a trader's finances, the associated loss of confidence is much harder to restore. A trader who has suffered serious losses will start doubting himself and his approach to trading. Very soon, he may decide to close his account and salvage the balance.

Selective Acceptance of System Signals

The trader might decide to stay on but trade hesitantly, perhaps second-guessing the trading system or being selective in accepting the signals it generates. This could be potentially disastrous, as the trader might go ahead with losing trades, ignoring the profitable ones!

System Switching

A despondent trader might decide to forsake a system and experiment with alternative systems, hoping eventually to find the "Perfect System". Through anxiety, such a trader forgets that no system is perfect under all market conditions. Lack of discipline and second-guessing of signals are the likely consequences of system switching.

MAINTAINING EMOTIONAL BALANCE

In a sense, a serious adversity might push a trader into an emotional rut by fostering some of the behavior patterns just outlined. As a general rule, the greater the unexpected adversity, the deeper the scar on the trading psyche: the higher the self-doubt and the greater the loss of confidence. The most effective way of maintaining emotional balance is to steer clear of errors of judgment with serious financial repercussions. Another solution is to reiterate some basic market truisms and to reinforce them with the help of statistics. That is the purpose of this section.

Back-to-Back Trades Are Unrelated

Often, a trader will be heard to remark that he does not care to trade a particular commodity because of the nasty setbacks he has suffered in this market. This is a good example of emotional trading, for in reality the market does not play favorites, just as the market does not take any hostages! If only a trader could treat back-to-back trades as discrete, independent events, the outcome of an earlier trade would in no way influence the trader's future responses. This is easier said than done, given that traders are human and have to contend with their emotional selves at all times. However, proving statistical independence between trade outcomes might help dissolve this mental block.

Trade outcomes may be analyzed using the one sample runs test given by Sidney Siegel.[1] A run is defined as a succession of identical outcomes that is followed and preceded by different outcomes or by no outcomes at all. Denoting a win by a +, and a loss by a −, the outcomes may look as follows:

$$+ + + - - - - + - + - - + + - - - + + - +$$

Here we have a total of 10 wins and 11 losses. The first three wins (+) constitute a run. Similarly, the next four losses (−) constitute yet another run. The following win is another run by itself, as is the subsequent losing trade. The total number of runs, r, is 11 in our example. Our null hypothesis (H_0) is that trade outcomes occurred in a random sequence. The alternative hypothesis (H_1) is that there was a pattern to the trade outcomes—that is, the outcomes were nonrandom. The dollar value of the profits and losses is irrelevant for this test of randomness of occurrences. We use the following formula to calculate the z statistic for the observed sequence of trades:

$$z = \frac{r - \left(\dfrac{2n_1 n_2}{n_1 + n_2} + 1 \right)}{\sqrt{\dfrac{2n_1 n_2 (2n_1 n_2 - n_1 - n_2)}{(n_1 + n_2)^2 (n_1 + n_2 - 1)}}}$$

where n_1 = the number of winning trades

n_2 = the number of losing trades

r = the number of runs observed in the sample

Compare the calculated z value with the tabulated z value given for a prespecified level of significance, typically 1 percent or 5 percent. Since H_1 does not predict the direction of the deviation from randomness, a two-tailed test of rejection is used.

A 1 percent level of significance implies that the theoretical z value encompasses 99 percent of the distribution under the bell-shaped curve.

[1] Sidney Siegel, *Nonparametric Statistics for the Behavioral Sciences* (New York: McGraw-Hill, 1956).

The theoretical or tabulated z value at the 1 percent level of significance for a two-tailed test is ± 2.58. Similarly, a 5 percent level of significance implies that the theoretical z value encompasses 95 percent of the distribution under the bell-shaped curve. The corresponding tabulated z value for a two-tailed test is ± 1.96.

If the calculated z value lies beyond the theoretical or tabulated value, there is reason to believe that the sequence of trade outcomes is significantly different from a random distribution. Accordingly, if the calculated z value exceeds $+2.58(+1.96)$ or falls below $-2.58(-1.96)$, the null hypothesis of randomness is rejected at the 1 percent (5 percent) level. However, if the calculated z value lies between ± 2.58 (± 1.96), the null hypothesis of randomness cannot be rejected at 1 percent (5 percent). At least 30 trades are needed to ensure the validity of the test results.

For purposes of illustration, we have analyzed the outcomes of trades generated by a three- and nine-day dual moving-average crossover system for three commodities over a two-year period, January 1987 to December 1988. The commodities studied are Eurodollars, Swiss francs, and the Standard & Poor's (S&P) 500 Index. The results are presented in Table 10.1. They reveal that wins and losses occur randomly across all three commodities at the 1 percent level of significance.

Looking for Trades with Positive Profit Expectation

Particularly worrisome is the phenomenon of withdrawing into one's shell, becoming "gun-shy" as it were, consequent upon a series of bad

Table 10.1   Testing for Randomness in the Sequence of Trade Outcomes

	Swiss Franc	S&P 500	Eurodollars
Total trades	66	73	62
Wins (n_1)	20	17	21
Losses (n_2)	46	56	41
Runs (r)	37	28	30
z, calculated	+2.39	+0.30	+0.35
z, table value at 1%	±2.58	±2.58	±2.58

Note: The three- and nine-day dual moving-average crossover system has been used over the period January 1987 to December 1988.

trades. Even if there is money in the trader's account, and his logical self senses a good trade emerging, his heart tends to pull him away from taking the plunge. In the process, the trader will most likely let many worthwhile opportunities slip by—an irrational move, given that these opportunities would have enabled the trader to recoup most or all of the earlier losses.

At the other end of the emotional scale, a trader might be tempted to trade, simply because she feels obliged to trade each day. A compulsive trader is as much a victim of emotional distress as is the gun-shy trader who cannot seem to execute when the system so demands. A compulsive trader is driven by the urge to trade and is mesmerized by unfolding price action. She feels she must trade every day, simply to justify her existence as a trader.

Perhaps the best way to overcome gun-shy behavior or the tendency to overtrade is to make an objective assessment of the expected profit of each trade. The expected profit on a trade is a function of (a) the probability of success, (b) the anticipated profit, and (c) the permissible loss. The formula for calculating the expected profit is

$$\text{Expected profit} = p(W) - (1 - p)L$$

where p = the probability of winning

$(1 - p)$ = the associated probability of losing

W = the dollar value of the anticipated win

L = the dollar value of the permissible loss

The greater the expected profit, the more desirable the trade. By the same token, if the expected profit is not large enough to recover the commissions charged to execute the trade, one would do well to refrain from the trade.

The only exception to this rule is when a trader is considering trading two negatively correlated markets concurrently. In such a case, it is conceivable that the optimal risk capital allocation across a portfolio of two negatively correlated commodities could exceed the sum of the optimal allocations for each commodity individually. This is notwithstanding the fact that one of the commodities has a negative expectation and would not qualify for consideration on its own merits.

The above formula presupposes that a trader has a clear idea of (a) the estimated reward on the trade, (b) the risk he or she is willing to assume to earn that reward, and (c) the odds of success. As a rule, system traders are not clear about the estimated reward on a trade. However, they are aware of the probability of success and the payoff ratio associated with the system over the most recent past. Using this historical information as a proxy for the future, they can calculate the expected trade profit, using a given system, as follows:

Expected profit $= [p(A + 1) - 1]$

where $p =$ the historical probability of success

   $A =$ the historical payoff ratio or the ratio of the dollars won on average for a \$1 loss

Once again, a system turning in a negative expected profit or an expected profit that barely recovers commissions should be avoided.

PUTTING IT ALL TOGETHER

Football coach Bear Bryant posted this sign outside his teams' lockers: "Cause something to happen." He believed that if a player did not cause something to happen, the other team would run all over him. Bryant did make something happen: He won more college football games than any other coach. For "other team" read "futures markets," and the analogy is equally applicable to futures trading. Yes, a trader can make something worthwhile happen in the futures markets, if he or she chooses to.

First, a trader must develop a game plan that is fanatical about controlling losses. Second, he or she must practice discipline to adhere to that game plan, constantly recalling that success is measured not by the number of times he or she called the market correctly but in terms of the growth in the account balance. Errors of judgment are inevitable, but their consequences can and must be controlled. If the trader does not take charge of losses, the losses will eventually force him or her out of the game. Controlling loss is easier said than done, but it is skill in this area that will determine whether the trader ends up as a winner or as yet another statistic.

Finally, the trader must learn to let logic rather than emotions dictate his or her trading decisions, constantly recalling that back-to-back trades are independent events: There are no permanently "bad" markets. Just as withdrawing from trading after a series of reverses does not help, compulsive overtrading in an attempt to recoup losses can hurt. One way to overcome gun-shy behavior or overtrading is to calculate the expected profit on each trade: If the number is a significant positive, go ahead with the trade; if the expected profit is barely enough to recover commissions, pass the trade.

Futures trading is one activity where performance is easy to measure and the report card is always in at the end of each trading day. In an activity where performance speaks far louder than words, it is hoped that this book will help the reader "speak" more eloquently than before!

A

Turbo Pascal 4.0 Program to Compute the Risk of Ruin

```
Program ruin;
    {[A+,T=3] Instruction to PasMat.}

    Uses
        Dos;

    Type
        String80 = String [80];

    Var
        Name: String80;
        Infile, Outfile: Text;
        C22, NSet, NSetL, Index: LongInt;
        BoundLower, BoundUpper, Cap, Capital, Del,
            Probability, ProbabilityWin, ProbabilityLose,
            TradeWin, TradeLose: Extended;
        Hour, Minute, Sec, Sec100, Year, Month, Day,
            DayOfWeek: Word;

    Begin
        Write(' Input file name: ');
        ReadLn(Name);
        Assign(Infile, Name);
        Reset(Infile);
        Write('Output file name: ');
```

```
ReadLn(Name);
Assign(Outfile, Name);
Rewrite(Outfile);
Randomize;
WriteLn;
Repeat
   GetTime(Hour, Minute, Sec, Sec100);
   GetDate(Year, Month, Day, DayOfWeek);
   ReadLn(Infile, Name);
   WriteLn(Outfile, Name);
   ReadLn(Infile, Capital, TradeWin, TradeLose,
         NSetL);
   WriteLn(Outfile);
   WriteLn(Outfile,
      'Probability of Win    Probability of Ruin');
   Del := 0.05;
   ProbabilityWin := 0.00;
   BoundLower := 0.0;
   BoundUpper := 100 * Capital;
   For Index := 0 to 17 do
      Begin
         ProbabilityWin := ProbabilityWin + Del;
         NSet := 0;
         C22 := 0;
         Repeat
            Cap := Capital;
            Inc(NSet);
            If (NSet / 10 = NSet Div 10) then
               Write(^M, 'Iteration Number ',
                     (NSet + (Index * NSetL)): 1, ' of ',
                     (18 * NSetL): 1);
            Repeat
               Probability := Random;
                 {random betweeen 0 and 1}
               If (Probability <= ProbabilityWin) then
                  Cap := Cap + TradeWin
               else
                  Begin
                     Cap := Cap + TradeLose;
                     If (Cap <= 0) then
                        Inc(C22)
                  End
```

```
                Until ((Cap >= BoundUpper)
                        or (Cap <= BoundLower))
            Until (NSet >= NSetL);
            ProbabilityLose := C22 / NSet;
            WriteLn(Outfile, '        ',
                    ProbabilityWin: 10: 8,
                    '          ', ProbabilityLose: 10: 8)
        End;
    WriteLn;
    WriteLn;
    WriteLn(Outfile);
    WriteLn('Starting at ', Hour: 2, ':', Minute: 2,
            ':', Sec: 2, ' on ', Month: 2, '/',
            Day, '/', Year);
    WriteLn(Outfile, 'Starting at ', Hour: 2, ':',
            Minute: 2, ':', Sec: 2, ' on ', Month: 2,
            '/', Day, '/', Year);
    GetTime(Hour, Minute, Sec, Sec100);
    GetDate(Year, Month, Day, DayOfWeek);
    WriteLn('  Ending at ', Hour: 2, ':', Minute: 2,
            ':', Sec: 2, ' on ', Month: 2, '/',
            Day, '/', Year);
    WriteLn;
    WriteLn(Outfile, '  Ending at ', Hour: 2, ':',
            Minute: 2, ':', Sec: 2, ' on ', Month: 2,
            '/', Day, '/', Year);
    WriteLn(Outfile)
  Until Eof(Infile);
  Close(Infile);
  Close(Outfile);
End.
```

B

BASIC Program to Compute the Risk of Ruin

```
001 REM THIS BASIC PROGRAM IS DESIGNED TO CALCULATE
    THE RISK OF RUIN
002 REM INPUTS: PROB. OF SUCCESS, PAYOFF RATIO,
    UNITS OF CAPITAL
007 OPEN "RUIN.OUT" FOR OUTPUT AS 1
010 PRINT  " INPUT CAPITAL: ";
020 INPUT CAPITAL
030 PRINT  " INPUT TRADEW: ";
040 INPUT TRADEW
050 PRINT  " INPUT TRADEL: ";
060 INPUT TRADEL
070 PRINT  " INPUT SETL: ";
080 INPUT SETL
081 NSETL = SETL
082 CLS:PRINT
083 CLS:PRINT #1,
085 PRINT    "CAPITAL     TRADEW          TRADEL        SETL "
091 PRINT #1, "CAPITAL      TRADEW          TRADEL        SETL "
092 PRINT  CAPITAL,TRADEW,TRADEL,SETL
095 PRINT #1,  CAPITAL,TRADEW,TRADEL,SETL
100 DEL = 0.05
110 PROW = 0
120 PRINT "  PROB(WIN)  PROB(RUIN)    TIME FOR COMPUTATION "
```

```
125 PRINT #1,  "  PROB(WIN)  PROB(RUIN)
    TIME FOR COMPUTATION "
130 FOR IPR = 1 TO 18
140 PROBW = PROBW + DEL
150 BOUNDL = 0
160 BOUNDU = 100* CAPITAL
170 NSET = 0
210 C22 = 0
211 WIN$ = "W"
212 LOSE$ = "L"
220 PROBL = 1 - PROBW
230 CAP = CAPITAL
240 NSET = NSET + 1
250 NTRADE = 0
260 X = RND
270 NTRADE = NTRADE + 1
280 PROB = X
290 IF( PROB <= PROBW ) THEN EVENT$ = WIN$
300 IF( PROB > PROBW ) THEN EVENT$ = LOSE$
310 IF( EVENT$ = WIN$ ) THEN CAP = CAP + TRADEW
320 IF( EVENT$ = LOSE$) THEN CAP = CAP + TRADEL
330 IF( EVENT$ = WIN$ ) THEN NWIN = NWIN + 1
340 IF( EVENT$ = LOSE$) THEN NLOS = NLOS + 1
350 RUIN = 0
360 IF( CAP   <=  0 ) THEN RUIN = 1
370 IF( CAP   <=  0 ) THEN NRUIN = NRUIN + 1
380 IF( EVENT = LOSE AND RUIN = 1 ) THEN C22 = C22 + 1
390 IF( CAP >= BOUNDU) THEN GO TO 420
400 IF( CAP <= BOUNDL) THEN GO TO 420
410 GO TO 260
420 IF( NSET >= NSETL ) THEN GO TO 460
430 NWIN = 0
440 NLOS = 0
450 GO TO 230
460 PROBR = C22/NSET
470 PRINT  PROBW, PROBR,  TIME$
475 PRINT #1,  PROBW, PROBR,  TIME$
480 NEXT IPR
490 CLOSE 1
500 END
```

C

Correlation Data for 24 Commodities

This Appendix presents correlation data for 24 commodities between 1983 and 1988. To ensure that correlations are not spurious, the sample period has been subdivided into three equal subperiods, 1983 to 1984, 1985 to 1986, and 1987 to 1988. A positive correlation over 0.80 in each of the three subperiods would suggest that the commodities are positively correlated. Similarly, a negative correlation below −0.80 in each of the three subperiods would suggest that the commodities are negatively correlated.

The trader should be wary of trading the same side of two positively correlated commodities. He or she should select the commodity that offers the highest reward potential. Alternatively, the trader might want to trade opposite sides of two positively correlated commodities; for example, either the Deutsche mark or the Swiss franc, but not both simultaneously. The trader could also spread the Deutsche mark and the Swiss franc, buying one and selling the other.

Using the same logic, it pays to be on the same side of two negatively correlated commodities. The rationale is that if one commodity fares poorly, the other will make up for the poor performance of the first.

Correlation Table for British Pound

	Correlation Coefficient			
	1983–88	1983–84	1985–86	1987–88
Swiss franc	0.901	0.973	0.809	0.913
Deutsche mark	0.889	0.947	0.800	0.928
Japanese yen	0.854	0.479	0.779	0.974
Gold (COMEX)	0.853	0.943	0.565	0.596
Copper	0.768	0.824	0.134	0.829
Sugar (world)	0.646	0.823	0.710	0.686
S&P 500 Stock Index	0.637	−0.046	0.754	−0.641
NYSE Composite Index	0.621	−0.024	0.753	−0.673
Treasury bonds	0.517	0.206	0.786	−0.507
Treasury bills	0.496	0.099	0.798	−0.176
Treasury notes	0.494	0.208	0.801	−0.534
Soymeal	0.494	0.854	0.588	0.881
Eurodollar	0.419	0.166	0.777	−0.423
Live cattle	0.266	−0.229	−0.559	0.600
Oats	0.076	−0.111	−0.825	0.498
Silver (COMEX)	0.068	0.851	−0.564	0.011
Soybeans	0.018	0.732	−0.754	0.882
Hogs	−0.042	−0.418	0.117	−0.229
Wheat (Chicago)	−0.359	0.327	−0.680	0.715
Wheat (Kansas City)	−0.374	0.297	−0.732	0.830
Corn	−0.435	0.830	−0.618	0.853
Soybean oil	−0.449	0.133	−0.803	0.859
Crude oil	−0.508	0.811	−0.609	−0.542

Correlation Table for Corn

	Correlation Coefficient			
	1983–88	1983–84	1985–86	1987–88
Wheat (Kansas City)	0.891	0.440	0.825	0.803
Soybean oil	0.886	0.573	0.871	0.848
Wheat (Chicago)	0.844	0.426	0.769	0.692
Soybeans	0.826	0.925	0.875	0.912
Crude oil	0.808	0.735	0.645	−0.423
Silver (COMEX)	0.673	0.658	0.596	0.145
Soymeal	0.436	0.865	−0.494	0.837
Oats	0.391	0.266	0.422	0.407
Live cattle	0.094	−0.126	0.369	0.704
Sugar (world)	0.072	0.577	−0.541	0.602
Hogs	−0.116	−0.103	−0.472	0.063
Copper	−0.233	0.611	0.421	0.614
Gold (COMEX)	−0.383	0.773	−0.862	0.503
British pound	−0.435	0.830	−0.618	0.853
Swiss franc	−0.726	0.846	−0.895	0.719
Deutsche mark	−0.743	0.830	−0.876	0.726
Japanese yen	−0.780	0.643	−0.849	0.866
Treasury bonds	−0.853	−0.153	−0.760	−0.477
S&P 500 Stock Index	−0.862	−0.283	−0.749	−0.523
Eurodollar	−0.866	−0.106	−0.839	−0.440
Treasury notes	−0.869	−0.156	−0.804	−0.514
NYSE Composite Index	−0.869	−0.281	−0.741	−0.548
Treasury bills	−0.897	−0.138	−0.853	−0.229

Correlation Table for Crude Oil

	Correlation Coefficient			
	1983–88	1983–84	1985–86	1987–88
Wheat (Kansas City)	0.843	0.423	0.818	−0.671
Corn	0.808	0.735	0.645	−0.423
Soybean oil	0.794	0.261	0.755	−0.619
Wheat (Chicago)	0.767	0.468	0.686	−0.697
Silver (COMEX)	0.631	0.862	0.824	0.547
Soybeans	0.593	0.632	0.474	−0.487
Oats	0.435	−0.135	0.519	−0.319
Soymeal	0.194	0.643	−0.729	−0.313
Live cattle	0.168	−0.287	0.533	−0.465
Hogs	−0.133	−0.325	−0.361	0.537
Sugar (world)	−0.141	0.660	−0.703	−0.769
Copper	−0.287	0.824	−0.031	−0.503
Gold (COMEX)	−0.380	0.877	−0.661	0.077
British pound	−0.508	0.811	−0.609	−0.542
Swiss franc	−0.736	0.769	−0.824	−0.633
Deutsche mark	−0.748	0.784	−0.836	−0.664
S&P 500 Stock Index	−0.777	−0.113	−0.910	0.611
NYSE Composite Index	−0.787	−0.098	−0.912	0.608
Japanese yen	−0.809	0.341	−0.880	−0.637
Eurodollar	−0.822	−0.110	−0.780	−0.204
Treasury bills	−0.851	−0.181	−0.792	−0.274
Treasury notes	−0.902	−0.042	−0.896	−0.179
Treasury bonds	−0.914	−0.025	−0.917	−0.195

Correlation Table for Copper (Standard)

	Correlation Coefficient			
	1983–88	1983–84	1985–86	1987–88
British pound	0.768	0.824	0.134	0.829
Gold (COMEX)	0.694	0.906	−0.188	0.678
Swiss franc	0.669	0.806	−0.132	0.905
Deutsche mark	0.658	0.800	−0.092	0.898
Japanese yen	0.641	0.254	−0.110	0.819
Sugar (world)	0.483	0.775	0.208	0.652
Soymeal	0.464	0.638	0.248	0.769
Oats	0.383	−0.233	−0.123	0.707
Live cattle	0.375	−0.217	−0.043	0.276
S&P 500 Stock Index	0.352	0.030	−0.037	−0.622
NYSE Composite Index	0.328	0.049	−0.030	−0.663
Treasury bills	0.251	0.120	−0.180	−0.183
Treasury bonds	0.190	0.274	−0.034	−0.497
Treasury notes	0.169	0.261	−0.059	−0.520
Eurodollar	0.165	0.201	−0.193	−0.424
Soybeans	0.135	0.521	0.268	0.651
Silver (COMEX)	0.100	0.937	0.224	−0.049
Wheat (Chicago)	−0.025	0.531	0.313	0.657
Wheat (Kansas City)	−0.059	0.355	0.250	0.714
Soybean oil	−0.127	0.019	0.118	0.717
Hogs	−0.202	−0.346	−0.483	−0.481
Corn	−0.233	0.611	0.421	0.614
Crude oil	−0.287	0.824	−0.031	−0.503

Correlation Table for Deutsche Mark

	Correlation Coefficient			
	1983–88	1983–84	1985–86	1987–88
Swiss franc	0.998	0.966	0.997	0.991
Japanese yen	0.983	0.642	0.981	0.933
British pound	0.889	0.947	0.800	0.928
S&P 500 Stock Index	0.857	−0.195	0.933	−0.766
NYSE Composite Index	0.846	−0.170	0.928	−0.796
Gold (COMEX)	0.841	0.893	0.875	0.561
Treasury bonds	0.748	0.048	0.938	−0.363
Treasury notes	0.734	0.053	0.964	−0.388
Treasury bills	0.724	−0.013	0.933	−0.041
Copper	0.658	0.800	−0.092	0.898
Eurodollar	0.651	0.035	0.922	−0.303
Sugar (world)	0.446	0.679	0.748	0.762
Live cattle	0.205	−0.101	−0.455	0.420
Soymeal	0.205	0.749	0.734	0.779
Hogs	0.099	−0.270	0.414	−0.447
Oats	−0.003	−0.089	−0.530	0.599
Silver (COMEX)	−0.222	0.785	−0.726	−0.132
Soybeans	−0.307	0.686	−0.800	0.739
Wheat (Chicago)	−0.596	0.297	−0.730	0.737
Wheat (Kansas City)	−0.643	0.222	−0.862	0.799
Soybean oil	−0.691	0.192	−0.932	0.787
Corn	−0.743	0.830	−0.876	0.726
Crude oil	−0.748	0.784	−0.836	−0.664

Correlation Table for Treasury Bonds

	Correlation Coefficient			
	1983–88	1983–84	1985–86	1987–88
Treasury notes	0.996	0.996	0.993	0.996
Treasury bills	0.942	0.876	0.928	0.842
Eurodollar	0.937	0.933	0.919	0.948
NYSE Composite Index	0.832	0.748	0.976	0.044
S&P 500 Stock Index	0.818	0.747	0.975	−0.004
Japanese yen	0.776	−0.295	0.950	−0.451
Deutsche mark	0.748	0.048	0.938	−0.363
Swiss franc	0.736	0.205	0.929	−0.394
British pound	0.517	0.206	0.786	−0.507
Gold (COMEX)	0.373	0.215	0.738	−0.826
Sugar (world)	0.206	0.580	0.775	−0.032
Copper	0.190	0.274	−0.034	−0.497
Hogs	0.064	−0.634	0.383	−0.078
Live cattle	−0.234	−0.175	−0.527	−0.284
Soymeal	−0.235	0.271	0.735	−0.617
Oats	−0.520	−0.091	−0.588	−0.544
Silver (COMEX)	−0.597	0.290	−0.849	−0.636
Soybeans	−0.655	−0.027	−0.669	−0.411
Wheat (Chicago)	−0.808	0.117	−0.734	−0.282
Corn	−0.853	−0.153	−0.760	−0.477
Soybean oil	−0.870	−0.486	−0.864	−0.316
Wheat (Kansas City)	−0.891	0.209	−0.871	−0.406
Crude oil	−0.914	−0.025	−0.917	−0.195

Correlation Table for Eurodollar

	Correlation Coefficient			
	1983–88	1983–84	1985–86	1987–88
Treasury bills	0.989	0.976	0.995	0.909
Treasury notes	0.953	0.937	0.946	0.945
Treasury bonds	0.937	0.933	0.919	0.948
NYSE Composite Index	0.777	0.589	0.887	0.000
S&P 500 Stock Index	0.762	0.589	0.890	−0.041
Japanese yen	0.692	−0.157	0.907	−0.364
Deutsche mark	0.651	0.035	0.922	−0.303
Swiss franc	0.641	0.195	0.928	−0.332
British pound	0.419	0.166	0.777	−0.423
Gold (COMEX)	0.266	0.158	0.839	−0.753
Copper	0.165	0.201	−0.193	−0.424
Sugar (world)	0.057	0.480	0.617	−0.042
Hogs	0.014	−0.503	0.478	−0.051
Live cattle	−0.236	−0.002	−0.501	−0.263
Soymeal	−0.353	0.292	0.554	−0.524
Oats	−0.547	0.034	−0.534	−0.484
Silver (COMEX)	−0.661	0.198	−0.700	−0.611
Soybeans	−0.718	0.057	−0.761	−0.319
Wheat (Chicago)	−0.804	0.060	−0.795	−0.262
Soybean oil	−0.821	−0.327	−0.829	−0.238
Crude oil	−0.822	−0.110	−0.780	−0.204
Corn	−0.866	−0.106	−0.839	−0.440
Wheat (Kansas City)	−0.883	0.148	−0.898	−0.370

Correlation Table for Gold (COMEX)

	Correlation Coefficient			
	1983–88	1983–84	1985–86	1987–88
Swiss franc	0.855	0.916	0.879	0.627
British pound	0.853	0.943	0.565	0.596
Deutsche mark	0.841	0.893	0.875	0.561
Japanese yen	0.769	0.367	0.835	0.553
Copper	0.694	0.906	−0.188	0.678
Sugar (world)	0.618	0.835	0.492	0.138
S&P 500 Stock Index	0.606	−0.014	0.745	−0.244
NYSE Composite Index	0.584	0.006	0.740	−0.299
Soymeal	0.554	0.796	0.522	0.656
Treasury bonds	0.373	0.215	0.738	−0.826
Treasury notes	0.353	0.208	0.791	−0.845
Oats	0.351	−0.139	−0.289	0.622
Treasury bills	0.342	0.086	0.841	−0.513
Live cattle	0.320	−0.287	−0.333	0.094
Silver (COMEX)	0.293	0.952	−0.440	0.641
Eurodollar	0.266	0.158	0.839	−0.753
Hogs	0.108	−0.437	0.439	−0.004
Soybeans	0.105	0.701	−0.734	0.409
Wheat (Chicago)	−0.269	0.440	−0.644	0.306
Wheat (Kansas City)	−0.280	0.367	−0.766	0.421
Soybean oil	−0.373	0.166	−0.765	0.339
Crude oil	−0.380	0.877	−0.661	0.077
Corn	−0.383	0.773	−0.862	0.503

Correlation Table for Japanese Yen

	Correlation Coefficient			
	1983–88	1983–84	1985–86	1987–88
Deutsche mark	0.983	0.642	0.981	0.933
Swiss franc	0.981	0.613	0.983	0.925
S&P 500 Stock Index	0.864	−0.363	0.949	−0.644
NYSE Composite Index	0.855	−0.350	0.945	−0.676
British pound	0.854	0.479	0.779	0.974
Treasury bonds	0.776	−0.295	0.950	−0.451
Gold (COMEX)	0.769	0.367	0.835	0.553
Treasury bills	0.764	−0.157	0.917	−0.138
Treasury notes	0.763	−0.279	0.963	−0.477
Eurodollar	0.692	−0.157	0.907	−0.364
Copper	0.641	0.254	−0.110	0.819
Sugar (world)	0.367	0.069	0.758	0.728
Live cattle	0.210	0.488	−0.438	0.630
Hogs	0.145	0.265	0.483	−0.237
Soymeal	0.129	0.375	0.756	0.835
Oats	−0.072	0.182	−0.573	0.521
Silver (COMEX)	−0.335	0.150	−0.794	−0.021
Soybeans	−0.366	0.493	−0.753	0.884
Wheat (Chicago)	−0.635	−0.047	−0.756	0.773
Wheat (Kansas City)	−0.682	−0.015	−0.881	0.871
Soybean oil	−0.707	0.373	−0.921	0.890
Corn	−0.780	0.643	−0.849	0.866
Crude oil	−0.809	0.341	−0.880	−0.637

Correlation Table for Live Cattle

	Correlation Coefficient			
	1983–88	1983–84	1985–86	1987–88
Oats	0.572	0.015	0.543	0.192
Copper	0.375	−0.217	−0.043	0.276
Wheat (Kansas City)	0.338	−0.402	0.647	0.678
Soymeal	0.321	−0.289	−0.135	0.461
Gold (COMEX)	0.320	−0.287	−0.333	0.094
Wheat (Chicago)	0.316	−0.410	0.671	0.563
Soybeans	0.303	−0.199	0.383	0.676
British pound	0.266	−0.229	−0.559	0.600
Hogs	0.230	0.531	0.139	0.038
Silver (COMEX)	0.216	−0.413	0.508	0.020
Japanese yen	0.210	0.488	−0.438	0.630
Soybean oil	0.210	−0.030	0.422	0.643
Swiss franc	0.208	−0.101	−0.454	0.393
Deutsche mark	0.205	−0.101	−0.455	0.420
Crude oil	0.168	−0.287	0.533	−0.465
Sugar (world)	0.098	−0.480	−0.396	0.450
Corn	0.094	−0.126	0.369	0.704
S&P 500 Stock Index	0.050	−0.292	−0.526	−0.175
NYSE Composite Index	0.028	−0.292	−0.530	−0.183
Treasury bills	−0.186	0.029	−0.525	−0.213
Treasury bonds	−0.234	−0.175	−0.527	−0.284
Eurodollar	−0.236	−0.002	−0.501	−0.263
Treasury notes	−0.245	−0.151	−0.513	−0.300

Correlation Table for Live Hogs

	Correlation Coefficient			
	1983–88	1983–84	1985–86	1987–88
Live cattle	0.230	0.531	0.139	0.038
S&P 500 Stock Index	0.151	−0.546	0.432	0.473
NYSE Composite Index	0.149	−0.549	0.425	0.476
Japanese yen	0.145	0.265	0.483	−0.237
Gold (COMEX)	0.108	−0.437	0.439	−0.004
Swiss franc	0.101	−0.345	0.437	−0.423
Deutsche mark	0.099	−0.270	0.414	−0.447
Treasury bonds	0.064	−0.634	0.383	−0.078
Treasury notes	0.059	−0.624	0.395	−0.085
Treasury bills	0.029	−0.417	0.446	−0.152
Oats	0.027	0.145	0.046	−0.478
Eurodollar	0.014	−0.503	0.478	−0.051
Soybeans	−0.026	−0.195	−0.186	0.022
British pound	−0.042	−0.418	0.117	−0.229
Soymeal	−0.051	−0.429	0.237	−0.099
Silver (COMEX)	−0.061	−0.495	−0.438	0.552
Soybean oil	−0.063	0.280	−0.288	−0.165
Corn	−0.116	−0.103	−0.472	0.063
Crude oil	−0.133	−0.325	−0.361	0.537
Wheat (Kansas City)	−0.186	−0.377	−0.437	−0.339
Wheat (Chicago)	−0.196	−0.176	−0.371	−0.382
Copper	−0.202	−0.346	−0.483	−0.481
Sugar (world)	−0.239	−0.660	0.036	−0.445

Correlation Table for Treasury Notes

	Correlation Coefficient			
	1983–88	1983–84	1985–86	1987–88
Treasury bonds	0.996	0.996	0.993	0.996
Treasury bills	0.955	0.879	0.953	0.822
Eurodollar	0.953	0.937	0.946	0.945
NYSE Composite Index	0.825	0.733	0.970	0.061
S&P 500 Stock Index	0.811	0.731	0.971	0.010
Japanese yen	0.763	−0.279	0.963	−0.477
Deutsche mark	0.734	0.053	0.964	−0.388
Swiss franc	0.722	0.206	0.956	−0.422
British pound	0.494	0.208	0.801	−0.534
Gold (COMEX)	0.353	0.208	0.791	−0.845
Copper	0.169	0.261	−0.059	−0.520
Sugar (world)	0.168	0.565	0.759	−0.043
Hogs	0.059	−0.624	0.395	−0.085
Live cattle	−0.245	−0.151	−0.513	−0.300
Soymeal	−0.273	0.265	0.725	−0.645
Oats	−0.541	−0.104	−0.577	−0.559
Silver (COMEX)	−0.621	0.276	−0.811	−0.644
Soybeans	−0.685	−0.033	−0.723	−0.436
Wheat (Chicago)	−0.817	0.091	−0.742	−0.292
Corn	−0.869	−0.156	−0.804	−0.514
Soybean oil	−0.877	−0.488	−0.888	−0.337
Wheat (Kansas City)	−0.901	0.196	−0.878	−0.426
Crude oil	−0.902	−0.042	−0.896	−0.179

Correlation Table for NYSE Composite Index

	Correlation Coefficient			
	1983–88	1983–84	1985–86	1987–88
S&P 500 Stock Index	0.999	0.991	1.000	0.997
Japanese yen	0.855	−0.350	0.945	−0.676
Deutsche mark	0.846	−0.170	0.928	−0.796
Treasury bonds	0.832	0.748	0.976	0.044
Swiss franc	0.828	−0.022	0.917	−0.776
Treasury notes	0.825	0.733	0.970	0.061
Treasury bills	0.816	0.533	0.892	−0.257
Eurodollar	0.777	0.589	0.887	0.000
British pound	0.621	−0.024	0.753	−0.673
Gold (COMEX)	0.584	0.006	0.740	−0.299
Copper	0.328	0.049	−0.030	−0.663
Sugar (world)	0.151	0.370	0.735	−0.753
Hogs	0.149	−0.549	0.425	0.476
Live cattle	0.028	−0.292	−0.530	−0.183
Soymeal	−0.162	0.050	0.710	−0.612
Oats	−0.248	0.016	−0.532	−0.499
Silver (COMEX)	−0.419	0.092	−0.855	0.358
Soybeans	−0.590	−0.164	−0.634	−0.592
Wheat (Chicago)	−0.775	0.134	−0.734	−0.698
Crude oil	−0.787	−0.098	−0.912	0.608
Soybean oil	−0.805	−0.421	−0.834	−0.679
Wheat (Kansas City)	−0.822	0.273	−0.874	−0.663
Corn	−0.869	−0.281	−0.741	−0.548

Correlation Table for Oats

	Correlation Coefficient			
	1983–88	1983–84	1985–86	1987–88
Soybeans	0.615	0.467	0.612	0.365
Wheat (Kansas City)	0.613	0.469	0.610	0.636
Wheat (Chicago)	0.596	0.409	0.643	0.612
Live cattle	0.572	0.015	0.543	0.192
Silver (COMEX)	0.557	−0.144	0.492	0.115
Soymeal	0.545	0.295	−0.465	0.578
Soybean oil	0.529	0.656	0.648	0.427
Crude oil	0.435	−0.135	0.519	−0.319
Corn	0.391	0.266	0.422	0.407
Copper	0.383	−0.233	−0.123	0.707
Gold (COMEX)	0.351	−0.139	−0.289	0.622
Sugar (world)	0.208	−0.032	−0.619	0.371
British pound	0.076	−0.111	−0.825	0.498
Hogs	0.027	0.145	0.046	−0.478
Swiss franc	0.007	−0.017	−0.559	0.636
Deutsche mark	−0.003	−0.089	−0.530	0.599
Japanese yen	−0.072	0.182	−0.573	0.521
S&P 500 Stock Index	−0.219	0.038	−0.528	−0.456
NYSE Composite Index	−0.248	0.016	−0.532	−0.499
Treasury bills	−0.500	0.095	−0.572	−0.307
Treasury bonds	−0.520	−0.091	−0.588	−0.544
Treasury notes	−0.541	−0.104	−0.577	−0.559
Eurodollar	−0.547	0.034	−0.534	−0.484

Correlation Table for Soybeans

	Correlation Coefficient			
	1983–88	1983–84	1985–86	1987–88
Corn	0.826	0.925	0.875	0.912
Soymeal	0.811	0.919	−0.443	0.886
Silver (COMEX)	0.788	0.627	0.471	−0.033
Soybean oil	0.788	0.703	0.884	0.948
Wheat (Kansas City)	0.780	0.565	0.719	0.815
Wheat (Chicago)	0.745	0.544	0.698	0.729
Oats	0.615	0.467	0.612	0.365
Crude oil	0.593	0.632	0.474	−0.487
Sugar (world)	0.425	0.597	−0.612	0.683
Live cattle	0.303	−0.199	0.383	0.676
Copper	0.135	0.521	0.268	0.651
Gold (COMEX)	0.105	0.701	−0.734	0.409
British pound	0.018	0.732	−0.754	0.882
Hogs	−0.026	−0.195	−0.186	0.022
Swiss franc	−0.281	0.746	−0.821	0.706
Deutsche mark	−0.307	0.686	−0.800	0.739
Japanese yen	−0.366	0.493	−0.753	0.884
S&P 500 Stock Index	−0.572	−0.156	−0.642	−0.573
NYSE Composite Index	−0.590	−0.164	−0.634	−0.592
Treasury bonds	−0.655	−0.027	−0.669	−0.411
Treasury notes	−0.685	−0.033	−0.723	−0.436
Treasury bills	−0.712	0.037	−0.787	−0.151
Eurodollar	−0.718	0.057	−0.761	−0.319

Correlation Table for Swiss Franc

	Correlation Coefficient			
	1983–88	1983–84	1985–86	1987–88
Deutsche mark	0.998	0.966	0.997	0.991
Japanese yen	0.981	0.613	0.983	0.925
British pound	0.901	0.973	0.809	0.913
Gold (COMEX)	0.855	0.916	0.879	0.627
S&P 500 Stock Index	0.840	−0.045	0.922	−0.741
NYSE Composite Index	0.828	−0.022	0.917	−0.776
Treasury bonds	0.736	0.205	0.929	−0.394
Treasury notes	0.722	0.206	0.956	−0.422
Treasury bills	0.714	0.139	0.940	−0.057
Copper	0.669	0.806	−0.132	0.905
Eurodollar	0.641	0.195	0.928	−0.332
Sugar (world)	0.472	0.786	0.733	0.720
Soymeal	0.237	0.846	0.715	0.763
Live cattle	0.208	−0.101	−0.454	0.393
Hogs	0.101	−0.345	0.437	−0.423
Oats	0.007	−0.017	−0.559	0.636
Silver (COMEX)	−0.196	0.804	−0.721	−0.051
Soybeans	−0.281	0.746	−0.821	0.706
Wheat (Chicago)	−0.586	0.324	−0.757	0.720
Wheat (Kansas City)	−0.628	0.292	−0.877	0.785
Soybean oil	−0.681	0.170	−0.937	0.753
Corn	−0.726	0.846	−0.895	0.719
Crude oil	−0.736	0.769	−0.824	−0.633

Correlation Table for Soymeal

	Correlation Coefficient			
	1983–88	1983–84	1985–86	1987–88
Soybeans	0.811	0.919	−0.443	0.886
Sugar (world)	0.765	0.814	0.780	0.540
Silver (COMEX)	0.714	0.731	−0.578	0.112
Gold (COMEX)	0.554	0.796	0.522	0.656
Oats	0.545	0.295	−0.465	0.578
British pound	0.494	0.854	0.588	0.881
Copper	0.464	0.638	0.248	0.769
Corn	0.436	0.865	−0.494	0.837
Wheat (Kansas City)	0.434	0.544	−0.462	0.737
Wheat (Chicago)	0.419	0.517	−0.314	0.624
Live cattle	0.321	−0.289	−0.135	0.461
Soybean oil	0.311	0.379	−0.775	0.791
Swiss franc	0.237	0.846	0.715	0.763
Deutsche mark	0.205	0.749	0.734	0.779
Crude oil	0.194	0.643	−0.729	−0.313
Japanese yen	0.129	0.375	0.756	0.835
Hogs	−0.051	−0.429	0.237	−0.099
S&P 500 Stock Index	−0.140	0.050	0.710	−0.576
NYSE Composite Index	−0.162	0.050	0.710	−0.612
Treasury bonds	−0.235	0.271	0.735	−0.617
Treasury notes	−0.273	0.265	0.725	−0.645
Treasury bills	−0.317	0.242	0.576	−0.292
Eurodollar	−0.353	0.292	0.554	−0.524

Correlation Table for Sugar (#11 World)

	Correlation Coefficient			
	1983–88	1983–84	1985–86	1987–88
Soymeal	0.765	0.814	0.780	0.540
British pound	0.646	0.823	0.710	0.686
Gold (COMEX)	0.618	0.835	0.492	0.138
Silver (COMEX)	0.486	0.855	−0.660	−0.447
Copper	0.483	0.775	0.208	0.652
Swiss franc	0.472	0.786	0.733	0.720
Deutsche mark	0.446	0.679	0.748	0.762
Soybeans	0.425	0.597	−0.612	0.683
Japanese yen	0.367	0.069	0.758	0.728
Oats	0.208	−0.032	−0.619	0.371
Treasury bonds	0.206	0.580	0.775	−0.032
Treasury notes	0.168	0.565	0.759	−0.043
S&P 500 Stock Index	0.161	0.353	0.735	−0.753
NYSE Composite Index	0.151	0.370	0.735	−0.753
Wheat (Chicago)	0.110	0.487	−0.480	0.825
Live cattle	0.098	−0.480	−0.396	0.450
Wheat (Kansas City)	0.074	0.476	−0.600	0.783
Treasury bills	0.073	0.397	0.648	0.102
Corn	0.072	0.577	−0.541	0.602
Eurodollar	0.057	0.480	0.617	−0.042
Soybean oil	−0.124	−0.048	−0.815	0.818
Crude oil	−0.141	0.660	−0.703	−0.769
Hogs	−0.239	−0.660	0.036	−0.445

Correlation Table for Soybean Oil

	Correlation Coefficient			
	1983–88	1983–84	1985–86	1987–88
Corn	0.886	0.573	0.871	0.848
Wheat (Kansas City)	0.868	0.410	0.804	0.876
Wheat (Chicago)	0.837	0.420	0.727	0.838
Crude oil	0.794	0.261	0.755	−0.619
Soybeans	0.788	0.703	0.884	0.948
Silver (COMEX)	0.535	0.134	0.697	−0.196
Oats	0.529	0.656	0.648	0.427
Soymeal	0.311	0.379	−0.775	0.791
Live cattle	0.210	−0.030	0.422	0.643
Hogs	−0.063	0.280	−0.288	−0.165
Sugar (world)	−0.124	−0.048	−0.815	0.818
Copper	−0.127	0.019	0.118	0.717
Gold (COMEX)	−0.373	0.166	−0.765	0.339
British pound	−0.449	0.133	−0.803	0.859
Swiss franc	−0.681	0.170	−0.937	0.753
Deutsche mark	−0.691	0.192	−0.932	0.787
Japanese yen	−0.707	0.373	−0.921	0.890
S&P 500 Stock Index	−0.795	−0.398	−0.840	−0.662
NYSE Composite Index	−0.805	−0.421	−0.834	−0.679
Eurodollar	−0.821	−0.327	−0.829	−0.238
Treasury bills	−0.833	−0.279	−0.855	−0.078
Treasury bonds	−0.870	−0.486	−0.864	−0.316
Treasury notes	−0.877	−0.488	−0.888	−0.337

Correlation Table for S&P 500 Stock Index

	Correlation Coefficient			
	1983–88	1983–84	1985–86	1987–88
NYSE Composite Index	0.999	0.991	1.000	0.997
Japanese yen	0.864	−0.363	0.949	−0.644
Deutsche mark	0.857	−0.195	0.933	−0.766
Swiss franc	0.840	−0.045	0.922	−0.741
Treasury bonds	0.818	0.747	0.975	−0.004
Treasury notes	0.811	0.731	0.971	0.010
Treasury bills	0.804	0.530	0.894	−0.286
Eurodollar	0.762	0.589	0.890	−0.041
British pound	0.637	−0.046	0.754	−0.641
Gold (COMEX)	0.606	−0.014	0.745	−0.244
Copper	0.352	0.030	−0.037	−0.622
Sugar (world)	0.161	0.353	0.735	−0.753
Hogs	0.151	−0.546	0.432	0.473
Live cattle	0.050	−0.292	−0.526	−0.175
Soymeal	−0.140	0.050	0.710	−0.576
Oats	−0.219	0.038	−0.528	−0.456
Silver (COMEX)	−0.399	0.079	−0.855	0.393
Soybeans	−0.572	−0.156	−0.642	−0.573
Wheat (Chicago)	−0.764	0.150	−0.737	−0.685
Crude oil	−0.777	−0.113	−0.910	0.611
Soybean oil	−0.795	−0.398	−0.840	−0.662
Wheat (Kansas City)	−0.808	0.308	−0.876	−0.640
Corn	−0.862	−0.283	−0.749	−0.523

Correlation Table for Silver (COMEX)

	Correlation Coefficient			
	1983–88	1983–84	1985–86	1987–88
Soybeans	0.788	0.627	0.471	−0.033
Soymeal	0.714	0.731	−0.578	0.112
Corn	0.673	0.658	0.596	0.145
Wheat (Kansas City)	0.659	0.456	0.771	−0.103
Crude oil	0.631	0.862	0.824	0.547
Wheat (Chicago)	0.613	0.577	0.692	−0.226
Oats	0.557	−0.144	0.492	0.115
Soybean oil	0.535	0.134	0.697	−0.196
Sugar (world)	0.486	0.855	−0.660	−0.447
Gold (COMEX)	0.293	0.952	−0.440	0.641
Live cattle	0.216	−0.413	0.508	0.020
Copper	0.100	0.937	0.224	−0.049
British pound	0.068	0.851	−0.564	0.011
Hogs	−0.061	−0.495	−0.438	0.552
Swiss franc	−0.196	0.804	−0.721	−0.051
Deutsche mark	−0.222	0.785	−0.726	−0.132
Japanese yen	−0.335	0.150	−0.794	−0.021
S&P 500 Stock Index	−0.399	0.079	−0.855	0.393
NYSE Composite Index	−0.419	0.092	−0.855	0.358
Treasury bonds	−0.597	0.290	−0.849	−0.636
Treasury notes	−0.621	0.276	−0.811	−0.644
Treasury bills	−0.659	0.117	−0.706	−0.558
Eurodollar	−0.661	0.198	−0.700	−0.611

CORRELATION DATA FOR 24 COMMODITIES

Correlation Table for Treasury Bills

	Correlation Coefficient			
	1983–88	1983–84	1985–86	1987–88
Eurodollar	0.989	0.976	0.995	0.909
Treasury notes	0.955	0.879	0.953	0.822
Treasury bonds	0.942	0.876	0.928	0.842
NYSE Composite Index	0.816	0.533	0.892	−0.257
S&P 500 Stock Index	0.804	0.530	0.894	−0.286
Japanese yen	0.764	−0.157	0.917	−0.138
Deutsche mark	0.724	−0.013	0.933	−0.041
Swiss franc	0.714	0.139	0.940	−0.057
British pound	0.496	0.099	0.798	−0.176
Gold (COMEX)	0.342	0.086	0.841	−0.513
Copper	0.251	0.120	−0.180	−0.183
Sugar (world)	0.073	0.397	0.648	0.102
Hogs	0.029	−0.417	0.446	−0.152
Live cattle	−0.186	0.029	−0.525	−0.213
Soymeal	−0.317	0.242	0.576	−0.292
Oats	−0.500	0.095	−0.572	−0.307
Silver (COMEX)	−0.659	0.117	−0.706	−0.558
Soybeans	−0.712	0.037	−0.787	−0.151
Wheat (Chicago)	−0.818	0.011	−0.805	−0.123
Soybean oil	−0.833	−0.279	−0.855	−0.078
Crude oil	−0.851	−0.181	−0.792	−0.274
Wheat (Kansas City)	−0.893	0.068	−0.905	−0.183
Corn	−0.897	−0.138	−0.853	−0.229

Correlation Table for Wheat (Chicago)

	Correlation Coefficient			
	1983–88	1983–84	1985–86	1987–88
Wheat (Kansas City)	0.964	0.817	0.954	0.950
Corn	0.844	0.426	0.769	0.692
Soybean oil	0.837	0.420	0.727	0.838
Crude oil	0.767	0.468	0.686	−0.697
Soybeans	0.745	0.544	0.698	0.729
Silver (COMEX)	0.613	0.577	0.692	−0.226
Oats	0.596	0.409	0.643	0.612
Soymeal	0.419	0.517	−0.314	0.624
Live cattle	0.316	−0.410	0.671	0.563
Sugar (world)	0.110	0.487	−0.480	0.825
Copper	−0.025	0.531	0.313	0.657
Hogs	−0.196	−0.176	−0.371	−0.382
Gold (COMEX)	−0.269	0.440	−0.644	0.306
British pound	−0.359	0.327	−0.680	0.715
Swiss franc	−0.586	0.324	−0.757	0.720
Deutsche mark	−0.596	0.297	−0.730	0.737
Japanese yen	−0.635	−0.047	−0.756	0.773
S&P 500 Stock Index	−0.764	0.150	−0.737	−0.685
NYSE Composite Index	−0.775	0.134	−0.734	−0.698
Eurodollar	−0.804	0.060	−0.795	−0.262
Treasury bonds	−0.808	0.117	−0.734	−0.282
Treasury notes	−0.817	0.091	−0.742	−0.292
Treasury bills	−0.818	0.011	−0.805	−0.123

Correlation Table for Wheat (Kansas City)

	Correlation Coefficient			
	1983–88	1983–84	1985–86	1987–88
Wheat (Chicago)	0.964	0.817	0.954	0.950
Corn	0.891	0.440	0.825	0.803
Soybean oil	0.868	0.410	0.804	0.876
Crude oil	0.843	0.423	0.818	−0.671
Soybeans	0.780	0.565	0.719	0.815
Silver (COMEX)	0.659	0.456	0.771	−0.103
Oats	0.613	0.469	0.610	0.636
Soymeal	0.434	0.544	−0.462	0.737
Live cattle	0.338	−0.402	0.647	0.678
Sugar (world)	0.074	0.476	−0.600	0.783
Copper	−0.059	0.355	0.250	0.714
Hogs	−0.186	−0.377	−0.437	−0.339
Gold (COMEX)	−0.280	0.367	−0.766	0.421
British pound	−0.374	0.297	−0.732	0.830
Swiss franc	−0.628	0.292	−0.877	0.785
Deutsche mark	−0.643	0.222	−0.862	0.799
Japanese yen	−0.682	−0.015	−0.881	0.871
S&P 500 Stock Index	−0.808	0.308	−0.876	−0.640
NYSE Composite Index	−0.822	0.273	−0.874	−0.663
Eurodollar	−0.883	0.148	−0.898	−0.370
Treasury bonds	−0.891	0.209	−0.871	−0.406
Treasury bills	−0.893	0.068	−0.905	−0.183
Treasury notes	−0.901	0.196	−0.878	−0.426

D
Dollar Risk Tables for 24 Commodities

This Appendix gives a percentile distribution of the daily/weekly true range in ticks across 24 commodities. It also defines the dollar value of a prespecified exposure in ticks resulting from trading anywhere from one to 10 contracts.

For example, a 52-tick exposure in the British pound is equivalent to a dollar risk of $650 for one contract. The same exposure amounts to a dollar risk of $3250 on five contracts and to $6500 on 10 contracts. Our analysis reveals that 40 percent of the daily true ranges for the pound between January 1980 and June 1988 have a tick value less than or equal to 52 ticks. 90 percent of the daily true ranges for the pound have a tick value of 117 ticks, or a risk exposure of $1463 on a one-contract basis. For five contracts, a 117-tick exposure would amount to $7313. For 10 contracts, the exposure would amount to $14,625.

The appendix could also be used to determine the number of contracts to be traded for a given aggregate dollar exposure and a permissible risk in ticks per contract. For example, assume that a trader wishes to risk $5000 to a British pound trade. The trader's permissible risk is 80 ticks per contract, which covers 70 percent of the distribution of all daily true ranges in our sample. This risk translates into $1000 per contract, allowing our trader to trade five contracts, for a total exposure of $5000.

Dollar Risk Table for British Pound Futures

Based on daily true ranges from January 1980 through June 1988

Percent of Days	Max Tick Range	Dollar Risk for 1 through 10 Contracts									
		1	2	3	4	5	6	7	8	9	10
		$	$	$	$	$	$	$	$	$	$
10	32	400	800	1200	1600	2000	2400	2800	3200	3600	4000
20	40	500	1000	1500	2000	2500	3000	3500	4000	4500	5000
30	45	563	1125	1688	2250	2813	3375	3938	4500	5063	5625
40	52	650	1300	1950	2600	3250	3900	4550	5200	5850	6500
50	60	750	1500	2250	3000	3750	4500	5250	6000	6750	7500
60	70	875	1750	2625	3500	4375	5250	6125	7000	7875	8750
70	80	1000	2000	3000	4000	5000	6000	7000	8000	9000	10000
80	93	1163	2325	3488	4650	5813	6975	8138	9300	10463	11625
90	117	1463	2925	4388	5850	7313	8775	10238	11700	13163	14625

Based on weekly true ranges from January 1980 through June 1988

Percent of Weeks	Max Tick Range	Dollar Risk for 1 through 10 Contracts									
		1	2	3	4	5	6	7	8	9	10
		$	$	$	$	$	$	$	$	$	$
10	92	1150	2300	3450	4600	5750	6900	8050	9200	10350	11500
20	108	1350	2700	4050	5400	6750	8100	9450	10800	12150	13500
30	123	1538	3075	4613	6150	7688	9225	10763	12300	13838	15375
40	140	1750	3500	5250	7000	8750	10500	12250	14000	15750	17500
50	160	2000	4000	6000	8000	10000	12000	14000	16000	18000	20000
60	177	2213	4425	6638	8850	11063	13275	15488	17700	19913	22125
70	202	2525	5050	7575	10100	12625	15150	17675	20200	22725	25250
80	230	2875	5750	8625	11500	14375	17250	20125	23000	25875	28750
90	282	3525	7050	10575	14100	17625	21150	24675	28200	31725	35250

Minimum price fluctuation of one tick, or $0.0002 per Pound, is equivalent to $12.50 per contract.

Dollar Risk Table for Corn Futures

Based on daily true ranges from January 1980 through June 1988

Percent of Days	Max Tick Range	Dollar Risk for 1 through 10 Contracts									
		1	2	3	4	5	6	7	8	9	10
		$	$	$	$	$	$	$	$	$	$
10	6	75	150	225	300	375	450	525	600	675	750
20	8	100	200	300	400	500	600	700	800	900	1000
30	9	113	225	338	450	563	675	788	900	1013	1125
40	10	125	250	375	500	625	750	875	1000	1125	1250
50	12	150	300	450	600	750	900	1050	1200	1350	1500
60	14	175	350	525	700	875	1050	1225	1400	1575	1750
70	16	200	400	600	800	1000	1200	1400	1600	1800	2000
80	20	250	500	750	1000	1250	1500	1750	2000	2250	2500
90	28	350	700	1050	1400	1750	2100	2450	2800	3150	3500

Based on weekly true ranges from January 1980 through June 1988

Percent of Weeks	Max Tick Range	Dollar Risk for 1 through 10 Contracts									
		1	2	3	4	5	6	7	8	9	10
		$	$	$	$	$	$	$	$	$	$
10	17	213	425	638	850	1063	1275	1488	1700	1913	2125
20	21	263	525	788	1050	1313	1575	1838	2100	2363	2625
30	25	313	625	938	1250	1563	1875	2188	2500	2813	3125
40	28	350	700	1050	1400	1750	2100	2450	2800	3150	3500
50	32	400	800	1200	1600	2000	2400	2800	3200	3600	4000
60	36	450	900	1350	1800	2250	2700	3150	3600	4050	4500
70	42	525	1050	1575	2100	2625	3150	3675	4200	4725	5250
80	51	638	1275	1913	2550	3188	3825	4463	5100	5738	6375
90	65	813	1625	2438	3250	4063	4875	5688	6500	7313	8125

Minimum price fluctuation of one tick, or 0.25 cents per bushel, is equivalent to $12.50 per contract.

DOLLAR RISK TABLES FOR 24 COMMODITIES

Dollar Risk Table for Crude Oil Futures

Based on daily true ranges from January 1980 through June 1988

Percent of Days	Max Tick Range	Dollar Risk for 1 through 10 Contracts									
		1	2	3	4	5	6	7	8	9	10
		$	$	$	$	$	$	$	$	$	$
10	14	140	280	420	560	700	840	980	1120	1260	1400
20	18	180	360	540	720	900	1080	1260	1440	1620	1800
30	21	210	420	630	840	1050	1260	1470	1680	1890	2100
40	25	250	500	750	1000	1250	1500	1750	2000	2250	2500
50	29	290	580	870	1160	1450	1740	2030	2320	2610	2900
60	34	340	680	1020	1360	1700	2040	2380	2720	3060	3400
70	40	400	800	1200	1600	2000	2400	2800	3200	3600	4000
80	50	500	1000	1500	2000	2500	3000	3500	4000	4500	5000
90	70	700	1400	2100	2800	3500	4200	4900	5600	6300	7000

Based on weekly true ranges from January 1980 through June 1988

Percent of Weeks	Max Tick Range	Dollar Risk for 1 through 10 Contracts									
		1	2	3	4	5	6	7	8	9	10
		$	$	$	$	$	$	$	$	$	$
10	38	380	760	1140	1520	1900	2280	2660	3040	3420	3800
20	48	480	960	1440	1920	2400	2880	3360	3840	4320	4800
30	60	600	1200	1800	2400	3000	3600	4200	4800	5400	6000
40	67	670	1340	2010	2680	3350	4020	4690	5360	6030	6700
50	77	770	1540	2310	3080	3850	4620	5390	6160	6930	7700
60	88	880	1760	2640	3520	4400	5280	6160	7040	7920	8800
70	103	1030	2060	3090	4120	5150	6180	7210	8240	9270	10300
80	128	1280	2560	3840	5120	6400	7680	8960	10240	11520	12800
90	171	1710	3420	5130	6840	8550	10260	11970	13680	15390	17100

Minimum price fluctuation of one tick, or $0.01 per barrel, is equivalent to $10.00 per contract.

Dollar Risk Table for Copper (Standard) Futures

Based on daily true ranges from January 1980 through June 1988

Percent of Days	Max Tick Range	Dollar Risk for 1 through 10 Contracts									
		1	2	3	4	5	6	7	8	9	10
		$	$	$	$	$	$	$	$	$	$
10	9	113	225	338	450	563	675	788	900	1013	1125
20	12	150	300	450	600	750	900	1050	1200	1350	1500
30	15	188	375	563	750	938	1125	1313	1500	1688	1875
40	18	225	450	675	900	1125	1350	1575	1800	2025	2250
50	22	275	550	825	1100	1375	1650	1925	2200	2475	2750
60	26	325	650	975	1300	1625	1950	2275	2600	2925	3250
70	32	400	800	1200	1600	2000	2400	2800	3200	3600	4000
80	42	525	1050	1575	2100	2625	3150	3675	4200	4725	5250
90	64	800	1600	2400	3200	4000	4800	5600	6400	7200	8000

Based on weekly true ranges from January 1980 through June 1988

Percent of Weeks	Max Tick Range	Dollar Risk for 1 through 10 Contracts									
		1	2	3	4	5	6	7	8	9	10
		$	$	$	$	$	$	$	$	$	$
10	28	350	700	1050	1400	1750	2100	2450	2800	3150	3500
20	35	438	875	1313	1750	2188	2625	3063	3500	3938	4375
30	42	525	1050	1575	2100	2625	3150	3675	4200	4725	5250
40	50	625	1250	1875	2500	3125	3750	4375	5000	5625	6250
50	56	700	1400	2100	2800	3500	4200	4900	5600	6300	7000
60	68	850	1700	2550	3400	4250	5100	5950	6800	7650	8500
70	83	1038	2075	3113	4150	5188	6225	7263	8300	9338	10375
80	104	1300	2600	3900	5200	6500	7800	9100	10400	11700	13000
90	170	2125	4250	6375	8500	10625	12750	14875	17000	19125	21250

Minimum price fluctuation of one tick, or 0.05 cents per pound, is equivalent to $12.50 per contract.

DOLLAR RISK TABLES FOR 24 COMMODITIES

Dollar Risk Table for Treasury Bond Futures

Based on daily true ranges from January 1980 through June 1988

Percent of Days	Max Tick Range	Dollar Risk for 1 through 10 Contracts									
		1	2	3	4	5	6	7	8	9	10
		$	$	$	$	$	$	$	$	$	$
10	14	438	875	1313	1750	2188	2625	3063	3500	3938	4375
20	17	531	1063	1594	2125	2656	3188	3719	4250	4781	5313
30	20	625	1250	1875	2500	3125	3750	4375	5000	5625	6250
40	23	719	1438	2156	2875	3594	4313	5031	5750	6469	7188
50	26	813	1625	2438	3250	4063	4875	5688	6500	7313	8125
60	30	938	1875	2813	3750	4688	5625	6563	7500	8438	9375
70	35	1094	2188	3281	4375	5469	6563	7656	8750	9844	10938
80	41	1281	2563	3844	5125	6406	7688	8969	10250	11531	12813
90	53	1656	3313	4969	6625	8281	9938	11594	13250	14906	16563

Based on weekly true ranges from January 1980 through June 1988

Percent of Weeks	Max Tick Range	Dollar Risk for 1 through 10 Contracts									
		1	2	3	4	5	6	7	8	9	10
		$	$	$	$	$	$	$	$	$	$
10	37	1156	2313	3469	4625	5781	6938	8094	9250	10406	11563
20	46	1438	2875	4313	5750	7188	8625	10063	11500	12938	14375
30	53	1656	3313	4969	6625	8281	9938	11594	13250	14906	16563
40	59	1844	3688	5531	7375	9219	11063	12906	14750	16594	18438
50	68	2125	4250	6375	8500	10625	12750	14875	17000	19125	21250
60	76	2375	4750	7125	9500	11875	14250	16625	19000	21375	23750
70	84	2625	5250	7875	10500	13125	15750	18375	21000	23625	26250
80	96	3000	6000	9000	12000	15000	18000	21000	24000	27000	30000
90	117	3656	7313	10969	14625	18281	21938	25594	29250	32906	36563

Minimum price fluctuation of one tick, or $\frac{1}{12}$ of one percentage point, is equivalent to $31.25 per contract.

Dollar Risk Table for Deutsche Mark Futures

Based on daily true ranges from January 1980 through June 1988

Percent of Days	Max Tick Range	Dollar Risk for 1 through 10 Contracts									
		1	2	3	4	5	6	7	8	9	10
		$	$	$	$	$	$	$	$	$	$
10	17	213	425	638	850	1063	1275	1488	1700	1913	2125
20	21	263	525	788	1050	1313	1575	1838	2100	2363	2625
30	24	300	600	900	1200	1500	1800	2100	2400	2700	3000
40	28	350	700	1050	1400	1750	2100	2450	2800	3150	3500
50	32	400	800	1200	1600	2000	2400	2800	3200	3600	4000
60	36	450	900	1350	1800	2250	2700	3150	3600	4050	4500
70	41	513	1025	1538	2050	2563	3075	3588	4100	4613	5125
80	48	600	1200	1800	2400	3000	3600	4200	4800	5400	6000
90	61	763	1525	2288	3050	3813	4575	5338	6100	6863	7625

Based on weekly true ranges from January 1980 through June 1988

Percent of Weeks	Max Tick Range	Dollar Risk for 1 through 10 Contracts									
		1	2	3	4	5	6	7	8	9	10
		$	$	$	$	$	$	$	$	$	$
10	47	588	1175	1763	2350	2938	3525	4113	4700	5288	5875
20	57	713	1425	2138	2850	3563	4275	4988	5700	6413	7125
30	66	825	1650	2475	3300	4125	4950	5775	6600	7425	8250
40	76	950	1900	2850	3800	4750	5700	6650	7600	8550	9500
50	82	1025	2050	3075	4100	5125	6150	7175	8200	9225	10250
60	90	1125	2250	3375	4500	5625	6750	7875	9000	10125	11250
70	107	1338	2675	4013	5350	6688	8025	9363	10700	12038	13375
80	132	1650	3300	4950	6600	8250	9900	11550	13200	14850	16500
90	160	2000	4000	6000	8000	10000	12000	14000	16000	18000	20000

Minimum price fluctuation of one tick, or $0.0001 per mark, is equivalent to $12.50 per contract.

Dollar Risk Table for Eurodollar Futures

Based on daily true ranges from December 1981 through June 1988

Percent of Days	Max Tick Range	Dollar Risk for 1 through 10 Contracts									
		1	2	3	4	5	6	7	8	9	10
		$	$	$	$	$	$	$	$	$	$
10	5	125	250	375	500	625	750	875	1000	1125	1250
20	7	175	350	525	700	875	1050	1225	1400	1575	1750
30	9	225	450	675	900	1125	1350	1575	1800	2025	2250
40	10	250	500	750	1000	1250	1500	1750	2000	2250	2500
50	12	300	600	900	1200	1500	1800	2100	2400	2700	3000
60	14	350	700	1050	1400	1750	2100	2450	2800	3150	3500
70	17	425	850	1275	1700	2125	2550	2975	3400	3825	4250
80	21	525	1050	1575	2100	2625	3150	3675	4200	4725	5250
90	29	725	1450	2175	2900	3625	4350	5075	5800	6525	7250

Based on weekly true ranges from December 1981 through June 1988

Percent of Weeks	Max Tick Range	Dollar Risk for 1 through 10 Contracts									
		1	2	3	4	5	6	7	8	9	10
		$	$	$	$	$	$	$	$	$	$
10	16	400	800	1200	1600	2000	2400	2800	3200	3600	4000
20	20	500	1000	1500	2000	2500	3000	3500	4000	4500	5000
30	24	600	1200	1800	2400	3000	3600	4200	4800	5400	6000
40	27	675	1350	2025	2700	3375	4050	4725	5400	6075	6750
50	31	775	1550	2325	3100	3875	4650	5425	6200	6975	7750
60	37	925	1850	2775	3700	4625	5550	6475	7400	8325	9250
70	44	1100	2200	3300	4400	5500	6600	7700	8800	9900	11000
80	57	1425	2850	4275	5700	7125	8550	9975	11400	12825	14250
90	77	1925	3850	5775	7700	9625	11550	13475	15400	17325	19250

Minimum price fluctuation of one tick, or 0.01 of one percentage point, is equivalent to $25.00 per contract.

Dollar Risk Table for Gold (COMEX) Futures

Based on daily true ranges from January 1980 through June 1988

Percent of Days	Max Tick Range	Dollar Risk for 1 through 10 Contracts									
		1	2	3	4	5	6	7	8	9	10
		$	$	$	$	$	$	$	$	$	$
10	24	240	480	720	960	1200	1440	1680	1920	2160	2400
20	32	320	640	960	1280	1600	1920	2240	2560	2880	3200
30	40	400	800	1200	1600	2000	2400	2800	3200	3600	4000
40	48	480	960	1440	1920	2400	2880	3360	3840	4320	4800
50	58	580	1160	1740	2320	2900	3480	4060	4640	5220	5800
60	70	700	1400	2100	2800	3500	4200	4900	5600	6300	7000
70	86	860	1720	2580	3440	4300	5160	6020	6880	7740	8600
80	110	1100	2200	3300	4400	5500	6600	7700	8800	9900	11000
90	155	1550	3100	4650	6200	7750	9300	10850	12400	13950	15500

Based on weekly true ranges from January 1980 through June 1988

Percent of Weeks	Max Tick Range	Dollar Risk for 1 through 10 Contracts									
		1	2	3	4	5	6	7	8	9	10
		$	$	$	$	$	$	$	$	$	$
10	70	700	1400	2100	2800	3500	4200	4900	5600	6300	7000
20	95	950	1900	2850	3800	4750	5700	6650	7600	8550	9500
30	110	1100	2200	3300	4400	5500	6600	7700	8800	9900	11000
40	126	1260	2520	3780	5040	6300	7560	8820	10080	11340	12600
50	146	1460	2920	4380	5840	7300	8760	10220	11680	13140	14600
60	175	1750	3500	5250	7000	8750	10500	12250	14000	15750	17500
70	204	2040	4080	6120	8160	10200	12240	14280	16320	18360	20400
80	255	2550	5100	7650	10200	12750	15300	17850	20400	22950	25500
90	345	3450	6900	10350	13800	17250	20700	24150	27600	31050	34500

Minimum price fluctuation of one tick, or $0.10 per troy ounce, is equivalent to $10.00 per contract.

Dollar Risk Table for Japanese Yen Futures

Based on daily true ranges from January 1980 through June 1988

Percent of Days	Max Tick Range	Dollar Risk for 1 through 10 Contracts									
		1	2	3	4	5	6	7	8	9	10
		$	$	$	$	$	$	$	$	$	$
10	14	175	350	525	700	875	1050	1225	1400	1575	1750
20	18	225	450	675	900	1125	1350	1575	1800	2025	2250
30	22	275	550	825	1100	1375	1650	1925	2200	2475	2750
40	25	313	625	938	1250	1563	1875	2188	2500	2813	3125
50	29	363	725	1088	1450	1813	2175	2538	2900	3263	3625
60	35	438	875	1313	1750	2188	2625	3063	3500	3938	4375
70	41	513	1025	1538	2050	2563	3075	3588	4100	4613	5125
80	49	613	1225	1838	2450	3063	3675	4288	4900	5513	6125
90	66	825	1650	2475	3300	4125	4950	5775	6600	7425	8250

Based on weekly true ranges from January 1980 through June 1988

Percent of Weeks	Max Tick Range	Dollar Risk for 1 through 10 Contracts									
		1	2	3	4	5	6	7	8	9	10
		$	$	$	$	$	$	$	$	$	$
10	43	538	1075	1613	2150	2688	3225	3763	4300	4838	5375
20	53	663	1325	1988	2650	3313	3975	4638	5300	5963	6625
30	63	788	1575	2363	3150	3938	4725	5513	6300	7088	7875
40	74	925	1850	2775	3700	4625	5550	6475	7400	8325	9250
50	85	1063	2125	3188	4250	5313	6375	7438	8500	9563	10625
60	99	1238	2475	3713	4950	6188	7425	8663	9900	11138	12375
70	113	1413	2825	4238	5650	7063	8475	9888	11300	12713	14125
80	134	1675	3350	5025	6700	8375	10050	11725	13400	15075	16750
90	172	2150	4300	6450	8600	10750	12900	15050	17200	19350	21500

Minimum price fluctuation of one tick, or $0.0001 per 100 yen, is equivalent to $12.50 per contract.

Dollar Risk Table for Live Cattle Futures

Based on daily true ranges from January 1980 through June 1988

Percent of Days	Max Tick Range	Dollar Risk for 1 through 10 Contracts									
		1	2	3	4	5	6	7	8	9	10
		$	$	$	$	$	$	$	$	$	$
10	19	190	380	570	760	950	1140	1330	1520	1710	1900
20	22	220	440	660	880	1100	1320	1540	1760	1980	2200
30	26	260	520	780	1040	1300	1560	1820	2080	2340	2600
40	29	290	580	870	1160	1450	1740	2030	2320	2610	2900
50	32	320	640	960	1280	1600	1920	2240	2560	2880	3200
60	37	370	740	1110	1480	1850	2220	2590	2960	3330	3700
70	42	420	840	1260	1680	2100	2520	2940	3360	3780	4200
80	48	480	960	1440	1920	2400	2880	3360	3840	4320	4800
90	57	570	1140	1710	2280	2850	3420	3990	4560	5130	5700

Based on weekly true ranges from January 1980 through June 1988

Percent of Weeks	Max Tick Range	Dollar Risk for 1 through 10 Contracts									
		1	2	3	4	5	6	7	8	9	10
		$	$	$	$	$	$	$	$	$	$
10	51	510	1020	1530	2040	2550	3060	3570	4080	4590	5100
20	61	610	1220	1830	2440	3050	3660	4270	4880	5490	6100
30	67	670	1340	2010	2680	3350	4020	4690	5360	6030	6700
40	74	740	1480	2220	2960	3700	4440	5180	5920	6660	7400
50	83	830	1660	2490	3320	4150	4980	5810	6640	7470	8300
60	91	910	1820	2730	3640	4550	5460	6370	7280	8190	9100
70	104	1040	2080	3120	4160	5200	6240	7280	8320	9360	10400
80	120	1200	2400	3600	4800	6000	7200	8400	9600	10800	12000
90	142	1420	2840	4260	5680	7100	8520	9940	11360	12780	14200

Minimum price fluctuation of one tick, or 0.025 cents per pound, is equivalent to $10.00 per contract.

Dollar Risk Table for Live Hog Futures

Based on daily true ranges from January 1980 through June 1988

Percent of Days	Max Tick Range	Dollar Risk for 1 through 10 Contracts									
		1	2	3	4	5	6	7	8	9	10
		$	$	$	$	$	$	$	$	$	$
10	22	220	440	660	880	1100	1320	1540	1760	1980	2200
20	25	250	500	750	1000	1250	1500	1750	2000	2250	2500
30	28	280	560	840	1120	1400	1680	1960	2240	2520	2800
40	32	320	640	960	1280	1600	1920	2240	2560	2880	3200
50	35	350	700	1050	1400	1750	2100	2450	2800	3150	3500
60	39	390	780	1170	1560	1950	2340	2730	3120	3510	3900
70	44	440	880	1320	1760	2200	2640	3080	3520	3960	4400
80	50	500	1000	1500	2000	2500	3000	3500	4000	4500	5000
90	58	580	1160	1740	2320	2900	3480	4060	4640	5220	5800

Based on weekly true ranges from January 1980 through June 1988

Percent of Weeks	Max Tick Range	Dollar Risk for 1 through 10 Contracts									
		1	2	3	4	5	6	7	8	9	10
		$	$	$	$	$	$	$	$	$	$
10	53	530	1060	1590	2120	2650	3180	3710	4240	4770	5300
20	62	620	1240	1860	2480	3100	3720	4340	4960	5580	6200
30	71	710	1420	2130	2840	3550	4260	4970	5680	6390	7100
40	79	790	1580	2370	3160	3950	4740	5530	6320	7110	7900
50	88	880	1760	2640	3520	4400	5280	6160	7040	7920	8800
60	95	950	1900	2850	3800	4750	5700	6650	7600	8550	9500
70	104	1040	2080	3120	4160	5200	6240	7280	8320	9360	10400
80	120	1200	2400	3600	4800	6000	7200	8400	9600	10800	12000
90	148	1480	2960	4440	5920	7400	8880	10360	11840	13320	14800

Minimum price fluctuation of one tick, or 0.025 cents per pound, is equivalent to $10.00 per contract.

Dollar Risk Table for Treasury Notes Futures

Based on daily true ranges from May 1982 through June 1988

Percent of Days	Max Tick Range	Dollar Risk for 1 through 10 Contracts									
		1	2	3	4	5	6	7	8	9	10
		$	$	$	$	$	$	$	$	$	$
10	9	281	563	844	1125	1406	1688	1969	2250	2531	2813
20	11	344	688	1031	1375	1719	2063	2406	2750	3094	3438
30	13	406	813	1219	1625	2031	2438	2844	3250	3656	4063
40	15	469	938	1406	1875	2344	2813	3281	3750	4219	4688
50	17	531	1063	1594	2125	2656	3188	3719	4250	4781	5313
60	20	625	1250	1875	2500	3125	3750	4375	5000	5625	6250
70	23	719	1438	2156	2875	3594	4313	5031	5750	6469	7188
80	26	813	1625	2438	3250	4063	4875	5688	6500	7313	8125
90	34	1063	2125	3188	4250	5313	6375	7438	8500	9563	10625

Based on weekly true ranges from May 1982 through June 1988

Percent of Weeks	Max Tick Range	Dollar Risk for 1 through 10 Contracts									
		1	2	3	4	5	6	7	8	9	10
		$	$	$	$	$	$	$	$	$	$
10	25	781	1563	2344	3125	3906	4688	5469	6250	7031	7813
20	30	938	1875	2813	3750	4688	5625	6563	7500	8438	9375
30	35	1094	2188	3281	4375	5469	6563	7656	8750	9844	10938
40	40	1250	2500	3750	5000	6250	7500	8750	10000	11250	12500
50	46	1438	2875	4313	5750	7188	8625	10063	11500	12938	14375
60	51	1594	3188	4781	6375	7969	9563	11156	12750	14344	15938
70	58	1813	3625	5438	7250	9063	10875	12688	14500	16313	18125
80	66	2063	4125	6188	8250	10313	12375	14438	16500	18563	20625
90	78	2438	4875	7313	9750	12188	14625	17063	19500	21938	24375

Minimum price fluctuation of one tick, or $\frac{1}{32}$ of one percentage point, is equivalent to $31.25 per contract.

Dollar Risk Table for NYSE Composite Index Futures

Based on daily true ranges from June 1983 through June 1988

Percent of Days	Max Tick Range	Dollar Risk for 1 through 10 Contracts									
		1	2	3	4	5	6	7	8	9	10
		$	$	$	$	$	$	$	$	$	$
10	15	375	750	1125	1500	1875	2250	2625	3000	3375	3750
20	19	475	950	1425	1900	2375	2850	3325	3800	4275	4750
30	22	550	1100	1650	2200	2750	3300	3850	4400	4950	5500
40	26	650	1300	1950	2600	3250	3900	4550	5200	5850	6500
50	30	750	1500	2250	3000	3750	4500	5250	6000	6750	7500
60	35	875	1750	2625	3500	4375	5250	6125	7000	7875	8750
70	41	1025	2050	3075	4100	5125	6150	7175	8200	9225	10250
80	51	1275	2550	3825	5100	6375	7650	8925	10200	11475	12750
90	66	1650	3300	4950	6600	8250	9900	11550	13200	14850	16500

Based on weekly true ranges from June 1983 through June 1988

Percent of Weeks	Max Tick Range	Dollar Risk for 1 through 10 Contracts									
		1	2	3	4	5	6	7	8	9	10
		$	$	$	$	$	$	$	$	$	$
10	40	1000	2000	3000	4000	5000	6000	7000	8000	9000	10000
20	47	1175	2350	3525	4700	5875	7050	8225	9400	10575	11750
30	54	1350	2700	4050	5400	6750	8100	9450	10800	12150	13500
40	61	1525	3050	4575	6100	7625	9150	10675	12200	13725	15250
50	69	1725	3450	5175	6900	8625	10350	12075	13800	15525	17250
60	80	2000	4000	6000	8000	10000	12000	14000	16000	18000	20000
70	94	2350	4700	7050	9400	11750	14100	16450	18800	21150	23500
80	120	3000	6000	9000	12000	15000	18000	21000	24000	27000	30000
90	155	3875	7750	11625	15500	19375	23250	27125	31000	34875	38750

Minimum price fluctuation of one tick, or 0.05 index points, is equivalent to $25.00 per contract.

Dollar Risk Table for Oats Futures

Based on daily true ranges from January 1980 through June 1988

Percent of Days	Max Tick Range	Dollar Risk for 1 through 10 Contracts									
		1	2	3	4	5	6	7	8	9	10
		$	$	$	$	$	$	$	$	$	$
10	10	125	250	375	500	625	750	875	1000	1125	1250
20	14	175	350	525	700	875	1050	1225	1400	1575	1750
30	18	225	450	675	900	1125	1350	1575	1800	2025	2250
40	22	275	550	825	1100	1375	1650	1925	2200	2475	2750
50	24	300	600	900	1200	1500	1800	2100	2400	2700	3000
60	30	375	750	1125	1500	1875	2250	2625	3000	3375	3750
70	34	425	850	1275	1700	2125	2550	2975	3400	3825	4250
80	42	525	1050	1575	2100	2625	3150	3675	4200	4725	5250
90	52	650	1300	1950	2600	3250	3900	4550	5200	5850	6500

Based on weekly true ranges from January 1980 through June 1988

Percent of Weeks	Max Tick Range	Dollar Risk for 1 through 10 Contracts									
		1	2	3	4	5	6	7	8	9	10
		$	$	$	$	$	$	$	$	$	$
10	32	400	800	1200	1600	2000	2400	2800	3200	3600	4000
20	42	525	1050	1575	2100	2625	3150	3675	4200	4725	5250
30	52	650	1300	1950	2600	3250	3900	4550	5200	5850	6500
40	60	750	1500	2250	3000	3750	4500	5250	6000	6750	7500
50	66	825	1650	2475	3300	4125	4950	5775	6600	7425	8250
60	74	925	1850	2775	3700	4625	5550	6475	7400	8325	9250
70	86	1075	2150	3225	4300	5375	6450	7525	8600	9675	10750
80	98	1225	2450	3675	4900	6125	7350	8575	9800	11025	12250
90	124	1550	3100	4650	6200	7750	9300	10850	12400	13950	15500

Minimum price fluctuation of one tick, or 0.25 cents per bushel, is equivalent to $12.50 per contract.

Dollar Risk Table for Soybeans Futures

Based on daily true ranges from January 1980 through June 1988

Percent of Days	Max Tick Range	Dollar Risk for 1 through 10 Contracts									
		1	2	3	4	5	6	7	8	9	10
		$	$	$	$	$	$	$	$	$	$
10	16	200	400	600	800	1000	1200	1400	1600	1800	2000
20	22	275	550	825	1100	1375	1650	1925	2200	2475	2750
30	26	325	650	975	1300	1625	1950	2275	2600	2925	3250
40	30	375	750	1125	1500	1875	2250	2625	3000	3375	3750
50	34	425	850	1275	1700	2125	2550	2975	3400	3825	4250
60	42	525	1050	1575	2100	2625	3150	3675	4200	4725	5250
70	50	625	1250	1875	2500	3125	3750	4375	5000	5625	6250
80	64	800	1600	2400	3200	4000	4800	5600	6400	7200	8000
90	92	1150	2300	3450	4600	5750	6900	8050	9200	10350	11500

Based on weekly true ranges from January 1980 through June 1988

Percent of Weeks	Max Tick Range	Dollar Risk for 1 through 10 Contracts									
		1	2	3	4	5	6	7	8	9	10
		$	$	$	$	$	$	$	$	$	$
10	43	538	1075	1613	2150	2688	3225	3763	4300	4838	5375
20	55	688	1375	2063	2750	3438	4125	4813	5500	6188	6875
30	66	825	1650	2475	3300	4125	4950	5775	6600	7425	8250
40	78	975	1950	2925	3900	4875	5850	6825	7800	8775	9750
50	88	1100	2200	3300	4400	5500	6600	7700	8800	9900	11000
60	104	1300	2600	3900	5200	6500	7800	9100	10400	11700	13000
70	124	1550	3100	4650	6200	7750	9300	10850	12400	13950	15500
80	153	1913	3825	5738	7650	9563	11475	13388	15300	17213	19125
90	198	2475	4950	7425	9900	12375	14850	17325	19800	22275	24750

Minimum price fluctuation of one tick, or 0.25 cents per bushel, is equivalent to $12.50 per contract.

Dollar Risk Table for Swiss Franc Futures

Based on daily true ranges from January 1980 through June 1988

Percent of Days	Max Tick Range	Dollar Risk for 1 through 10 Contracts									
		1	2	3	4	5	6	7	8	9	10
		$	$	$	$	$	$	$	$	$	$
10	24	300	600	900	1200	1500	1800	2100	2400	2700	3000
20	29	363	725	1088	1450	1813	2175	2538	2900	3263	3625
30	34	425	850	1275	1700	2125	2550	2975	3400	3825	4250
40	38	475	950	1425	1900	2375	2850	3325	3800	4275	4750
50	44	550	1100	1650	2200	2750	3300	3850	4400	4950	5500
60	49	613	1225	1838	2450	3063	3675	4288	4900	5513	6125
70	56	700	1400	2100	2800	3500	4200	4900	5600	6300	7000
80	66	825	1650	2475	3300	4125	4950	5775	6600	7425	8250
90	82	1025	2050	3075	4100	5125	6150	7175	8200	9225	10250

Based on weekly true ranges from January 1980 through June 1988

Percent of Weeks	Max Tick Range	Dollar Risk for 1 through 10 Contracts									
		1	2	3	4	5	6	7	8	9	10
		$	$	$	$	$	$	$	$	$	$
10	64	800	1600	2400	3200	4000	4800	5600	6400	7200	8000
20	82	1025	2050	3075	4100	5125	6150	7175	8200	9225	10250
30	92	1150	2300	3450	4600	5750	6900	8050	9200	10350	11500
40	103	1288	2575	3863	5150	6438	7725	9013	10300	11588	12875
50	116	1450	2900	4350	5800	7250	8700	10150	11600	13050	14500
60	128	1600	3200	4800	6400	8000	9600	11200	12800	14400	16000
70	149	1863	3725	5588	7450	9313	11175	13038	14900	16763	18625
80	171	2138	4275	6413	8550	10688	12825	14963	17100	19238	21375
90	213	2663	5325	7988	10650	13313	15975	18638	21300	23963	26625

Minimum price fluctuation of one tick, or $0.0001 per Swiss franc, is equivalent to $12.50 per contract.

Dollar Risk Table for Soymeal Futures

Based on daily true ranges from January 1980 through June 1988

Percent of Days	Max Tick Range	Dollar Risk for 1 through 10 Contracts									
		1	2	3	4	5	6	7	8	9	10
		$	$	$	$	$	$	$	$	$	$
10	12	120	240	360	480	600	720	840	960	1080	1200
20	15	150	300	450	600	750	900	1050	1200	1350	1500
30	18	180	360	540	720	900	1080	1260	1440	1620	1800
40	22	220	440	660	880	1100	1320	1540	1760	1980	2200
50	25	250	500	750	1000	1250	1500	1750	2000	2250	2500
60	30	300	600	900	1200	1500	1800	2100	2400	2700	3000
70	36	360	720	1080	1440	1800	2160	2520	2880	3240	3600
80	47	470	940	1410	1880	2350	2820	3290	3760	4230	4700
90	65	650	1300	1950	2600	3250	3900	4550	5200	5850	6500

Based on weekly true ranges from January 1980 through June 1988

Percent of Weeks	Max Tick Range	Dollar Risk for 1 through 10 Contracts									
		1	2	3	4	5	6	7	8	9	10
		$	$	$	$	$	$	$	$	$	$
10	35	350	700	1050	1400	1750	2100	2450	2800	3150	3500
20	42	420	840	1260	1680	2100	2520	2940	3360	3780	4200
30	50	500	1000	1500	2000	2500	3000	3500	4000	4500	5000
40	58	580	1160	1740	2320	2900	3480	4060	4640	5220	5800
50	67	670	1340	2010	2680	3350	4020	4690	5360	6030	6700
60	80	800	1600	2400	3200	4000	4800	5600	6400	7200	8000
70	98	980	1960	2940	3920	4900	5880	6860	7840	8820	9800
80	120	1200	2400	3600	4800	6000	7200	8400	9600	10800	12000
90	152	1520	3040	4560	6080	7600	9120	10640	12160	13680	15200

Minimum price fluctuation of one tick, or $0.10 per ton, is equivalent to $10.00 per contract.

Dollar Risk Table for Sugar (#11 World) Futures

Based on daily true ranges from January 1980 through June 1988

Percent of Days	Max Tick Range	Dollar Risk for 1 through 10 Contracts									
		1	2	3	4	5	6	7	8	9	10
		$	$	$	$	$	$	$	$	$	$
10	11	123	246	370	493	616	739	862	986	1109	1232
20	15	168	336	504	672	840	1008	1176	1344	1512	1680
30	18	202	403	605	806	1008	1210	1411	1613	1814	2016
40	21	235	470	706	941	1176	1411	1646	1882	2117	2352
50	25	280	560	840	1120	1400	1680	1960	2240	2520	2800
60	30	336	672	1008	1344	1680	2016	2352	2688	3024	3360
70	39	437	874	1310	1747	2184	2621	3058	3494	3931	4368
80	57	638	1277	1915	2554	3192	3830	4469	5107	5746	6384
90	100	1120	2240	3360	4480	5600	6720	7840	8960	10080	11200

Based on weekly true ranges from January 1980 through June 1988

Percent of Weeks	Max Tick Range	Dollar Risk for 1 through 10 Contracts									
		1	2	3	4	5	6	7	8	9	10
		$	$	$	$	$	$	$	$	$	$
10	32	358	717	1075	1434	1792	2150	2509	2867	3226	3584
20	40	448	896	1344	1792	2240	2688	3136	3584	4032	4480
30	47	526	1053	1579	2106	2632	3158	3685	4211	4738	5264
40	54	605	1210	1814	2419	3024	3629	4234	4838	5443	6048
50	62	694	1389	2083	2778	3472	4166	4861	5555	6250	6944
60	74	829	1658	2486	3315	4144	4973	5802	6630	7459	8288
70	93	1042	2083	3125	4166	5208	6250	7291	8333	9374	10416
80	133	1490	2979	4469	5958	7448	8938	10427	11917	13406	14896
90	248	2778	5555	8333	11110	13888	16666	19443	22221	24998	27776

Minimum price fluctuation of one tick, or 0.01 cents per pound, is equivalent to $11.20 per contract.

Dollar Risk Table for Soybean Oil Futures

Based on daily true ranges from January 1980 through June 1988

Percent of Days	Max Tick Range	Dollar Risk for 1 through 10 Contracts									
		1	2	3	4	5	6	7	8	9	10
		$	$	$	$	$	$	$	$	$	$
10	18	108	216	324	432	540	648	756	864	972	1080
20	23	138	276	414	552	690	828	966	1104	1242	1380
30	28	168	336	504	672	840	1008	1176	1344	1512	1680
40	33	198	396	594	792	990	1188	1386	1584	1782	1980
50	38	228	456	684	912	1140	1368	1596	1824	2052	2280
60	45	270	540	810	1080	1350	1620	1890	2160	2430	2700
70	54	324	648	972	1296	1620	1944	2268	2592	2916	3240
80	69	414	828	1242	1656	2070	2484	2898	3312	3726	4140
90	90	540	1080	1620	2160	2700	3240	3780	4320	4860	5400

Based on weekly true ranges from January 1980 through June 1988

Percent of Weeks	Max Tick Range	Dollar Risk for 1 through 10 Contracts									
		1	2	3	4	5	6	7	8	9	10
		$	$	$	$	$	$	$	$	$	$
10	50	300	600	900	1200	1500	1800	2100	2400	2700	3000
20	61	366	732	1098	1464	1830	2196	2562	2928	3294	3660
30	72	432	864	1296	1728	2160	2592	3024	3456	3888	4320
40	81	486	972	1458	1944	2430	2916	3402	3888	4374	4860
50	95	570	1140	1710	2280	2850	3420	3990	4560	5130	5700
60	110	660	1320	1980	2640	3300	3960	4620	5280	5940	6600
70	130	780	1560	2340	3120	3900	4680	5460	6240	7020	7800
80	158	948	1896	2844	3792	4740	5688	6636	7584	8532	9480
90	218	1308	2616	3924	5232	6540	7848	9156	10464	11772	13080

Minimum price fluctuation of one tick, or 0.01 cents per pound, is equivalent to $6.00 per contract.

Dollar Risk Table for S&P 500 Stock Index Futures

Based on daily true ranges from May 1982 through June 1988

Percent of Days	Max Tick Range	Dollar Risk for 1 through 10 Contracts									
		1	2	3	4	5	6	7	8	9	10
		$	$	$	$	$	$	$	$	$	$
10	26	650	1300	1950	2600	3250	3900	4550	5200	5850	6500
20	32	800	1600	2400	3200	4000	4800	5600	6400	7200	8000
30	37	925	1850	2775	3700	4625	5550	6475	7400	8325	9250
40	44	1100	2200	3300	4400	5500	6600	7700	8800	9900	11000
50	50	1250	2500	3750	5000	6250	7500	8750	10000	11250	12500
60	57	1425	2850	4275	5700	7125	8550	9975	11400	12825	14250
70	68	1700	3400	5100	6800	8500	10200	11900	13600	15300	17000
80	82	2050	4100	6150	8200	10250	12300	14350	16400	18450	20500
90	107	2675	5350	8025	10700	13375	16050	18725	21400	24075	26750

Based on weekly true ranges from May 1982 through June 1988

Percent of Weeks	Max Tick Range	Dollar Risk for 1 through 10 Contracts									
		1	2	3	4	5	6	7	8	9	10
		$	$	$	$	$	$	$	$	$	$
10	69	1725	3450	5175	6900	8625	10350	12075	13800	15525	17250
20	80	2000	4000	6000	8000	10000	12000	14000	16000	18000	20000
30	92	2300	4600	6900	9200	11500	13800	16100	18400	20700	23000
40	104	2600	5200	7800	10400	13000	15600	18200	20800	23400	26000
50	117	2925	5850	8775	11700	14625	17550	20475	23400	26325	29250
60	135	3375	6750	10125	13500	16875	20250	23625	27000	30375	33750
70	157	3925	7850	11775	15700	19625	23550	27475	31400	35325	39250
80	205	5125	10250	15375	20500	25625	30750	35875	41000	46125	51250
90	252	6300	12600	18900	25200	31500	37800	44100	50400	56700	63000

Minimum price fluctuation of one tick, or 0.05 index points, is equivalent to $25.00 per contract.

Dollar Risk Table for Silver (COMEX) Futures

Based on daily true ranges from January 1980 through June 1988

Percent of Days	Max Tick Range	Dollar Risk for 1 through 10 Contracts									
		1	2	3	4	5	6	7	8	9	10
		$	$	$	$	$	$	$	$	$	$
10	65	325	650	975	1300	1625	1950	2275	2600	2925	3250
20	90	450	900	1350	1800	2250	2700	3150	3600	4050	4500
30	117	585	1170	1755	2340	2925	3510	4095	4680	5265	5850
40	150	750	1500	2250	3000	3750	4500	5250	6000	6750	7500
50	180	900	1800	2700	3600	4500	5400	6300	7200	8100	9000
60	220	1100	2200	3300	4400	5500	6600	7700	8800	9900	11000
70	290	1450	2900	4350	5800	7250	8700	10150	11600	13050	14500
80	395	1975	3950	5925	7900	9875	11850	13825	15800	17775	19750
90	550	2750	5500	8250	11000	13750	16500	19250	22000	24750	27500

Based on weekly true ranges from January 1980 through June 1988

Percent of Weeks	Max Tick Range	Dollar Risk for 1 through 10 Contracts									
		1	2	3	4	5	6	7	8	9	10
		$	$	$	$	$	$	$	$	$	$
10	175	875	1750	2625	3500	4375	5250	6125	7000	7875	8750
20	235	1175	2350	3525	4700	5875	7050	8225	9400	10575	11750
30	310	1550	3100	4650	6200	7750	9300	10850	12400	13950	15500
40	399	1995	3990	5985	7980	9975	11970	13965	15960	17955	19950
50	460	2300	4600	6900	9200	11500	13800	16100	18400	20700	23000
60	575	2875	5750	8625	11500	14375	17250	20125	23000	25875	28750
70	750	3750	7500	11250	15000	18750	22500	26250	30000	33750	37500
80	970	4850	9700	14550	19400	24250	29100	33950	38800	43650	48500
90	1300	6500	13000	19500	26000	32500	39000	45500	52000	58500	65000

Minimum price fluctuation of one tick, or 0.10 cents per troy ounce, is equivalent to $5.00 per contract.

Dollar Risk Table for Treasury Bills Futures

Based on daily true ranges from January 1980 through June 1988

Percent of Days	Max Tick Range	Dollar Risk for 1 through 10 Contracts									
		1	2	3	4	5	6	7	8	9	10
		$	$	$	$	$	$	$	$	$	$
10	6	150	300	450	600	750	900	1050	1200	1350	1500
20	8	200	400	600	800	1000	1200	1400	1600	1800	2000
30	10	250	500	750	1000	1250	1500	1750	2000	2250	2500
40	12	300	600	900	1200	1500	1800	2100	2400	2700	3000
50	14	350	700	1050	1400	1750	2100	2450	2800	3150	3500
60	18	450	900	1350	1800	2250	2700	3150	3600	4050	4500
70	25	625	1250	1875	2500	3125	3750	4375	5000	5625	6250
80	33	825	1650	2475	3300	4125	4950	5775	6600	7425	8250
90	45	1125	2250	3375	4500	5625	6750	7875	9000	10125	11250

Based on weekly true ranges from January 1980 through June 1988

Percent of Weeks	Max Tick Range	Dollar Risk for 1 through 10 Contracts									
		1	2	3	4	5	6	7	8	9	10
		$	$	$	$	$	$	$	$	$	$
10	16	400	800	1200	1600	2000	2400	2800	3200	3600	4000
20	21	525	1050	1575	2100	2625	3150	3675	4200	4725	5250
30	25	625	1250	1875	2500	3125	3750	4375	5000	5625	6250
40	29	725	1450	2175	2900	3625	4350	5075	5800	6525	7250
50	35	875	1750	2625	3500	4375	5250	6125	7000	7875	8750
60	47	1175	2350	3525	4700	5875	7050	8225	9400	10575	11750
70	61	1525	3050	4575	6100	7625	9150	10675	12200	13725	15250
80	81	2025	4050	6075	8100	10125	12150	14175	16200	18225	20250
90	105	2625	5250	7875	10500	13125	15750	18375	21000	23625	26250

Minimum price fluctuation of one tick, or 0.01 of one percentage point, is equivalent to $25.00 per contract.

Dollar Risk Table for Wheat (Chicago) Futures

Based on daily true ranges from January 1980 through June 1988

Percent of Days	Max Tick Range	Dollar Risk for 1 through 10 Contracts									
		1	2	3	4	5	6	7	8	9	10
		$	$	$	$	$	$	$	$	$	$
10	12	150	300	450	600	750	900	1050	1200	1350	1500
20	14	175	350	525	700	875	1050	1225	1400	1575	1750
30	16	200	400	600	800	1000	1200	1400	1600	1800	2000
40	18	225	450	675	900	1125	1350	1575	1800	2025	2250
50	21	263	525	788	1050	1313	1575	1838	2100	2363	2625
60	24	300	600	900	1200	1500	1800	2100	2400	2700	3000
70	28	350	700	1050	1400	1750	2100	2450	2800	3150	3500
80	32	400	800	1200	1600	2000	2400	2800	3200	3600	4000
90	42	525	1050	1575	2100	2625	3150	3675	4200	4725	5250

Based on weekly true ranges from January 1980 through June 1988

Percent of Weeks	Max Tick Range	Dollar Risk for 1 through 10 Contracts									
		1	2	3	4	5	6	7	8	9	10
		$	$	$	$	$	$	$	$	$	$
10	31	388	775	1163	1550	1938	2325	2713	3100	3488	3875
20	37	463	925	1388	1850	2313	2775	3238	3700	4163	4625
30	43	538	1075	1613	2150	2688	3225	3763	4300	4838	5375
40	48	600	1200	1800	2400	3000	3600	4200	4800	5400	6000
50	53	663	1325	1988	2650	3313	3975	4638	5300	5963	6625
60	60	750	1500	2250	3000	3750	4500	5250	6000	6750	7500
70	67	838	1675	2513	3350	4188	5025	5863	6700	7538	8375
80	76	950	1900	2850	3800	4750	5700	6650	7600	8550	9500
90	94	1175	2350	3525	4700	5875	7050	8225	9400	10575	11750

Minimum price fluctuation of one tick. or 0.25 cents per bushel. is equivalent to $12.50 per contract.

Dollar Risk Table for Wheat (Kansas City) Futures

Based on daily true ranges from January 1980 through June 1988

Percent of Days	Max Tick Range	Dollar Risk for 1 through 10 Contracts									
		1	2	3	4	5	6	7	8	9	10
		$	$	$	$	$	$	$	$	$	$
10	6	75	150	225	300	375	450	525	600	675	750
20	8	100	200	300	400	500	600	700	800	900	1000
30	10	125	250	375	500	625	750	875	1000	1125	1250
40	12	150	300	450	600	750	900	1050	1200	1350	1500
50	14	175	350	525	700	875	1050	1225	1400	1575	1750
60	16	200	400	600	800	1000	1200	1400	1600	1800	2000
70	19	238	475	713	950	1188	1425	1663	1900	2138	2375
80	24	300	600	900	1200	1500	1800	2100	2400	2700	3000
90	32	400	800	1200	1600	2000	2400	2800	3200	3600	4000

Based on weekly true ranges from January 1980 through June 1988

Percent of Weeks	Max Tick Range	Dollar Risk for 1 through 10 Contracts									
		1	2	3	4	5	6	7	8	9	10
		$	$	$	$	$	$	$	$	$	$
10	18	225	450	675	900	1125	1350	1575	1800	2025	2250
20	23	288	575	863	1150	1438	1725	2013	2300	2588	2875
30	28	350	700	1050	1400	1750	2100	2450	2800	3150	3500
40	33	413	825	1238	1650	2063	2475	2888	3300	3713	4125
50	39	488	975	1463	1950	2438	2925	3413	3900	4388	4875
60	46	575	1150	1725	2300	2875	3450	4025	4600	5175	5750
70	52	650	1300	1950	2600	3250	3900	4550	5200	5850	6500
80	60	750	1500	2250	3000	3750	4500	5250	6000	6750	7500
90	82	1025	2050	3075	4100	5125	6150	7175	8200	9225	10250

Minimum price fluctuation of one tick, or 0.25 cents per bushel, is equivalent to $12.50 per contract.

E

Analysis of Opening Prices for 24 Commodities

This Appendix analyzes the location of up and down periods for 24 commodities. An up period is one where the close price is higher than the opening price. A down period is one where the close price is lower than the opening price. The analysis is conducted separately for daily and weekly data. A percentile distribution is provided for (a) the difference between the open and the low, for up periods, and (b) the difference between the high and the open, for down periods.

For example, in 90 percent of the up days analyzed for the British pound, the opening price was found to be within 32 ticks of the daily low. In 90 percent of the down weeks analyzed for the British pound, the opening price was found to be within 85 ticks of the weekly high.

Analysis of Opening Prices for British Pound Futures

Analysis for Up Periods

Difference in Ticks[a] between
the Open (O) and the Low (L)

Percent of Total Obs.	Daily Data (O − L) in Ticks	Weekly Data (O − L) in Ticks
10	2	2
20	5	7
30	7	10
40	10	15
50	12	20
60	15	28
70	18	37
80	23	50
90	32	75

Analysis for Down Periods

Difference in Ticks[a] between
the High (H) and the Open (O)

Percent of Total Obs.	Daily Data (H − O) in Ticks	Weekly Data (H − O) in Ticks
10	2	3
20	5	7
30	5	12
40	10	18
50	12	25
60	15	32
70	18	42
80	23	58
90	32	85

Based on price data from January 1980 through June 1988.

[a]Minimum price fluctuation of one tick, or $0.0002 per Pound, is equivalent to $12.50 per contract.

Analysis of Opening Prices for Corn Futures

Analysis for Up Periods

Difference in Ticks[a] between
the Open (O) and the Low (L)

Percent of Total Obs.	Daily Data (O − L) in Ticks	Weekly Data (O − L) in Ticks
10	0	0
20	0	2
30	1	3
40	2	4
50	3	6
60	3	7
70	4	9
80	5	12
90	8	18

Analysis for Down Periods

Difference in Ticks[a] between
the High (H) and the Open (O)

Percent of Total Obs.	Daily Data (H − O) in Ticks	Weekly Data (H − O) in Ticks
10	0	0
20	0	2
30	1	2
40	1	4
50	2	6
60	2	7
70	4	11
80	4	13
90	7	18

Based on price data from January 1980 through June 1988.

[a]Minimum price fluctuation of one tick. or 0.25 cents per bushel. is equivalent to $12.50 per contract.

Analysis of Opening Prices for Crude Oil Futures

Analysis for Up Periods

Difference in Ticks[a] between
the Open (O) and the Low (L)

Percent of Total Obs.	Daily Data (O − L) in Ticks	Weekly Data (O − L) in Ticks
10	0	0
20	1	5
30	3	8
40	5	10
50	6	12
60	7	14
70	9	20
80	11	28
90	17	47

Analysis for Down Periods

Difference in Ticks[a] between
the High (H) and the Open (O)

Percent of Total Obs.	Daily Data (H − O) in Ticks	Weekly Data (H − O) in Ticks
10	0	1
20	1	3
30	2	5
40	4	7
50	5	12
60	7	17
70	9	20
80	12	26
90	18	38

Based on price data from January 1980 through June 1988.

[a] Minimum price fluctuation of one tick, or $0.01 per barrel, is equivalent to $10.00 per contract.

Analysis of Opening Prices
for Copper (Standard) Futures

Analysis for Up Periods

Difference in Ticks[a] between
the Open (O) and the Low (L)

Percent of Total Obs.	Daily Data (O − L) in Ticks	Weekly Data (O − L) in Ticks
10	0	0
20	0	2
30	0	4
40	1	6
50	2	10
60	4	14
70	5	18
80	8	28
90	14	44

Analysis for Down Periods

Difference in Ticks[a] between
the High (H) and the Open (O)

Percent of Total Obs.	Daily Data (H − O) in Ticks	Weekly Data (H − O) in Ticks
10	0	1
20	1	4
30	2	5
40	4	7
50	4	10
60	6	14
70	8	17
80	10	22
90	16	29

Based on price data from January 1980 through June 1988.

[a]Minimum price fluctuation of one tick, or 0.05 cents per pound, is equivalent to $12.50 per contract.

Analysis of Opening Prices
for Treasury Bond Futures

Analysis for Up Periods

Difference in Ticks[a] between
the Open (O) and the Low (L)

Percent of Total Obs.	Daily Data (O − L) in Ticks	Weekly Data (O − L) in Ticks
10	0	2
20	1	4
30	2	6
40	4	9
50	5	12
60	6	16
70	8	20
80	10	27
90	14	36

Analysis for Down Periods

Difference in Ticks[a] between
the High (H) and the Open (O)

Percent of Total Obs.	Daily Data (H − O) in Ticks	Weekly Data (H − O) in Ticks
10	0	0
20	2	3
30	3	6
40	4	8
50	5	11
60	7	14
70	8	19
80	11	27
90	15	39

Based on price data from January 1980 through June 1988.

[a]Minimum price fluctuation of one tick, or $1/32$ of one percentage point, is equivalent to $31.25 per contract.

Analysis of Opening Prices
for Deutsche Mark Futures

Analysis for Up Periods

Difference in Ticks[a] between
the Open (O) and the Low (L)

Percent of Total Obs.	Daily Data (O − L) in Ticks	Weekly Data (O − L) in Ticks
10	1	2
20	2	4
30	3	7
40	4	9
50	6	13
60	7	18
70	9	22
80	12	31
90	17	40

Analysis for Down Periods

Difference in Ticks[a] between
the High (H) and the Open (O)

Percent of Total Obs.	Daily Data (H − O) in Ticks	Weekly Data (H − O) in Ticks
10	1	2
20	2	4
30	4	6
40	5	9
50	6	11
60	7	15
70	9	20
80	12	29
90	17	39

Based on price data from January 1980 through June 1988.

[a]Minimum price fluctuation of one tick, or $0.0001 per mark, is equivalent to $12.50 per contract.

Analysis of Opening Prices for Eurodollar Futures

Analysis for Up Periods

Difference in Ticks[a] between
the Open (O) and the Low (L)

Percent of Total Obs.	Daily Data (O − L) in Ticks	Weekly Data (O − L) in Ticks
10	0	0
20	1	2
30	1	3
40	2	4
50	2	5
60	3	7
70	4	9
80	5	11
90	7	18

Analysis for Down Periods

Difference in Ticks[a] between
the High (H) and the Open (O)

Percent of Total Obs.	Daily Data (H − O) in Ticks	Weekly Data (H − O) in Ticks
10	0	0
20	0	2
30	1	3
40	1	5
50	2	6
60	3	8
70	4	10
80	5	14
90	7	20

Based on price data from December 1981 through June 1988.

[a]Minimum price fluctuation of one tick, or 0.01 of one percentage point, is equivalent to $25.00 per contract.

Analysis of Opening Prices for Gold (COMEX) Futures

Analysis for Up Periods

Percent of Total Obs.	Difference in Ticks[a] between the Open (O) and the Low (L)	
	Daily Data (O − L) in Ticks	Weekly Data (O − L) in Ticks
10	0	3
20	3	10
30	5	15
40	9	20
50	10	25
60	15	35
70	19	45
80	26	70
90	40	110

Analysis for Down Periods

Percent of Total Obs.	Difference in Ticks[a] between the High (H) and the Open (O)	
	Daily Data (H − O) in Ticks	Weekly Data (H − O) in Ticks
10	0	3
20	4	6
30	5	10
40	8	18
50	10	24
60	14	30
70	18	40
80	25	60
90	35	90

Based on price data from January 1980 through June 1988.

[a]Minimum price fluctuation of one tick, or $0.10 per troy ounce, is equivalent to $10.00 per contract.

Analysis of Opening Prices for Japanese Yen Futures

Analysis for Up Periods

Difference in Ticks[a] between
the Open (O) and the Low (L)

Percent of Total Obs.	Daily Data (O − L) in Ticks	Weekly Data (O − L) in Ticks
10	1	2
20	2	4
30	3	8
40	4	10
50	5	13
60	7	17
70	9	22
80	12	27
90	15	37

Analysis for Down Periods

Difference in Ticks[a] between
the High (H) and the Open (O)

Percent of Total Obs.	Daily Data (H − O) in Ticks	Weekly Data (H − O) in Ticks
10	0	2
20	2	5
30	3	6
40	4	9
50	6	13
60	7	16
70	9	22
80	12	31
90	18	44

Based on price data from January 1980 through June 1988.

[a]Minimum price fluctuation of one tick, or $0.0001 per 100 yen, is equivalent to $12.50 per contract.

Analysis of Opening Prices for Live Cattle Futures

Analysis for Up Periods

Difference in Ticks[a] between
the Open (O) and the Low (L)

Percent of Total Obs.	Daily Data (O − L) in Ticks	Weekly Data (O − L) in Ticks
10	0	2
20	2	5
30	4	9
40	5	13
50	6	18
60	8	22
70	10	29
80	13	36
90	17	50

Analysis for Down Periods

Difference in Ticks[a] between
the High (H) and the Open (O)

Percent of Total Obs.	Daily Data (H − O) in Ticks	Weekly Data (H − O) in Ticks
10	0	2
20	2	4
30	4	8
40	5	11
50	6	14
60	8	18
70	10	21
80	13	28
90	17	38

Based on price data from January 1980 through June 1988.

[a]Minimum price fluctuation of one tick. or 0.025 cents per pound. is equivalent to $10.00 per contract.

Analysis of Opening Prices for Live Hog Futures

Analysis for Up Periods

Difference in Ticks[a] between the Open (O) and the Low (L)

Percent of Total Obs.	Daily Data (O − L) in Ticks	Weekly Data (O − L) in Ticks
10	0	2
20	2	6
30	4	8
40	5	12
50	7	16
60	9	22
70	12	28
80	14	34
90	20	44

Analysis for Down Periods

Difference in Ticks[a] between the High (H) and the Open (O)

Percent of Total Obs.	Daily Data (H − O) in Ticks	Weekly Data (H − O) in Ticks
10	0	2
20	2	4
30	4	8
40	5	12
50	7	18
60	9	24
70	12	28
80	14	34
90	19	43

Based on price data from January 1980 through June 1988.

[a]Minimum price fluctuation of one tick, or 0.025 cents per pound, is equivalent to $10.00 per contract.

Analysis of Opening Prices
for Treasury Notes Futures

Analysis for Up Periods

Difference in Ticks[a] between
the Open (O) and the Low (L)

Percent of Total Obs.	Daily Data (O − L) in Ticks	Weekly Data (O − L) in Ticks
10	0	1
20	1	2
30	1	4
40	2	5
50	3	7
60	4	9
70	5	13
80	7	18
90	9	25

Analysis for Down Periods

Difference in Ticks[a] between
the High (H) and the Open (O)

Percent of Total Obs.	Daily Data (H − O) in Ticks	Weekly Data (H − O) in Ticks
10	0	2
20	1	3
30	2	5
40	2	6
50	3	8
60	4	10
70	6	13
80	7	16
90	10	25

Based on price data from May 1982 through June 1988.

[a] Minimum price fluctuation of one tick, or $\frac{1}{32}$ of one percentage point, is equivalent to $31.25 per contract.

Analysis of Opening Prices for NYSE Composite Index Futures

Analysis for Up Periods

Difference in Ticks[a] between the Open (O) and the Low (L)

Percent of Total Obs.	Daily Data (O − L) in Ticks	Weekly Data (O − L) in Ticks
10	1	3
20	2	5
30	4	8
40	5	12
50	6	15
60	8	19
70	10	25
80	14	31
90	20	41

Analysis for Down Periods

Difference in Ticks[a] between the High (H) and the Open (O)

Percent of Total Obs.	Daily Data (H − O) in Ticks	Weekly Data (H − O) in Ticks
10	1	1
20	2	4
30	3	7
40	4	9
50	6	11
60	7	15
70	10	18
80	13	21
90	19	29

Based on price data from June 1983 through June 1988.

[a] Minimum price fluctuation of one tick, or 0.05 index points, is equivalent to $25.00 per contract.

Analysis of Opening Prices for Oats Futures

Analysis for Up Periods

Difference in Ticks[a] between
the Open (O) and the Low (L)

Percent of Total Obs.	Daily Data (O − L) in Ticks	Weekly Data (O − L) in Ticks
10	0	0
20	0	2
30	0	4
40	2	8
50	4	12
60	4	16
70	6	20
80	10	26
90	14	36

Analysis for Down Periods

Difference in Ticks[a] between
the High (H) and the Open (O)

Percent of Total Obs.	Daily Data (H − O) in Ticks	Weekly Data (H − O) in Ticks
10	0	0
20	0	2
30	0	4
40	2	8
50	4	10
60	4	16
70	8	20
80	10	28
90	16	44

Based on price data from January 1980 through June 1988.

[a]Minimum price fluctuation of one tick, or 0.25 cents per bushel, is equivalent to $12.50 per contract.

Analysis of Opening Prices for Soybeans Futures

Analysis for Up Periods

Difference in Ticks[a] between
the Open (O) and the Low (L)

Percent of Total Obs.	Daily Data (O − L) in Ticks	Weekly Data (O − L) in Ticks
10	0	0
20	0	4
30	2	8
40	4	10
50	6	16
60	8	22
70	12	26
80	15	42
90	22	62

Analysis for Down Periods

Difference in Ticks[a] between
the High (H) and the Open (O)

Percent of Total Obs.	Daily Data (H − O) in Ticks	Weekly Data (H − O) in Ticks
10	0	0
20	1	6
30	3	10
40	5	12
50	7	18
60	10	22
70	12	26
80	16	36
90	24	52

Based on price data from January 1980 through June 1988.

[a] Minimum price fluctuation of one tick, or 0.25 cents per bushel, is equivalent to $12.50 per contract.

Analysis of Opening Prices for Swiss Franc Futures

Analysis for Up Periods

Difference in Ticks[a] between
the Open (O) and the Low (L)

Percent of Total Obs.	Daily Data (O − L) in Ticks	Weekly Data (O − L) in Ticks
10	1	4
20	2	7
30	5	10
40	6	13
50	8	18
60	11	24
70	13	29
80	17	40
90	24	58

Analysis for Down Periods

Difference in Ticks[a] between
the High (H) and the Open (O)

Percent of Total Obs.	Daily Data (H − O) in Ticks	Weekly Data (H − O) in Ticks
10	1	3
20	3	5
30	5	9
40	7	11
50	9	17
60	11	23
70	13	32
80	17	40
90	23	65

Based on price data from January 1980 through June 1988.

[a]Minimum price fluctuation of one tick, or $0.0001 per Swiss franc, is equivalent to $12.50 per contract.

Analysis of Opening Prices for Soymeal Futures

Analysis for Up Periods

Difference in Ticks[a] between
the Open (O) and the Low (L)

Percent of Total Obs.	Daily Data (O − L) in Ticks	Weekly Data (O − L) in Ticks
10	0	0
20	0	4
30	2	7
40	3	10
50	5	13
60	6	17
70	8	21
80	11	29
90	17	41

Analysis for Down Periods

Difference in Ticks[a] between
the High (H) and the Open (O)

Percent of Total Obs.	Daily Data (H − O) in Ticks	Weekly Data (H − O) in Ticks
10	0	0
20	0	2
30	0	4
40	2	5
50	3	8
60	5	11
70	7	16
80	10	23
90	15	35

Based on price data from January 1980 through June 1988.

[a]Minimum price fluctuation of one tick, or $0.10 per ton, is equivalent to $10.00 per contract.

Analysis of Opening Prices
for Sugar (#11 World) Futures

Analysis for Up Periods

Difference in Ticks[a] between
the Open (O) and the Low (L)

Percent of Total Obs.	Daily Data (O − L) in Ticks	Weekly Data (O − L) in Ticks
10	0	0
20	0	3
30	0	5
40	1	7
50	3	10
60	5	15
70	6	20
80	10	29
90	15	45

Analysis for Down Periods

Difference in Ticks[a] between
the High (H) and the Open (O)

Percent of Total Obs.	Daily Data (H − O) in Ticks	Weekly Data (H − O) in Ticks
10	2	2
20	2	4
30	4	6
40	5	10
50	6	12
60	8	15
70	10	21
80	15	29
90	25	43

Based on price data from January 1980 through June 1988.

[a]Minimum price fluctuation of one tick, or 0.01 cents per pound, is equivalent to $11.20 per contract.

Analysis of Opening Prices for Soybean Oil Futures

Analysis for Up Periods

Difference in Ticks[a] between
the Open (O) and the Low (L)

Percent of Total Obs.	Daily Data (O − L) in Ticks	Weekly Data (O − L) in Ticks
10	0	1
20	1	4
30	3	7
40	5	12
50	7	17
60	9	23
70	12	32
80	15	40
90	24	55

Analysis for Down Periods

Difference in Ticks[a] between
the High (H) and the Open (O)

Percent of Total Obs.	Daily Data (H − O) in Ticks	Weekly Data (H − O) in Ticks
10	0	0
20	0	3
30	1	5
40	3	8
50	5	15
60	7	22
70	10	30
80	15	40
90	22	53

Based on price data from January 1980 through June 1988.

[a]Minimum price fluctuation of one tick, or 0.01 cents per pound, is equivalent to $6.00 per contract.

Analysis of Opening Prices for S&P 500 Stock Index Futures

Analysis for Up Periods

Difference in Ticks[a] between
the Open (O) and the Low (L)

Percent of Total Obs.	Daily Data (O − L) in Ticks	Weekly Data (O − L) in Ticks
10	1	4
20	3	8
30	6	12
40	8	16
50	10	22
60	13	29
70	16	36
80	22	44
90	30	58

Analysis for Down Periods

Difference in Ticks[a] between
the High (H) and the Open (O)

Percent of Total Obs.	Daily Data (H − O) in Ticks	Weekly Data (H − O) in Ticks
10	1	5
20	3	10
30	5	16
40	8	20
50	10	25
60	12	28
70	16	34
80	20	44
90	30	58

Based on price data from May 1982 through June 1988.

[a]Minimum price fluctuation of one tick, or 0.05 index points, is equivalent to $25.00 per contract.

Analysis of Opening Prices
for Silver (COMEX) Futures

Analysis for Up Periods

Difference in Ticks[a] between
the Open (O) and the Low (L)

Percent of Total Obs.	Daily Data (O − L) in Ticks	Weekly Data (O − L) in Ticks
10	0	0
20	0	15
30	9	30
40	15	40
50	25	60
60	35	80
70	50	110
80	70	170
90	100	270

Analysis for Down Periods

Difference in Ticks[a] between
the High (H) and the Open (O)

Percent of Total Obs.	Daily Data (H − O) in Ticks	Weekly Data (H − O) in Ticks
10	0	0
20	10	15
30	20	30
40	25	40
50	35	60
60	50	95
70	69	130
80	90	190
90	140	295

Based on price data from January 1980 through June 1988.

[a]Minimum price fluctuation of one tick, or 0.10 cents per troy ounce, is equivalent to $5.00 per contract.

Analysis of Opening Prices for Treasury Bills Futures

Analysis for Up Periods

Difference in Ticks[a] between
the Open (O) and the Low (L)

Percent of Total Obs.	Daily Data (O − L) in Ticks	Weekly Data (O − L) in Ticks
10	0	1
20	1	2
30	1	4
40	2	5
50	3	7
60	3	9
70	4	12
80	6	18
90	10	28

Analysis for Down Periods

Difference in Ticks[a] between
the High (H) and the Open (O)

Percent of Total Obs.	Daily Data (H − O) in Ticks	Weekly Data (H − O) in Ticks
10	0	0
20	1	2
30	1	2
40	2	4
50	3	5
60	3	6
70	5	9
80	7	14
90	12	23

Based on price data from January 1980 through June 1988.

[a] Minimum price fluctuation of one tick, or 0.01 of one percentage point, is equivalent to $25.00 per contract.

Analysis of Opening Prices
for Wheat (Chicago) Futures

Analysis for Up Periods

Difference in Ticks[a] between
the Open (O) and the Low (L)

Percent of Total Obs.	Daily Data (O − L) in Ticks	Weekly Data (O − L) in Ticks
10	0	0
20	0	2
30	2	4
40	2	7
50	4	9
60	5	11
70	6	16
80	8	21
90	12	28

Analysis for Down Periods

Difference in Ticks[a] between
the High (H) and the Open (O)

Percent of Total Obs.	Daily Data (H − O) in Ticks	Weekly Data (H − O) in Ticks
10	0	0
20	1	3
30	2	5
40	3	8
50	4	11
60	5	14
70	6	20
80	8	24
90	12	34

Based on price data from January 1980 through June 1988.

[a]Minimum price fluctuation of one tick, or 0.25 cents per bushel, is equivalent to $12.50 per contract.

Analysis of Opening Prices for
Wheat (Kansas City) Futures

Analysis for Up Periods

Difference in Ticks[a] between
the Open (O) and the Low (L)

Percent of Total Obs.	Daily Data (O − L) in Ticks	Weekly Data (O − L) in Ticks
10	0	0
20	0	1
30	0	2
40	1	3
50	2	5
60	2	7
70	3	10
80	5	14
90	8	20

Analysis for Down Periods

Difference in Ticks[a] between
the High (H) and the Open (O)

Percent of Total Obs.	Daily Data (H − O) in Ticks	Weekly Data (H − O) in Ticks
10	0	0
20	0	2
30	1	3
40	2	4
50	2	7
60	3	9
70	4	12
80	6	14
90	8	22

Based on price data from January 1980 through June 1988.

[a]Minimum price fluctuation of one tick, or 0.25 cents per bushel, is equivalent to $12.50 per contract.

F

Deriving Optimal Portfolio Weights: A Mathematical Statement of the Problem

Minimize

$$S_p^2 = \sum_i (w_i)^2 s_i^2 + \sum_i \sum_j (w_i)(w_j) s_{ij}$$

subject to the following constraints:

$$R_p = \sum_i w_i r_i = T$$

$$\sum_i w_i = 1$$

$$w_i \geq 0$$

where R_p = portfolio expected return

r_i = expected return on commodity i

w_i = proportion of risk capital allocated to i

s_p^2 = portfolio variance

s_i^2 = variance of returns on commodity i

s_{ij} = covariance between returns on i and j

T = prespecified portfolio return target

INDEX

SOFTWARE FOR MONEY MANAGEMENT STRATEGIES

Programs in the package include:

(i)   Correlation analysis;
(ii) Effective exposure analysis;
(iii) Risk of ruin analysis;
(iv) Optimal allocation of capital; and
(v)   Avoiding Bull and Bear Traps.

The programs operationalize some of the key concepts presented in the book. They are designed to run on an IBM or an IBM compatible personal computer and are available on 3.5-inch or 5.25-inch diskettes. The cost of a demonstration diskette is a nonrefundable $25. This fee will be applied toward the purchase price of the software should the software be ordered within 30 days of ordering the demonstration diskette. Please add $3 for postage and handling. Illinois residents should include 8 percent sales tax. Checks should be drawn in favor of Money Management Strategies.

Mail your check, clearly specifying your diskette preference, to:

Money Management Strategies
Post Box 59592
Chicago, IL 60659-0592

LaVergne, TN USA
02 November 2009

162815LV00003B/106/A